The Challenge of Transnational Private Regulation: Conceptual and Constitutional Debates

T0374571

Edited by

Colin Scott, Fabrizio Cafaggi, and Linda Senden

This edition first published 2011
Editorial organization © 2011 Cardiff University Law School
Chapters © 2011 by the chapter author

Blackwell Publishing was acquired by John Wiley & Sons in February 2007. Blackwell's publishing programme has been merged with Wiley's global Scientific, Technical, and Medical business to form Wiley-Blackwell.

Editorial Offices
350 Main Street, Malden, MA 02148-5020, USA
9600 Garsington Road, Oxford OX4 2DQ, UK

For details of our global editorial offices, for customer services, and for information about how to apply for permission to reuse the copyright material in this book please see our website at www.wiley.com/wiley-blackwell

Registered Office
John Wiley & Sons Ltd, The Atrium, Southern Gate, Chichester, West Sussex PO19 8SQ.

Library of Congress Cataloging-in-Publication Data
Library of Congress Cataloging-in-Publication data is available for this book.

A catalogue record for this title is available from the British Library.

ISBN: 9781444339277

Set in the United Kingdom by Godiva Publishing Services Ltd
Printed in Singapore by Fabulous Printers Pte Ltd

Contents

JOURNAL OF LAW AND SOCIETY
VOLUME 38, NUMBER 1, MARCH 2011
ISSN: 0263-323X, pp. 1–19

The Conceptual and Constitutional Challenge of Transnational Private Regulation

COLIN SCOTT,* FABRIZIO CAFAGGI,** AND LINDA SENDEN***

Transnational private regulation (TPR) is a key aspect of contemporary governance. At first glance TPR regimes raise significant problems of legitimacy because of a degree of detachment from traditional government mechanisms. A variety of models have emerged engaging businesses, associations of firms, and NGOs, sometimes in hybrid form and often including governmental actors. Whilst the linkage to electoral politics is a central mechanism of legitimating governance activity, we note there are also other mechanisms including proceduralization and potentially also judicial accountability. But these public law forms do not exhaust the set of such mechanisms, and we consider also the contribution of private law forms and social and competitive structures which may support forms of legitimation. The central challenge identified concerns the possibility of reconceptualizing the global public sphere so as better to embrace TPR regimes in their myriad forms, so that they are recognized as having similar potential for legitimacy as national and international governmental bodies and regulation.

INTRODUCTION

It has been widely observed that governance powers that were once considered the prerogative of the nation state have emerged in a form where they are exercised by actors distinct from national governments. This transformation has involved both a shift of power towards international

* *UCD School of Law, University College Dublin, Belfield, Dublin 4, Ireland*
colin.scott@ucd.ie
** *Faculty of Law, University of Trento and Department of Law, European University Institute, I-50014 San Domenico di Fiesole (FI), Italy*
fabrizio.cafaggi@eui.eu
*** *Department of European and International Public Law, Tilburg Law School, Tilburg University, P.O. Box 90153, 5000 LE, Tilburg, The Netherlands*
l.a.j.senden@uvt.nl

governance bodies and also to non-governmental bodies.[1] This diffusion of governance power is widely associated with processes of globalization which, though they do not render national governments powerless, nevertheless throw up challenges of coordination and regulation which national governments, acting on their own, cannot effectively address. International governmental organizations such as those associated with the European Union, the Organisation for Economic Cooperation and Development and the United Nations, and many other treaty-based organizations, derive a good deal of their governance capacity in their decision making and their legitimacy from the direct participation of, or delegation from, national governments. Much of the implementation of such governance regimes does, in any case, fall to national governments. Transnational and non-governmental regulatory power does not so obviously have linkages to the electoral politics associated with national governments. Arguably transnational private regulation (TPR) presents a greater challenge in terms of its constitutional standing and legitimacy.

Constitutional problems of TPR are accentuated within more state-centred conceptions of constitutional governance. If we are to follow the exercise of power beyond nation-state institutions, this argues for adopting a more pluralist conception of constitutionalism which gives greater recognition to the diversity of institutional structures. Within such a pluralist approach, governance forms range from those associated with traditional electoral politics through inter-governmental activity to complete self-governance regimes.[2] Such a pluralist approach has the potential not only to embrace the activities of private actors, but also the instruments of private law and, in particular, the contracts upon which much of this regulatory activity is dependent for its normative effects.[3]

The articles in this collection are part of a larger project investigating the emergence, legitimacy, and effectiveness of transnational private regulatory regimes (TPRERs), funded by the Hague Institute for the Internationalization of Law.[4] The project investigates the claims to legitimacy and effectiveness of TPR regimes across different sectors by combining theoretical and empirical research. In this article, we offer an introduction to the constitutional challenges associated with TPR. We first discuss the variety of transnational private regulatory regimes which come within our conception of the phenomenon. This requires an examination of distinctions and commonalities between public and private actions. A central question in the

---

1 A.C. Cutler, V. Haufler, and T. Porter, *Private Authority and International Affairs* (1999).
2 N. Walker, 'The Idea of Constitutional Pluralism' (2002) 65 *Modern Law Rev.* 317–59, at 341.
3 O. Perez, 'Using Private-Public Linkages to Regulate Environmental Conflicts: The Case of International Construction Contracts' (2002) 29 *J. of Law and Society* 77–110.
4 Further details may be found on the project website at <www.privateregulation.eu>.

examination of non-state regulation is the extent to which private regulation may be conceived of as serving collective interests. We then examine how each of the different types of regimes addresses core regulatory tasks of setting and enforcing norms. A variety of models have emerged engaging businesses, associations of firms and NGOs, sometimes in hybrid form and often including governmental actors[5]. Whilst the linkage to electoral politics is a central mechanism of legitimating governance activity there are clearly other mechanisms relating to proceduralization and potentially also to judicial accountability. But these public law forms do not exhaust the set of such mechanisms, and we consider also the contribution of private law forms and cooperative and competitive structures which may support similar legitimating functions. Accordingly, the constitutional standing of TPRERs is considered from the perspective of the variety of mechanisms through which legitimacy may be achieved for private regulation.

KEY CONCEPTS OF TRANSNATIONAL PRIVATE REGULATION AND THE CONSTITUTIONAL CHALLENGE

The concept of transnational private regulation emerged, it has been claimed, to capture the idea of governance regimes which take the form of 'coalitions of nonstate actors which codify, monitor, and in some cases certify firms' compliance with labor, environmental, human rights, or other standards of accountability'.[6] They are transnational, rather than international, in the sense that their effects cross borders, but are not constituted through the cooperation of states as reflected in treaties (the latter being the principal territory of international law).[7] They are nonstate (or private, as we prefer) in the sense that key actors in such regimes include both civil society or non-governmental organizations (NGOs) and firms (both individually and in associations).

Such regimes address activities characterized in some instances by market-oriented needs for intervention and coordination, as with technical standards regimes,[8] but also provide a response to broader political conflicts

---

5 B. Kingsbury, N. Krisch, and R.B Stewart, 'The Emergence of Global Administrative Law' (2005) 68 *Law and Contemporary Problems* 15–61; S. Cassese, 'Administrative Law Without the State? The Challenge of Global Regulation' (2005) 37 *New York University J. of International Law and Politics* 663–94.

6 T. Bartley, 'Institutional Emergence in an Era of Globalization: The Rise of Transnational Private Regulation of Labor and Environmental Conditions' (2007) 113 *Am. J. of Sociology* 297–351, at 298.

7 M.L. Djelic and K.S. Andersson, 'Introduction: A World of Governance: The Rise of Transnational Regulation' in *Transnational Governance: Institutional Dynamics of Regulation*, eds. M.L Djelic and K.S. Andersson (2006) 4.

8 N. Brunsson and B. Jacobsson, 'The Contemporary Expansion of Standardization' in *A World of Standards*, eds. N. Brunsson, B. Jacobsson, et al. (2000).

over the appropriate balance between states and markets in determining such matters as entitlements to the protection of human rights and conservation of the environment.[9] Thus, while standardization regimes might be evaluated to some extent by reference to market criteria, there is arguably a stronger political component to regimes which may be characterized as constituting global points of connection between civil society, business, and government and, indeed, global governance without global government. For some, this political engagement between civil society and government, represented in this case at transnational level, merits discussion and investigation of the emergence of a 'new public sphere'.[10] Recent activity, engaging NGOs, governments, and businesses in respect of employment rights provides a key example.[11] This point is well demonstrated by Fiona de Londras's contribution to this volume in which she argues that threats to human rights generated by the delegated activities of private airlines cannot be adequately addressed by conventional litigation strategies but are likely to require more institutionalized and hybrid responses drawing in both NGOs and associations of firms and governments in developing and implementing appropriate protective norms. Her approach involves a critical examination of the capacity for governance within the aviation industry, largely over technical matters, which might be turned towards effectively addressing human rights concerns. An underlying question in her approach is whether there are some activities for which privatization of provision and regulation are inappropriate. This is not simply a question of the limits to legitimate transfer to private firms of state functions, an issue that has been explored in the case of privatization of prisons,[12] but also the appropriate role and limits of *private* regulation over such privatized activities. De Londras's claim that the institutional structures of private regulation, established to address issues of technical standards and safety, might be turned to address human rights issues is made not because of some normative superiority of such private regulation but, rather, because this is where the capacity for such oversight is best developed.

The emergence of TPR regimes may produce transfers of power and authority from state to international level and from public to private, affecting traditional conceptions of sovereignty and self-determination.[13]

---

9 Bartley, op. cit., n. 6, p. 299.
10 M. Castells, 'The New Public Sphere: Global Civil Society, Communication Networks and Global Governance' (2008) 616 *Annals of the Am. Academy of Political and Social Science* 78–93, at 80, 89.
11 D. O'Rourke, 'Multi-stakeholder Regulation: Privatizing or Socializing Global Labor Standards?' (2006) 34 *World Development* 899–918.
12 R. Harding, *Private Prisons and Public Accountability* (1997).
13 N. McCormick, 'Beyond the Sovereign State' (1993) 56 *Modern Law Rev.* 1–18; N. Rose and M. Valverde, 'Governed by Law?' (1998) 7 *Social and Legal Studies* 541–51; F. Cafaggi, 'The New Foundations of Transnational Private Regulation (in this volume, pp. 23–5).

Frequently built on mixed, co-regulatory bases, private regulatory regimes exhibit a different structure at national and international level, due predominantly to the weaker governmental dimension at the global level. These developments have been subject to criticisms in literature and by policy makers, focusing on their lack of legitimacy. The emergence of powerful private regulators operating transnationally clearly raises challenges for ideas of constitutionalism which remain substantially rooted in electoral politics at national level and attached to the ambition to control governmental and legislative power by reference to principles concerned with the rule of law.[14] However, we should recognize that theories of sovereignty and nation state have been able to operate alongside powerful transnational governance regimes of earlier eras, including the power of the Roman Catholic church and of large multinational enterprises and their predecessors in the great trading companies.[15] Furthermore, the centrality of the state to contemporary constitutional governance has been increasingly challenged by the emergence of both international and private governance regimes.[16]

For some, the idea of private regulatory power, particularly where it involves a degree of self-regulation, is tantamount to deregulation or an abdication of regulation. On the contrary, we believe that it is a form of regulation which can significantly enhance capacity for developing and implementing public-regarding norms, although requiring investigation as to its effects and effectiveness. We note that the standing and legitimacy of private regulation varies across different countries even within the European Union. For example, whereas self-regulation is well accepted and integrated into wider regimes of regulatory governance in the United Kingdom, the legitimacy of self-regulation is more fragile in some member states and also in the United States.

The principal objections to self-regulation at both national and supranational level include claims that such regimes are likely to be programmed to be soft or ineffective or, where they are effective, this is to enhance the position of regime members so as to cartelize a market, with not only positive effects for participants but also negative effects for others (both competitors and consumers). Indeed, it has been suggested that the existence of a TPR regime may indicate an absence of competition between firms within a sector.[17] The dismissal of non-state regulation on the grounds that it serves only private interests through ineffectiveness, cartelization or capture is too simple. In her contribution to this volume, Imelda Maher critically

---

14 J. Murkens, 'The Quest for Constitutionalism in UK Public Law Discourse' (2009) 29 *Oxford J. of Legal Studies* 427–55.
15 P. Drahos, 'The Regulation of Public Goods' (2004) 7 *J. of International Economic Law* 321–39, at 323.
16 McCormick, op. cit., n. 13; Walker, op. cit., n. 2.
17 D. Mügge, 'Private-Public Puzzles: Inter-Firm Competition and Transnational Private Regulation' (2006) 11 *New Political Economy* 177–200, at 172.

evaluates the modern tendency of competition law policies and agencies to operate a more or less blanket prohibition on cartel agreements, and asks what conditions would be required to satisfy some form of public interest justification for a cartel? She notes that in some contexts, notably export cartels, agreements lawfully evade such prohibitions without state involvement, while others seem to require public sanction and oversight to render them lawful, generating a hybrid form of regulation. Within this discussion there is potential for competition law to offer a means to regulate, in the public interest, private regulation through cartels, as an alternative to prohibition.

The promulgation and enforcement of norms are usually regarded as being public goods, in the sense that the taking of the benefits by one person does not reduce the stock of benefits available to others (non-rivalry) and that no one can be excluded from the benefits (non-excludability).[18] Indeed, it is possible to characterize much TPR as constituting the de-centred regulation of public goods associated with the good order of society, whether such outcomes are intended or not.[19] In principle it makes no difference to the public-good qualities of effective norms whether they are publicly or privately promulgated. Put another way, private regulation need not simply be about the production of club goods (that is, norms which benefit the members of a regime only) and purely private goods. An important question is to what extent can public goods, such as effective regulation, be privately produced? For some, the absence of an effective incentive structure for private provision of global public goods is problematic.[20] This is an issue we address in the next section.

THE EMERGENCE OF TRANSNATIONAL PRIVATE REGULATORY REGIMES

In many instances, the production of effective private regulation is very closely tied to the interests of those putting the regime forward. This is a central theme of Elinor Ostrom's research on self-organizing responses to problems associated with common resource goods (and the problem of excessive exploitation of commonly owned resources, the commons, more generally), such as fisheries. It may be in the interests of one person to take all the fish they can, but the aggregate welfare of all is affected by overfishing. An apparent paradox identified by Ostrom is the demonstration that market failures associated with excessive depletion of common resources

18 A. Katz, 'Taking Private Ordering Seriously' (1996) 144 *University of Pennsylvania Law Rev.* 1745–63, at 1749.
19 Drahos, op. cit., n. 15.
20 A.C. Cutler, 'The Legitimacy of Private Transnational Governance: Experts and the Transnational Market for Force' (2010) 8 *Social & Economic Rev.* 157–85, at 176.

6

may be effectively addressed through action by the very same market actors whose conduct caused the problem, but now acting collectively rather than individually.[21] Whilst in some instances it may be sufficient for the affected actors to act collectively (and differently from how they might act individually), in other instances the collective action challenges are too great. Classically, we might think of the necessary response as being governmental. But a major reason for the emergence of TPR regimes is that NGOs seek to address the costs of economic activity which cannot be addressed effectively by the actors involved alone, collectively or individually. The problem of the commons is not restricted to such local issues as fisheries, but extends also to global issues, notably climate change.[22] Extending beyond the problem of the commons, we should consider the ways in which private interests are pursued and served through private regulation, and the extent to which the relationships to government, to market, and to communities support and incentivize effective regulation, serving some version of the public interest.

These issues of purposes and effects of private regulation are closely linked to questions of the emergence of regimes. We conceive of regulatory regimes, following Eberlein and Grande, as 'the full set of actors, institutions, norms and rules that are of importance for the process and the outcome of [...] regulation in a given sector'.[23] Many regimes are driven by market concerns, but market incentives to private regulation are not of one type. Standardization processes, for example, are chiefly linked to problems of coordination in markets.[24] Producers want to be able to use each others' components in production and to assure consumers that products from different producers will work together. There is a market incentive to develop and follow standards, and the market punishes those who do not follow them.

Quite distinct from the coordination issue, firms may self-regulate to address reputational issues in the market. Thus, individual and collective firm responses to concerns about poor working conditions in the garment manufacturing industry have involved seeking to establish credible regimes to develop and implement higher standards so as to protect market position in industrialized countries.[25] This latter motivation hints at the position of

21 E. Ostrom, *Governing the Commons: The Evolution of Institutions for Collective Action* (1990).
22 W.D. Nordhaus, *Managing the Global Commons: The Economics of Climate Change* (1994); F. Haines and N. Reichman, 'The Problem that is Global Warming' (2008) 30 *Law & Policy* 385–93.
23 B. Eberlein and E. Grande, 'Beyond Delegation: Transnational Regulatory Regimes and the EU Regulatory State' (2005) 12 *J. of European Public Policy* 89–112, at 91.
24 K. Tamm Hallström, *Organizing International Standardization: ISO and IASC in Quest of Authority* (2004).
25 D. O'Rourke, 'Outsourcing Regulation: Analyzing Non-Governmental Systems of Labor Standards and Monitoring' (2003) 49 *Policy Studies J.* 1–29.

firms within communities and is reminiscent of the idea that firms in extractive industries such as logging and mining are dependent on a 'social licence to operate'[26] which, though it may be implicit, has significant consequences for firms when it is deemed to be breached. This may result in some institutionalization of private regulatory capacity over the issues at the level of individual firms or trade associations.

In some sectors, it has fallen to NGOs to find ways to address social problems created by firms, for example, respecting human rights and the environment. Organizations such as Amnesty International and the Rainforest Alliance reflect and channel public concerns about human rights and the environment respectively, and have become important sources of standards and monitoring over multinational enterprises in particular. Many more NGOs have transnational reach in regimes which they lead, increasingly with some engagement of governmental and/or industry actors.[27] Such engaged leadership of NGOs is exemplified by, for example, the activities of the Forest Stewardship Council discussed in the article in this volume by Bomhoff and Meuwese. Though TPR regimes sometimes emerge without government involvement, governments have the capacity to stimulate and steer such regimes through a variety of actions, including giving statutory recognition to private regimes and threatening legislative intervention. In some instances it is the weaknesses of national governments, particularly in developing economies, which stimulate the emergence of TPRs to address matters which national governments cannot effectively address. The capacity to steer trans-national actors is arguably greater for inter-governmental actors than for national governments. The EU institutions, for example, have made increasing reference to regimes which link public encouragement to private capacity, under the rubric of co-regulation, as a means to regulating more effectively with less use of public resources.[28] Such regimes are increasingly likely to be both hybrid, involving both governmental and non-state actors, and also multi-level, involving national, European, and international levels.[29]

A central example is provided by self-regulation in the area of advertising. In operational terms, advertising self-regulation occurs in many member states as a privately organized and national regime.[30] However, the European

---

26 N. Gunningham, R. Kagan, and D. Thornton, 'Social License and Environmental Protection: Why Businesses Go Beyond Compliance' (2004) 29 *Law and Social Inquiry* 307–42.

27 K. Abbott and D. Snidal, 'The Governance Triangle: Regulatory Standards Institutions and the Shadow of the State' in *The Politics of Global Regulation*, eds. W. Mattli and N. Wood (2009).

28 L. Senden, 'Soft Law, Self-Regulation and Co-Regulation in European Law – Where do they Meet?' (2005) 9 *Electronic J. of Comparative Law*.

29 F. Cafaggi, 'Rethinking self-regulation in European Private Law' in *Reframing Self-Regulation in European Private Law*, ed. F. Cafaggi (2006).

30 European Advertising Standards Alliance (EASA), *Blue Book 6: Advertising Self-Regulation in Europe and Beyond* (2010).

8

Commission has been heavily involved in encouraging a transnational private organization, the European Advertising Standards Alliance, to promote more uniform and stringent models of self-regulation and regulatory standards through the national private regimes.[31] The common reference point for the standardization of national codes is the Consolidated Code of Advertising and Communications Marketing Practice promulgated by the International Chamber of Commerce.[32] In turn, legislative measures, such as the Unfair Commercial Practices Directive (Directive 2005/29/EC) both encourage the engagement of stakeholders in the promulgation of self-regulatory codes (recital 20) and require member states to penalize through legislation the abuse of self-regulatory codes by businesses (article 6(2)(b)).[33]

PATTERNS OF TRANSNATIONAL PRIVATE REGULATION

Whilst TPR regimes do, by definition, share important elements of trans-national reach and leadership by non-governmental actors, their legal forms are diverse. Some TPRERs are based on organizational forms such as companies, and others on contractual forms, both associational and bilateral. Amongst the companies, corporate social responsibility (CSR) regimes frequently involve the self-regulation of the company itself, whereas the adoption of externally set standards and certification or assurance processes involves companies in specifying and enforcing regulatory standards for other companies. Whereas associations do, in many cases, comprise member companies of the regulated industry, with a strong self-regulatory element, in some instances associations bring together a wider range of stakeholders, as with the case of the Forest Stewardship Council which is led by environmental NGOs. GlobalGap, the private food standards organization, is led by representatives of major retailers.[34] Producer companies comprise the primary target of regulation and, increasingly, are represented within the association.

With the practices of individual firms involving corporate governance, key issues concern the sources of the norms which they follow and the mechanisms through which compliance is overseen. Corporate governance norms have emerged in recent years through the activities of various private committees, but have been given some official force through reference to some or all of their requirements in national corporate law regimes.

---

31 European Commission, *Self-Regulation in the EU Advertising Sector: A Report of Some Discussion Among Interested Parties* (2006) 12–13.
32 EASA, op. cit., n. 30, pp. 22–7.
33 F. Cafaggi, 'Private Regulation in European Private Law' in *Towards a Civil Code*, eds. A.S. Hartkamp et al. (2010, 4th edn.) ch. 5.
34 T. Havinga, 'Private Regulation of Food Safety by Supermarkets' (2006) 28 *Law & Policy* 515–33.

Oversight and enforcement has been in part a matter for companies themselves, through their executive and non-executive directors. Often ethical committees have been created independent from the management to oversee the implementation of codes of conducts. But shareholders have assumed increasing prominence, frequently acting through associational groups, in steering firms towards compliance with key corporate governance norms.[35] The increasing importance of private regulation has promoted important changes in the corporate governance structure of multinational enterprises to promote responsiveness towards stakeholders affected by the activity of the corporation.

With multinational enterprises generally, both in their own corporate governance activities, and in their relationships to others, whether in bilateral or associational contracts, there are significant distinctions in the market position of different firms. Proximity to final consumers has the potential to create market pressure on businesses to adopt and implement private regulatory regimes. Private regulators such as NGOs may exert greater pressure because labelling and other marketing mechanisms affecting reputation can be used as a competitive tool. In some instances where consumer pressure is absent, investors may exert a degree of oversight over company practices through investment decisions generally and negotiation with companies through investor associations, a growing trend in the environmental protection area.[36]

Governments also have increasingly sought to assert at least limited enforcement capacity over firms' compliance with privately promulgated corporate governance norms. Thus corporate governance is frequently a multi-level and hybrid affair. As Peer Zumbansen notes in his contribution, corporate governance regimes exemplify contemporary challenges to legal centralism, and require a more pluralistic conception of both law making and law enforcement in the corporate sphere. Such regimes typically comprise both hard and soft law instruments, a theme central to other articles in this volume, notably that of Fabrizio Cafaggi. It is significant that corporate governance and even bilateral contracting practices of companies should increasingly be regarded as not wholly private matters for companies themselves but, rather, representative of hybrid governance arrangements in which a public dimension to corporate activities is recognized. Conventional private law devices have been transformed to perform regulatory functions at the global level. A new body of rules and practices has emerged. Associational regimes in which businesses (and sometimes others, including governmental actors) work together to create regulatory arrangements raise rather different issues, but which may be equally characterized in terms of

---

35 B.J. Richardson, *Socially Responsible Investment Law: Regulating the Unseen Polluters* (2008).
36 B.J. Richardson, *Environmental Regulation Through Financial Organisation: Comparative Perspectives on the Industrialised Nations* (2002).

asking to what extent such arrangements should be regarded as private or public matters. It is striking how little scrutiny associations with regulatory purposes and/or effects have had from competition law institutions, a lacuna which Imelda Maher's article seeks to remedy. From a constitutional perspective, questions for such associational regimes include the extent to which they are representative and inclusive, transparent in their policy making, and respectful of rule of law norms in their enforcement activity.

A third form of transnational private governance is based neither on single entities nor associations of interested firms but, rather, has a broader form bringing together NGOs and, with increasing frequency, governmental and/ or business actors, a phenomenon referred to as the 'governance triangle'.[37] Standards regimes are one form for such organizations, originating in industry-based, but non-associational activities which are more frequently engaging non-industry actors within their processes. Environmental and labour rights regimes operating transnationally are increasingly characterized by such multiple representation. Elaborating on this theme, Cafaggi gives particular emphasis to the hybrid nature of much TPR, involving the mixing of public and private legal instruments and collaboration between governmental and non-governmental actors. While the use of the term of TPR has become a common one, it also becomes very clear from his contribution that there is no question of a strict public-private divide in transnational governance, but that the relationship between the public and private spheres is intertwined and is being transformed in a variety of ways.

Hybridity is an important theme not only in respect of standard setting, but also with respect to monitoring and enforcement, a relatively neglected topic in the literature on transnational governance generally.[38] Within research on regulation it has been widely noted that enforcement tends to emphasize advice and persuasion by enforcement agencies and that this may be effective where there is capacity to escalate enforcement strategies to include more stringent measures such as prosecution and licence revocation.[39] This pyramidal model of enforcement has been extended in ways which are promising for hybrid governance regimes, to recognize the potential for third-party enforcement, such as where businesses, trade associations, and NGOs become involved in enforcing, using powers delegated by legislative bodies or rights assigned to them under contracts.[40] In many TPRERs, enforcement in a conventional sense has limited application since

---

37 Abbott and Snidal, op. cit., n. 27.
38 F. Cafaggi (ed.), *The Enforcement of Transnational Private Regulation* (2011, forthcoming).
39 I. Ayres and J. Braithwaite, *Responsive Regulation: Transcending the Deregulation Debate* (1992).
40 P. Grabosky, 'Discussion Paper: Inside the Pyramid: Towards a Conceptual Framework for the Analysis of Regulatory Systems' (1997) 25 *International J. of Sociology and Law* 195–201.

11

businesses adopt standards voluntarily and they are, in a sense, judged by the market in terms of the acceptability of their compliance. However the importance of checking for compliance is recognized within many regimes and it is not unusual to find contractual requirements on businesses that they engage third parties to certify compliance.[41] Where participation in a TPRER is less than voluntary, then more conventional bilateral monitoring and enforcement may apply, though, as with many international regulatory regimes, it is frequently the case that the standard setting and the enforcement are organizationally distinct functions with the enforcement being carried out at national or sub-national level. There is, for example, relatively little direct involvement of the International Chamber of Commerce or the European Advertising Standards Alliance in the enforcement of advertising rules which they are involved in designing, nor is GlobalGap directly involved in enforcing its standards on food producers.[42] Rather, the rules are adopted and enforced by others, national self-regulatory bodies in the case of advertising, and large retailers in the case of foods standards. Thus an evaluation of the effectiveness of enforcement is likely to depend substantially on an analysis of the activities of firms, associations, and NGOs operating more locally.

CONSTITUTIONALISM AND TRANSNATIONAL PRIVATE REGULATION

Questions of legitimacy of regulatory governance are not restricted to private regulatory regimes, but are raised also by the tendency within public regimes to distance regulatory decision making from elected politicians. Within public international law, the relationship between legitimacy and constitutionalism has been much discussed.[43] In the European Union, for example, extensive delegation of apparently technical decision making to expert committees ('comitology') exemplifies this problem.[44] To the extent that transnational and private regulatory regimes are assessed by reference to traditional constitutional criteria, they are liable to magnify such issues. For this reason, the emergence of transnational governance generally has stimulated greater attention to more pluralist conceptions of constitutionalism

---

41 M. Blair, C.A. Williams, and L.W. Lin, 'The New Role for Assured Services in Global Commerce' (2007) 33 *J. of Corporate Law* 325–60.
42 T. Havinga, 'Private Regulation of Food Safety By Supermarkets' (2006) 28 *Law & Policy* 515–33.
43 A. von Bogdandy, P. Dann, and M. Goldmann, 'Developing the Publicness of Public International Law: Towards a Legal Framework for Global Governance Activities' (2008) 9 *German Law J.* 1375–400.
44 C. Joerges and E. Vos, *EU Committees: Social Regulation, Law and Politics* (1999); M. Pollack, 'Control Mechanism or Deliberative Democracy?: Two Images of Comitology' (2003) 36 *Comparative Political Studies* 125–55.

12

which emphasize the constitutional potential of private activities where there are plausible claims to authority and common identity within a social or economic group.[45] Within such a perspective, interdependence through the creation of networks, competitive processes, and the potential for judicial accountability may be as important sources of legitimacy as the ballot box.

Thinking about regulation generally, we can distinguish processes for setting norms from monitoring and enforcement. The constitutional significance of the distinction is that the former function involves a role conventionally understood as reserved to legislative institutions, while the latter is conventionally associated with the executive (and sometimes also the judicial) branch of government. Accordingly, the different elements of regulatory regimes throw up different sorts of problems. In private regimes, separation of functions and powers is not the rule. The integration within a single body of different functions can decrease independence and increase conflicts of interests. In his contribution, Cafaggi suggests that separation of regulatory functions can address some of these problems: depending on the various regulatory relationships, different governance responses should be provided in order to increase accountability without decreasing effectiveness.

Concerning the setting of norms, constitutionalism is associated with the idea not only that laws should be made by elected legislatures, and not by delegated bodies, but also that lawmakers should be subject to constraints on the content of the laws they pass (ensuring, for example, compliance with human rights norms, and other rule of law principles such as the rule against retrospective legislation). Many jurisdictions allow for a scrutiny of the lawfulness of legislative acts by a constitutional or supreme court. Accordingly, private law making within TPR regimes raises the problem not only of delegation, but also and distinctly, that scrutiny of such private law making may not apply or involve the range of norms and judicial procedures which are applied to parliamentary legislation. In their contribution to this volume, Casey and Scott address this issue in an exploration of alternative mechanisms through which the legitimacy of norms is supported within TPR regimes. Research in a number of regimes is suggestive of deliberate attempts to construct legitimacy and to prioritize certain forms of legitimacy over others in particular instances. Normative legitimacy is closely tied to the appropriateness of processes in terms of such matters as inclusion and transparency. Pragmatic legitimacy is more closely allied to output measures of legitimacy concerned with the acceptance of the effectiveness of a regime. Clearly there may be a trade-off between process and output, for example, because the prioritization of normative legitimacy slows down or increases costs thereby adversely affecting outcomes. Casey and Scott consider also a third possible basis for legitimacy based in a sense that it is

45 Walker, op. cit., n. 2.

13

not possible to think how things could be done otherwise ('cognitive legitimacy').[46]

The legitimacy of regulatory governance generally is frequently understood in terms of a dichotomy between democratic and expert governance. The non-majoritarian character of much regulatory governance is, for some, a virtue and a source of legitimacy based on technical expertise and relative insulation from political interference.[47] The sometimes fragile legitimacy based on such expertise, with evaluation at least to some extent geared towards the outputs and effects of a regime rather than the processes, has nevertheless involved also a degree of dependence on the democratic origins and accountability of public regimes, and frequently also the fact that senior officials are appointed by elected politicians. The absence of such national democratic elements within most TPRERs is likely to make the technocratic basis of legitimacy more fragile and is suggestive of the need for alternative modes of constitutional evaluation.[48]

As regards the power to make legislation, the constitutional attachment to the legislature is derived from the link of the legislature to the *demos* through elections. However, it is arguable that the focus on electoral politics constitutes a privileging of *one form* of governance which complies with a meta-principle of the right to self-governance, and that other mechanisms of self-governance should be given equal prominence. A theory of constitutional private legislation might, then, look to other forms of self-governance including more direct ways to identify and engage those affected by governance decisions. This is frequently more challenging for TPR regimes than it would be in national contexts, since stakeholders are likely to be widely diffused and may be difficult to identify.[49] However, there is emerging a theory of legitimate global civil society premised on the donations by, and volunteering of, participants. Many TPRERs exemplify tendencies towards the creation of networks of action by global civil-society actors, in areas such as environmental protection and labour.[50] Others have referred to self-governance as a constitutional principle to ground the foundations of TPR.[51] A central challenge for contemporary constitutional

---

46 J. Black, 'Constructing and Contesting Legitimacy and Accountability in Polycentric Regulatory Regimes' (2008) *Regulation & Governance* 137–64; M. Suchman, 'Managing Legitimacy: Strategic and Institutional Approaches' (1995) 20 *Academy of Management Rev.* 571–610.

47 M. Everson and G. Majone, 'Institutional Reform: Independent Agencies, Oversight, Coordination and Procedural Control' in *Governance in the European Union*, eds. O.D. Schutter, N. Lebessis, and J. Paterson (2001); M. Thatcher and A.S. Sweet, 'Theory and Practice of Delegation to Non-Majoritarian Institutions' (2002) 25 *West European Politics* 1–22.

48 Cutler, op. cit., n. 20.

49 id., pp. 174–5.

50 Castells, op. cit., n. 10; D. Vogel, 'The Private Regulation of Global Conduct' in Mattli and Woods, op. cit., n. 27.

51 Cafaggi, op. cit., n. 29.

14

theory is to adapt its thinking to accommodate claims that such phenomena may constitute a new form of global democratic governance. This is of importance not only because of the spontaneous emergence of global civil-society actors but, more critically, because delegation by governments to such actors represents a central alternative to inter-governmental responses to global governance problems.[52] The legitimacy of monitoring and enforcement functions is amenable to being addressed not only through participation, but also through institutionalization both of processes and norms for scrutiny.

One very important difference between the public and the private at transnational level is that the former operates within a regime of attributed competences while the latter more frequently exercises original rule-making power based on freedom of contract and association.[53] In some instances powers may be delegated by international organizations directly by treaties. In this vein, one set of responses to the challenges of TPRERs asserts the potential of applying public-law models of transparency and accountability to non-state and mixed actors within a model of global administrative law (GAL).[54] One line of development in this literature is to argue that a wide range of activities which might once have been thought of as private should be regarded as public in character and therefore amenable to public-law controls, whether at domestic[55] or global level.[56] We contend that this strategy is but one among many instruments provided by the toolbox of public and private law to increase legitimacy. Private organizations engage a large number of tools to empower members and stakeholders with control over their activity in order to increase organizational accountability. When regimes are composed of several organizations, control emerges from both cooperation and competition. The formation of private regulatory networks produces mutual control: the competition for members or, more broadly, regulatees can increase the standards to the extent that information is adequate to support the making of choices. The use of public oversight and procedural rules is one among the many potential strategies that TPR can use to increase accountability without reducing effectiveness.

A particular issue which is being addressed within the research project on TPR from which this article is drawn is the prominent role of private-law instruments generally, and contracts in particular. Should contractual

---

52 Castells, op. cit., no. 10; Vogel, op. cit., n. 50, p. 8.
53 F. Cafaggi, 'Private Regulation and European Legal Integration' in *The Regulatory State,* eds. D. Oliver, T. Prosser, and R. Rawlings (2010).
54 Kingsbury et al., op. cit., n. 5; C. Harlow, 'Global Administrative Law: The Quest for Principles and Values' (2006) 17 *European J. of International Law* 187–214.
55 J. Freeman, 'Extending Public Law Norms Through Privatization' (2003) 116 *Harvard Law Rev.* 1285–352; C. Harlow, 'The "Hidden Paw" of the State and the Publicisation of Private Law' in *A Simple Common Lawyer: Essays in Honour of Michael Taggart,* eds. D. Dyzenhaus, M. Hunt, and G. Huscroft (2009).
56 von Bogdandy et al., op. cit., n. 43.

15

governance increasingly be regarded as public in character? It may be that the exclusive focus of public law processes on the state is simply a hangover from the Westphalian state model and to the extent that such a model is rendered obsolete by governance changes, then public law oversight should be reconceived. Such an approach requires a rethinking of the public-private divide and also some caution against the risks of excessive legalization. These themes are addressed in the contribution of Jacco Bomhoff and Anne Meuwese to this volume. They find a good deal of common ground in two alternative approaches or 'lenses' for viewing TPR, one based in the ideas of private international law and the other in the development and operation of policies of better regulation. Both approaches are, in a sense, meta-regulatory in that they offer both norms and procedures, somewhat distinct from the GAL approach, through which oversight of aspects of TPR regimes might be achieved.

The case for a meta-regulatory approach need not be tied exclusively to legal oversight,[57] as Bomhoff and Meuwese suggest in their search for meta-norms. Better regulation policies, in particular, give some priority to seeking alternatives to legal control. An alternative approach, canvassed in this volume, emphasizes both the modes of control and accountability which are emergent in regimes rooted in market and community activities, and the potential for reconceptualizing the effects of networks in governing network participants in a manner which is quite distinct from traditional public law modes. This approach addresses the shift from hierarchical to heterarchic governance and recognizes the need to reconceptualize the bases of legitimacy for such regimes at both national and supranational level.[58] The central question is whether TPRERs can or should be analogized to traditional institutional actors domestically and internationally. In their contribution to this volume, Deirdre Curtin and Linda Senden make a case for developing an accountability perspective on TPRERs. They explore the distinctiveness of these regimes and, in particular, the extent to which accountability should be pursued as a virtue, and what this may entail in terms of applying traditional accountability mechanisms to TPR regimes and developing alternatives. Besides social accountability devices, the search for such alternative modes offers at least two distinct alternatives to the top-down approach to the control and accountability of TPRs. The first is rooted in choice and the second in networks of mutuality.

Choice, though not uncritically accepted,[59] is a central value within market-based governance regimes. The performance and accountability of

57 C. Scott, 'Reflexive Governance, Meta-Regulation and Corporate Social Responsibility: The Heineken Effect?' in *Perspectives on Corporate Social Responsibility*, eds. N. Boeger, R. Murray, and C. Villiers (2008).

58 G. Teubner, 'Breaking Frames: The Global Interplay of Legal and Social Systems' (1997) 45 *Am. J. of Comparative Law* 149–69.

59 B. Barry, 'Chance, Choice and Justice' in *Contemporary Political Philosophy: An Anthology*, eds. R. Goodin and P. Pettit (2006).

actors is driven, at least in theory, by the observation that those who use their services have options to exit and take services from others.[60] Within private regulation, regulatees may have choice about who regulates them,[61] whilst beneficiaries of regulation, such as consumers, may similarly have choices as to which self-regulatory regime they are protected by, by virtue of their product choices. Systems of mutual recognition also offer choices as to which of a variety of level of standards should be adopted because of a commitment to recognize each of the diverse sets of valid standards across all the mutually recognizing jurisdictions.[62] There may be a further element of choice offered *within* regimes. If choice is pursued as a value, a key question is how to make regimes choice-enhancing and support this with the possibility of exit. That there may be competitive effects does not, of course, preclude a role for governmental actors in stimulating or participating in such regimes. Competition between public and private regimes has received some analysis in respect of provision of public services such as rail and air transport,[63] but rather less attention in respect of regulation. Where neither form of control is feasible, the participation of governmental actors through competition may provide an alternative. Such competition may be direct or indirect, as where governments give recognition to some but not other private regulators. Imelda Maher alludes to this possibility in the context of the EU prohibition on cartels as a form of TPRER. Notwithstanding this, it is illustrated that the Commission may, instead, make provision for 'regulatory frameworks' affording legitimacy to similar forms of horizontal cooperation between firms, amounting to a TPRER, where these are seen to deliver public benefits.

Networks of mutuality are rooted in the interdependence of actors, as with standards regimes. In an extreme case of interdependence, United States nuclear power operators faced the likely destruction of their industry should one of their number cause an accident through failure to follow self-regulatory rules.[64] Many regimes exhibit interdependence not only between regulatees but also between regulatees and those protected by the regime. Evaluation of such regimes involves consideration of the extent to which they promote a thicker form of proceduralization.[65] Giving voice in such context is not simply about expressing preferences, but also learning about

---

60 A.O. Hirschman, *Exit, Voice and Loyalty: Responses to Decline in Firms, Organizations and States* (1970).
61 Cafaggi, op. cit., n. 29; A. Ogus, 'Re-Thinking Self-Regulation' (1995) 15 *Oxford J. of Legal Studies* 97–108.
62 Cafaggi, id.; Bomhoff and Meuwese in this volume, p. 161.
63 M. Bishop, J. Kay, and C. Mayer, *Privatization and Economic Performance* (1994).
64 J. Rees, *Hostages of Each Other: The Transformation of Nuclear Safety Since Three Mile Island* (1994).
65 J. Black, 'Proceduralizing Regulation: Part I' (2000) 20 *Oxford J. of Legal Studies* 597–614; J. Black, 'Proceduralizing Regulation: Part II' (2001) 21 *Oxford J. of Legal Studies* 33–58.

the preferences of others, the varieties of perspectives on the problem the regimes addresses, and the potential for rethinking not only the rules and instruments of the regime, but also its objectives.[66] Such an approach may be tied to the idea, discussed above, of developing novel forms of democratic governance, at transnational level, which are not tied to national electoral politics.

CONCLUSIONS

The emergence and increasing significance of transnational private regulatory regimes presents many challenges. Perhaps the central challenge identified in this article concerns the possibility of reconceptualizing the global public sphere so as better to embrace TPR regimes in their myriad forms, such that they are recognized as having similar potential for legitimacy as national and international governmental bodies. Such recognition raises challenges for TPR regimes to develop strategically their own institutional structures and processes, and also their links to others, notably governments, as part of that underpinning.

A central issue emerging from processes of globalization generally concerns the role of the state. Whilst the 'myth of the powerless state'[67] has been effectively challenged, the nature of state activity is being transformed by international and transnational activity. Much of the emphasis in discussion of these issues has focused on the effects of international governance on state capacity and the increasing interdependence of states in fields such as financial regulation. TPRERs raise different sorts of issues concerning the role of the state. We suggest that just as international organizations might increasingly use their capacity for steering or 'orchestration' to enrol the capacity of private actors in transnational governance,[68] so also may national governments enhance the range of their activities, complementing participation in international governance with direct engagement with TPR. It has long been observed that national governments make extensive use of transnational corporate capacity, for example, by enrolling airlines in immigration control and banks in monitoring and reporting money laundering.[69] A wider recognition of both the effectiveness and legitimacy potential for such engagement with transnational private regulatory capacity might underpin stronger

---

66 C. Scott, 'Reflexive Governance, Regulation and Meta-Regulation: Control or Learning?' in *Reflexive Governance: Redefining the Public Interest in a Pluralistic World*, eds. O. de Schutter and J. Lenoble (2010).

67 L. Weiss, *The Myth of the Powerless State* (1998).

68 K.W. Abbott and D. Snidal, 'International Regulation Without International Government: Improving IO Performance Through Orchestration' (2010) 5 *Rev. of International Organization* 315–44.

69 J. Gilboy, 'Implications of "Third Party" Involvement in Enforcement: The INS, Illegal Travellers, and International Airlines' (1997) 31 *Law and Society Rev.* 505–30.

18

engagement with both NGO-led and business-led TPRERs.[70] Increasing emphasis on TPRERs is part of a wider set of changes within which national governments are seen less as representative of sovereign states and more as central actors in national, transnational, and international governance.

If the constitutional standing and legitimacy of TPRERs can be effectively resolved, the potential benefits for governance are significant. The remoteness of global regulation from electoral politics has inhibited inter-governmental regulatory governance from achieving similar legitimacy to national regulatory regimes and, to some extent, undermined claims to effectiveness also. The necessity for TPRERs to find alternative sources of legitimacy based in procedural and other mechanisms may enable them to achieve stronger legitimacy than inter-governmental regimes. It is not unreasonable to hypothesize that the combination of direct participation of market actors and the interdependence of such actors with both NGOs and governments within many TPRERs has the potential to combine advantages both for effectiveness and legitimacy as compared with inter-governmental regimes.

---

70 D. Vogel, 'The Private Regulation of Global Corporate Conduct: Achievements and Limitations' (2010) 49 *Business & Society* 68–87.

19

JOURNAL OF LAW AND SOCIETY
VOLUME 38, NUMBER 1, MARCH 2011
ISSN: 0263-323X, pp. 20–49

New Foundations of Transnational Private Regulation

FABRIZIO CAFAGGI*

In section I of this article, the factors driving towards the emergence of new transnational private regulation (TPR) are identified in comparison with, on the one hand, merchant law and, on the other, international public regimes. In section II, the focus is on the private sphere, looking at both the different conflicts of interests arising in the regulatory relationships and the need for governance responses. In section III, institutional complementarity between public and private regimes is examined. In light of this approach, the claim that differences between public and private at the global level exist is substantiated. The public-private divide is analysed, comparing the domestic and the transnational level. Four different models of interaction are identified: hybridization, collaborative law-making, coordination, and competition. Section IV summarizes the results of the analysis, reconsidering the boundaries between public and private at transnational level.

INTRODUCTION

Transnational private regulation (TPR) constitutes a new body of rules, practices, and processes, created primarily by private actors, firms, NGOs, independent experts like technical standard setters and epistemic communi-

* Faculty of Law, University of Trento and Department of Law, European University Institute, I-50014 San Domenico di Fiesole (FI), Italy
fabrizio.cafaggi@eui.eu

This paper is part of a wider research project that I coordinate at the EUI\RSCAS on 'The Constitutional Foundations of Transnational Private Regulation. Governance Design', supported by HIIL. Information and papers on the research project can be found at <www.privateregulation.eu>. I developed this paper while teaching a course on transnational regulation in the fall of 2009 at NYU School of Law and a seminar at EUI in the fall of 2010. I am also thankful for conversations with Eyal Benvenisti, Cindy Estlund, Katharina Pistor, and Dick Stewart who provided me with a rich and stimulating intellectual environment. Thanks to Linda Senden, Colin Scott, Peer Zumbansen and, in particular, to Tony Prosser for useful comments on previous drafts and to Federica Casarosa and Rebecca Schmidt for research and editorial assistance. The usual disclaimer applies.

ties, either exercising autonomous regulatory power or implementing delegated power, conferred by international law or by national legislation. Its recent growth reflects, first, a reallocation of regulatory power from the domestic to the global sphere and, second, a redistribution between public and private regulators. When in place, TPR produces strong distributive effects both among private actors and between them and nation states. It differs both from global public regulation and from conventional forms of private rule making identifiable with the merchant law. The main differences concern both actors and effects.

TPR differs from international regulation primarily because rule making is not based on states' legislation. It is, rather, centred around private actors, interacting with international organizations (IO) and intergovernmental organizations (IGO). This is not to say that states do not take part in and are not affected by TPR. TPR emphasizes to a greater extent the role of the state as a rule taker as opposed to a rule maker.[1] It produces direct effects on participants to the regime without the need for states' legislative inter-mediation. However, it still lacks a comprehensive and integrated set of common principles. The toolbox of regulatory instruments differs significantly from that developed in the domain of public international law. Private regulatory regimes are sector specific, driven by different constituencies often conflicting because they protect divergent interests. Standards are generally stricter than those defined by international public organizations, when they exist. The complementarity between public and private often encompasses multiple standards, where the public provides minimum mandatory common standards and the private voluntary stricter ones.

TPR endorses a broad definition of the private sphere, going beyond industry to include NGO-led regulators and multi-stakeholder organizations. New players have entered the regulatory space: in particular NGOs, who are generally outside the domain of merchant law or functionally equivalent forms of private law making. TPR overcomes the traditional limitations that exist in the relationship between regulators and regulated, thereby departing also from conventional self-regulatory regimes. It can be identified in very different forms, ranging from those fostered by trade associations and market players to those promoted by NGOs and trade unions.[2] It comprises:
(i)   regulatory frameworks concerning individual enterprises, promoted by shareholders or by other stakeholders;
(ii) the product and process regulation of small enterprises by large multinational corporations along the supply chain;

---

1   For this distinction and its implications see J. Braithwaite, *Regulatory Capitalism* (2008).
2   Different goals are pursued by these two forms. Individual firms often regulate to promote product differentiation, and trade associations to standardize and make rules uniform, sometimes creating barriers to entry for newcomers.

(iii) the regulation of financial aspects of firms governed by rating agencies and accounting firms;

(iv) the regulation of transnational employment standards promoted by unions and international organizations such as ILO;

(v) the regulation of environmental aspects.

TPR is generally voluntary, mirroring domestic private regulation. Parties who wish to join the regulatory bodies participating in the regime are free to do so, however once they are in, they are legally bound and violation of the rules is subject to legal sanctions.[3] This freedom can be partially limited when participation in a private regime and compliance with its standards is the condition for access to other regimes which provide market opportunities for the regulated entities. Often, subscription to a regime or compliance with a set of standards condition the access to the market or the ability to compete, thereby reducing the freedom to choose. Voluntariness can be undermined by public intervention changing the regime from voluntary to compulsory. Less frequent than those observed at the domestic level are the examples of delegated private regulation to be found at the transnational level, where an explicit act of delegation by an IO or an IGO empowers a private body with regulatory power and makes the regime mandatory for the regulated entities. More diffused are the examples of retrospective judicially recognized private regulation, when domestic courts recognize privately produced standards as part of customary public or private (international) law, making it binding.

TPR, like many international regimes, produces direct effects beyond the signatories or members of the organization. The effects of these regulatory regimes are far-reaching, going well beyond the sphere of the members of the regulatory body. This produces a knock-on effect on the behaviour of a wide number of regulated parties and beneficiaries which have not given their consent beforehand to the rules they are subject to. The conventional principles of contract law and those of private organizations are useful (though inadequate) in describing these new forms and need to be rethought and transformed to accommodate the regulatory functions.[4] Unlike public international law where *jus cogens* and custom operate as spreading mechanisms to produce legal effects on all states beyond the signatories, TPR has not yet developed common principles with general binding effects; rather, each sector has devised its own tools.[5]

TPR subscribes to a comprehensive concept of regulation which includes

---

3 This definition differs from that of standards adopted in the Agreement on Technical Barriers to Trade (TBT) under Annex 1.

4 The inadequacies of private law for regulatory purposes are examined by H. Collins, *Regulating Contracts* (1999).

5 An interesting comparison, beyond the scope of this paper, concerns the function of public interest norms in public international law and that of public function\public interest in transnational private regulation.

22

both responses to market/government failures and distributional effects.[6] It starts from the conventional definition that includes rule-making, monitoring, and enforcement. It focuses on how shifting from public to private and from domestic to transnational may redistribute financial resources and institutional capabilities from developed to developing economies and, within the latter, among different stakeholders. It does not subscribe to a notion of regulation which necessarily restricts and limits private parties' freedom; it seeks to distinguish between capability-enhancing and capability-reducing regulatory regimes.

This paper proceeds as follows. In section I, the factors driving towards the emergence of new TPR are identified in comparison with, on the one hand, merchant law and, on the other, international public regimes. In section II, the focus is on the private sphere, looking at both the different conflicts of interests arising in the regulatory relationships and the need for governance responses. In section III, institutional complementarity between public and private regimes is examined. In light of this approach, the claim that differences between public and private at the global level exist is substantiated. The public-private divide is analysed, comparing the domestic and the transnational level. Four different models of interaction are identified: hybridization, collaborative law-making, coordination, and competition. Section IV summarizes the results of the analysis, reconsidering the boundaries between public and private at transnational level.

I. THE EMERGENCE OF NEW TPR: DRIVERS AND PATTERNS

The growth of TPR is often associated, if not made dependent upon, the shortcomings of the regulatory state as a global regulator.[7] These weaknesses fostered the emergence of international institutions in the first half of the last century, followed by the development of transnational private regulators in the second half and, particularly, in the last quarter of the twentieth century.[8]

---

6 See J. Stiglitz, 'Regulation and failure' in *New Perspectives on Regulation*, eds. D. Moss and J. Cisternino (2009) 12.

7 See K.W. Abbott and D. Snidal, 'Governance triangle' in *The Politics of Global Regulation*, eds. W. Mattli and N. Woods (2009) 50. On the correlation between globalization and the increasing power of transnational private actors, see A.C. Cutler, *Private Power and Global Authority: Transnational Merchant Law in the Global Political Economy* (2003).

8 The increasing influence of private power in the global sphere has been observed for a long time. See Y. Dezalay and B.G. Garth, *Dealing in Virtue. International Arbitration and the Construction of a Transnational Legal Order* (1996); Cutler, id.; S. Sassen, *Territory, Authority, and Rights from Medieval to Assemblages* (2006); G.P. Callies and P.C. Zumbansen, *Rough Consensus and Running Code* (2010). The question had been already debated in the thirties in the United States with the pioneering work of Jaffe. See L. Jaffe, 'Law Making by Private Groups' (1937) 51 *Harvard Law Rev.* 201–53, at 213.

The transformations brought about by the new private regulatory regimes have also modified the unit of analysis, moving from regulatory state to regulatory capitalism.[9] This change concerns not only rule making but also compliance and enforcement.[10]

The increasing role of non-state regulators, both at domestic and transnational level, has not cancelled the differences between private and public but has forced a reconsideration of their functions and the boundaries between the two spheres.[11] In particular, it obliges one to ask whether private transnational institutions should be considered as alternatives to international organizations or whether they complement them at the global level and, in a multi-level structure, nation states at domestic level.[12] Clearly the answer to this question depends on the degree of assimilation between public and private that is believed to exist.[13] The consolidation of effective TPR frequently occurs when strong public institutions are in place to complement rather than supplement public regulation at the domestic level.[14] Thence effective private regulation often consolidates in combination with strong public institutions. However, it is also possible that TPR precedes the creation of public regimes when, in order to fill regulatory gaps, private organizations design new markets and new institutions to be later supplanted by hybrids.

The emergence of a new generation of TPR is linked to different factors: some are related to the institutional dimension, others more to the economic consequences of market and trade integration.[15] Market liberalization and the

---

9 See D. Levi-Faur and J. Jordana, 'The Rise of Regulatory Capitalism: The Global Diffusion of a New Order' (2005) 598 Annals of the Am. Academy of Political and Social Sci. 200–17; D. Levi-Faur, 'Varieties of Regulatory Capitalism: Sectors and Nations in the Making of a New Global Order' (2006) 19 Governance 363–6, at 363.

10 See Braithwaite, op. cit., n. 1, p. 185 ff.

11 The presence of non-state actors in the global governance system is seen by many as a characteristic of global governance. See A. von Bogdandy, P. Dann, and M. Goldmann, 'Developing the Publicness of Public International Law: Towards a Legal Framework for Global Governance Activity' (2008) 9 German Law J. 1375–400, at 1378 ff.

12 See Abbott and Snidal, op. cit., n. 7, p. 66.

13 Those who claim that private actors exercising regulatory authority should be considered functionally equivalent to public actors and thus be subject to the same regime erase the complementarity. My claim is that functional – let alone structural – assimilation is a mistake and the distinction between public and private should be maintained even within a common set of principles concerning compliance with democracy and the rule of law.

14 Food safety provides a good illustration of a much wider phenomenon which concerns many sectors.

15 See G.K. Hadfield, 'The Public and Private in the Provision of Law for Global Transactions' in Contractual Certainty in International Trade: Empirical Studies and Theoretical Debates on Institutional Support for Global Economic Exchanges, ed. V. Gessner (2009); J. Davis, 'Privatizing the Adjudication of International Commercial Disputes: The Relevance of Organizational Form' in The Enforcement of Transnational Private Regulation, ed. F. Cafaggi (2011, forthcoming).

24

diffusion of universal fundamental rights have been powerful drivers of transnational regulation, generating sector-specific regimes, often in conflict. In many instances, they develop to increase prevention and deterrence for risk that can no longer be monitored and managed.[16] Consensus exists over the weaknesses of nation states in regulating markets that operate across state boundaries.[17] Similarly, the difficulties of individual states in securing compliance with fundamental rights have been underlined.[18] Divergences emerge in relation to the role of states in trans-nationalized regulation.[19] Some believe that they lose their intended role to become rule takers; others claim that they maintain a dominant position.[20] The list that follows exemplifies some of the factors contributing to the emergence and consolidation of TPR.

1. The need for international harmonization

The most frequently identified rationale is the need to overcome normative fragmentation of market regulation, often associated with divergent state legislation.[21] Sometimes, however, TPR reacts to divergent private regulatory regimes in place at the local level by generating new uniform private rules at the transnational level.[22] The creation of a TPR may thus be a response to either the multiplication of private regimes or diverging domestic public legislation. The harmonization of rules, within which private harmonization has gained importance, constitutes one response to normative fragmentation. Harmonization may be driven by general objectives or by specific ones. The fragmentation of state legislation, for example, constitutes a barrier to trade and one that has been tackled by trade regimes, promoting standardization. Delegation to IGO constitutes a different partial response to fragmentation. However, this delegation is often limited to standard setting with limited implementation capacity.[23]

16   This is clear in the area of product safety and in particular that of food safety. See C. Coglianese, A. Finkel, and D. Zaring (eds.), *Import Safety. Regulatory Governance in the Global Economy* (2009).
17   See B. Kingsbury, N. Krisch, and R.B. Stewart, 'The Emergence of Global Administrative Law' (2005) 68 *Law and Contemporary Problems* 15–62, at 16; Abbot and Snidal, op. cit., n. 7.
18   See J. Ruggie, *Protect, Respect and Remedy: a Framework for Business and Human Rights* (2008).
19   See A.C. Cutler, V. Haufler, and T. Porter, *Private Authority and International Affairs* (1999); Cutler, op. cit., n. 7; Sassen, op. cit., n. 8.
20   D. Drezner, *All Politics is Global* (2007).
21   See W. Leebron, 'Lying Down with Procrustes: An Analysis of Harmonization Claims' in *Economic Analysis of Fair Trade and Harmonization*, eds. J. Baghwati and R.E. Hudec (1996) 41.
22   Legal harmonization by private parties can translate into an agreement similar to a treaty or the creation of an organization comparable to an IO or an IGO.
23   Abbott and Snidal, op. cit., n. 7, p. 67. But see, in relation to ILO, L.R. Helfer, 'Monitoring Compliance with Unratified Treaties: The ILO Experience' (2008) 71 *Law and Contemporary Problems* 193–218.

A more recent phenomenon is the proliferation of TPR at the global level.[24] Many competing TPRs have emerged in the area of food safety and that of environmental protection, with numerous certification processes, applying different standards to same products or processes.[25] Even within the global dimension, the initial response to local fragmentation through the emergence of transnational regulation has changed into a different form of international fragmentation, driven by private regulatory competition. We therefore observe a shift from local to global fragmentation within the private field, the former primarily territorial, the latter predominantly functional.

2. The weaknesses of states as global rule-makers

Public regulation by states through international treaties has proven difficult to achieve and even when international standards exist, they are rarely uniformly implemented.[26] Often, though not always, TPR emerges as a response to intergovernmental failures, such as the inability to reach political consensus over a proposed international treaty. Evidence suggests that failure to reach political consensus over treaty-based solutions has triggered TPR.[27] In the environmental field, the failures of the Rio Conference in 1992 facilitated the emergence of private NGO-led forestry protection regimes. Another example can be seen in the emerging private carbon-trading systems that complement the existing pattern of regimes regulating climate change counter-measures.[28]

3. The weaknesses of state regulation in monitoring compliance with international standards

State institutions are not only often ineffective rule makers but they are also poor at monitoring and enforcing violations of transnational regimes.[29]

---

24 See D. Vogel, 'The Private Regulation of Global Corporate Conduct' in Mattli and Woods, op. cit., n. 7, pp. 151 ff., highlighting differences from conventional self-regulation; also pp. 156 ff. In a different perspective, see A. Peters et al. (eds.), *Non-State Actors as Standard Setters* (2009).

25 See E. Meidinger, 'Private Import Safety Regulation and Transnational New Governance' in Coglianese et al. (eds.), op. cit., n. 16, p. 233.

26 See, generally, Abbott and Snidal, op. cit., n. 7, pp. 59, 67.

27 There is wide consensus over the birth of private forestry certification systems. See, for an overview, E.E. Meidinger, 'The Administrative Law of Global Private – Public Regulation: the Case of Forestry' (2006) 17 *European J. of International Law* 47–87.

28 See R.O. Keohane and D.G. Victor, *The Regime Complex for Climate Change* (2010) 26.

29 These difficulties, among other factors, have lead to the supply-chain approach in food safety where direct responsibility for ensuring safety has been distributed among the private operators of the supply chain. See S. Henson and J. Humphrey,

Therefore, the effectiveness of states' implementation is often questioned.[30] Frequently transnational rule making is complemented by domestic administrative and judicial enforcement giving rise to vertical complementarity between private and public. The use of domestic monitoring frequently brings about conflicting results which contradict the fundamental rationales of transnationalizing regulation.[31] Localized monitoring follows the incentives of individual states or litigants in courts which may not be aligned with those of transnational regimes. Monitoring resources might be deployed to promote domestic interests at the expense of the protection of the global common good, as the experience of environmental regulation shows. This is not to say that domestic monitoring and enforcement does not or should not play a role. On the contrary, the role of national courts is quite significant. However, it is important to recognize its limitations. Food safety and financial markets provide illustrations of how countries importing goods and capital may be unable to control violations that have occurred in exporting states.[32] States' implementation of transnational regulation may be biased. The emergence of TPR with innovative implementation techniques attempts to respond to these shortcomings.

4. *The weaknesses of public international law*

The weakness of individual states and the necessity of multilateral responses contributed to the growth of international law beyond its conventional domains at the beginning of the twentieth century.[33] The dynamics of

The Impacts of Private Food Safety Standards on the Food Chain and on Public Standard-Setting Processes (2009); OECD, 'Final Report on Private Standards and the Shaping of the Agro-Food System', AGR/CA/APM (2006) 9/FINAL (2006).

30 See the critique of conventional international law and its weaknesses by Kingsbury et al., op. cit., n. 17, p. 15; B. Kingsbury and N. Krisch, 'Introduction: Global Governance and Global Administrative Law in the International Legal Order' (2006) 17 *European J. of International Law* 1–13; von Bogdandy et al., op. cit., n. 11; B. Kingsbury, 'The Concept of "Law" in Global Administrative Law' (2009) 20 *European J. of International Law* 23–57, and responses by A. Somek, 'The Concept of "Law" in Global Administrative Law: A Reply to Benedict Kingsbury' (2009) 20 *European J. of International Law* 985–95 and Ming-Sung Kuo, 'The Concept of "Law" in Global Administrative Law: A Reply to Benedict Kingsbury' (2009) 20 *European J. of International Law* 997–1004.

31 See F. Cafaggi, 'Enforcing Transnational Private Regulation' and R. Stewart, 'Enforcement of Transnational Public Regulation' in Cafaggi, op. cit., n. 15.

32 Food safety crises in the nineties showed that importing states were unable to control food safety hazards and changed the approach, placing monitoring responsibility on the supply chain. This shift in monitoring policies from public to private produced additional transformations in rule making, increasing transnational private regulation by retailers. See Henson and Humphrey, op. cit., n. 29 and, for a broader picture, Coglianese et al., op. cit., n. 16.

33 M. Koskenniemi, 'History of International Law since World War II' in *Max Planck Encyclopedia of International Law* (2007).

27

regulatory power transfers, from the nation-states to international organizations, has profoundly changed since then.[34] The central role of domestic executives and IGOs has been partly substituted by the creation of networks and other forms of international players outside the conventional forms recognized by public international law.[35]

The international system is still based on the assumption that state responsibility is the primary factor in ensuring effective incentives to implement transnational regulation. The limits of a system based on state responsibility in ensuring the effectiveness of the regulatory regimes suggest (i) the necessity of overcoming the state's normative intermediation problems and (ii) of establishing the direct applicability of transnational regimes towards parties affected by the regulatory processes.[36] The limits of international law and, in particular, the inability of non-state actors and international public entities to regulate rule making has generated a number of effects.[37] On the one hand, a transformation of the public sphere can be observed with the emergence of new bodies, applying new principles of global administrative law (GAL).[38] On the other hand, these limitations have favoured the development and consolidation of TPR.

5. Technology

Another factor contributing to the growth of TPR is the development of new technologies that redistribute rule-making power in favour of private actors and transform the role of the nation state.[39] ICT and, in particular, internet regulation provides an illustration of the role of technology in shifting rule-making power from national to transnational and from public to private.[40] In fact, the characteristic feature is that of hybridity. The conflict and the subsequent agreement between Google and the People's Republic of China

---

34 J.E. Alvarez, *International Organizations as Law Makers* (2006).
35 A.-M. Slaughter, *A New World Order* (2004); A.-M. Slaughter, 'Global Government Networks, Global Information Agencies, and Disaggregated Democracy' (2003) 24 *Michigan J. of International Law* 1041–76.
36 id. (2003), p. 1056. On legitimacy deficits of such networks in general, see S. Picciotto, 'Networks in International Economic Integration: Fragmented States and the Dilemmas of Neo-liberalism' (1996) 17 *Northwestern J. of International Law and Business* 1014–56, at 1045.
37 Kingsbury et al., op. cit., n. 17; A. Cassese, 'Administrative Law Without the State? The Challenge of Global Regulation' (2005) 37 *J. of International Law and Politics* 663–94; von Bogdandy et al., op. cit., n. 11, pp. 1375 ff.
38 See Kingsbury, id., p. 17.
39 Cassese, op. cit., n. 37.
40 See R. Deibert, J. Palfrey, R. Rohozinski, and J. Zittrain (eds.), *Access Denied, The Practice and Policy of Global Internet Filtering* (2008); Y. Benkler, *The Wealth of Networks: How Social Production Transforms Markets and Freedom* (2006); D. Tambini, D. Leonardi, and C. Marsden, *Codifying Cyberspace – Communications Self-Regulation in the Age of Internet Convergence* (2008).

28

highlights new modes of regulation at the global level based on contracts between multinational firms and states.

IPR constitutes another area where international public goods and states' interests can collide.[41] Although it is clear that states maintain a significant role, especially in relation to security and the protection of fundamental rights, the regulatory patterns show an increasingly transnational private dimension.[42]

6. Technical standards

Technical standards have long been produced by private actors at the international level. They do not constitute a factor in the emergence of private regulation as such but influence the emergence of private regulatory regimes. In particular, they play a role in the development of new forms of private regulation. Transnational public and private regulation in relation to safety have, for example, adopted a supply-chain approach driven by the use of technical standards difficult for states to monitor. The boundaries between normative and technical standards have blurred and, even if they can still be kept distinct, the impact of technical standardization on private regulation is strong. Technical standardization bodies have increased their influence on regulatory regimes, moving from product to process standards and broadening of quality management standards. Private regulation often represents a combination of different standards, some of them directly produced by the private regulator, others by the technical standard-setters, subsequently endorsed or adopted by private regulators.[43]

Technical standards, produced by private or hybrid organizations, affect several dimensions of TPR: they contribute to a reduction of differences across sectors since there is a common denominator for technical standards concerning quality management control and they also reduce the distance between public and private transnational regulation. Often, both public and private bodies refer to the same technical standards, as the examples of food safety, environmental protection, and corporate social responsibility demonstrate.

7. Governance of distributional effects

The development of TPR produces important distributional effects connected with the costs of regulation and its impact. These effects cannot be

---

41 See the different contributions in K.E. Maskus and J.H. Reichmann, *International Public Goods and Transfer of Technology under a Globalized Intellectual Property Regime* (2005).
42 See Mattli and Woods, op. cit., n. 7.
43 Examples range from ISO to professional standards like those drafted by IASB in the accounting profession.

29

governed only by the fiscal policies of nation states. There is a cost transfer from states to private actors but also from Western developed economies to southern developing economies.[44] Symmetrically, there is a transfer of power from southern states to private actors in developed economies with the emerging role of BRIC (Brazil, Russia, India, and China).[45] The internalization of distributional effects has produced different responses. Sometimes, other private regimes have been created to manage distributional effects. For example, many NGO-led regimes have emerged to provide distributional responses to public and private trade regimes. In other instances, internal governance structures have tried to govern the redistribution of resources and capabilities. Specialized IGOs continue to play an important role in ensuring the growth of regulatory capabilities but are increasingly supported by new private actors.

A second distributional effect is related to the impact of private regulation and the distribution of rule-making power on market structures, particularly on the degree of market concentration and the distribution of market power among private actors according to the size of the regulated firms. Therefore, there are the distributional consequences of a reallocation of regulatory powers but also effects on the size of firms. It is difficult, if not impossible, for small suppliers to afford the costs of private regulation rendering it impossible to gain or maintain market access. As a result, private regulation increases the power and the market share of significantly sized suppliers and reduces the market share of small ones, driving some of them away.[46]

These factors are, at the same time, both causes and effects; they constitute, and may trigger in the future, the emergence of new regimes and institutions to address uneven distribution.[47]

---

44 The example of food safety is paramount. See Codex Alimentarius Commission (CAC), *Joint FAO/WHO Food Standard Programme: Considerations of the Impact of Private Standards* (2010), at <http://www.fsis.usda.gov/PDF/2010-CAC/cac33_13e.pdf>.

45 Private regulation is designed by associations mainly controlled by private actors, businesses, and NGOs located in Western countries, but it is implemented and monitored in developing economies. Thus the costs of compliance is often shifted to suppliers upstream and then partly transferred to final consumers in the West.

46 There is relative widespread consensus over the distributional effects of private regulation although the measurement of the effects vary significantly sector by sector. See, in the field of food safety, OECD, op. cit., n. 30; Henson and Humphrey, op. cit., n. 29; Y. Amekawa, 'Reflections on the Growing Influence of Good Agricultural Practices in the Global South' (2009) 22 *J. of Agricultural and Environmental Ethics* 531–57; L. Busch and C. Bain, 'New! Improved? The Transformation of the Global Agrifood System' (2004) 39 *Rural Sociology* 321–46. In the environmental field, for carbon footprint labelling, see S.G. Mayson, 'Carbon Footprint Labelling in Climate Finance' in *Climate Finance*, eds. R.B Stewart, B. Kingsbury, and B. Rudyk (2009) 283.

47 See F. Cafaggi and K. Pistor, 'The Distributional Effects of TPR', unpublished paper on file with the author.

II. DISENTANGLING THE PRIVATE SPHERE: EXPLORING CONFLICTS OF INTEREST AND RESPONSES FROM GOVERNANCE REGIMES

By now it should be clear that the private sphere is not homogeneous and needs to be disentangled.[48] TPR encompasses numerous regimes, reflecting the complexity of the private sphere.[49] Some are mainly driven by industries; some are promoted by NGOs, others by the joint endeavour of industry and NGOs, often complemented by public intervention, giving rise to tripartite or multiparty agreements.[50] While at first sight they are all governed by private actors, they pursue different objectives and incorporate multiple dimensions and degrees of public interest, depending on the composition of their respective governance bodies and the effects they have on the general public. Plurality of interests often translates into different regulatory strategies or a concentration on different stages of the regulatory process. As we shall see, while industry-driven regimes focus more on rule-making, NGO-led regulators are primarily concerned with firms' compliance and frequently deploy certification.[51] These differences are often reflected in the choice of governance models and enforcement mechanisms, particularly in the balance between judicial and non-judicial enforcement.[52] The relevance of governance in TPR highlights the necessity to include it as an additional dimension together with procedural and functional aspects in an inclusive approach to accountability.

Private actors have different, often conflicting, incentives for the creation and implementation of transnational private regimes. Their preferences may differ not only concerning the choice of the optimal level between state, regional, and global but also in relation to the normative architecture to be adopted by the specific regime. Certainly NGO-led private regulatory regimes differ remarkably from traditional forms of private rule making, but even industry-driven regimes, focused on regulatory needs, present very different features from those conventionally associated with merchant law.[53]

---

48 See Vogel, op. cit., n. 24, p. 156; D. Vogel, 'Private Global Business Regulation' (2008) 11 *Annual Rev. of Pol. Sci.* 261–82; G.C. Shaffer, 'How Business Shapes Law: A Socio Legal Framework' (2009) 42 *Connecticut Law Rev.* 147–84. In a different and closer perspective to the text, see D. Levi-Faur, 'The Global Diffusion of Regulatory Capitalism' (2005) 598 *Annals of the Am. Academy of Pol. and Social Sci.* 12–32.

49 For an interesting conceptual map, see Abbott and Snidal, op. cit., n. 7, pp. 57–62.

50 The tripartite model is frequent in the sector of labour and employment but it has also application in that of environment and food safety. The unilateral model is diffused in the area of financial regulation and e-commerce.

51 Compare, for example, Forest Stewardship Council or Marine Stewardship Council with IFRS in the accounting profession or IATA in the air transport.

52 See Cafaggi, op. cit., n. 31.

53 The differences are wider with the so-called European continental view and more limited with the American perspective where differences within merchant law are widely recognized.

31

Conflicts are not restricted to the different components of the private sphere but also within them. Within NGOs, conflicts may arise between value-based and interest-based organizations.[54]

In order to demonstrate how the combinations among private actors may lead to different regimes and, in particular, different governance structures, I build on the concept of regulatory relationship developed in earlier work.[55] This includes not only the regulator and the regulated but also the beneficiaries of the regulatory process, those who are supposed to benefit from compliance with the regulation and are harmed by their violations.

The use of a regulatory relationship structure, one which includes the beneficiaries, redefines the nature of responsiveness and the means through which effectiveness of the regulation should be measured. Effectiveness does not only measure regulatees' compliance but looks at the effects of the regulatory process on the final beneficiaries.[56]

The four following illustrations depict the different regulatory relationships depending on the dominant actors within the regulatory body; their brief description suggests the implications for rule making and conflicts of interest. The range of examples offered below is meant to illustrate that governance models have common features across sectors.

1. *Industry-driven*

This model represents an ideal type of structure where the regulator and regulated coincide whereas the beneficiaries are outside the regulatory body, that is, they are not members but are affected by the regulatory process. It is the opposite of a public regulation structure in which the regulator and regulated have to differ and capture of the regulator by the regulatees is one of the main governance problems.[57]

Examples of this model are trade associations regulating the conduct of their members or industry cartels created by market players. They often concur and the choice between the two variants is dependent upon the market structure and the representation and governance model of the associations.[58]

---

54 See Abbott and Snidal, op. cit., n. 7, p. 61.
55 See F. Cafaggi (ed.), *Reframing Self-Regulation in European Private Law* (2006) 3 and, for a more recent elaboration, F. Cafaggi, 'Governance of Transnational Private Regulation' in *Handbook of Governance*, ed. D. Levi-Faur (2011, forthcoming).
56 See F. Cafaggi, 'Compliance and Effectiveness in Transnational Private Regulation', on file with the author.
57 Differentiation does not imply lack of dialogue. The increased need for responsiveness has changed the regulatory model in the public domain, increasing forms of dialogue between the regulator and the regulated.
58 The hypothesis to be verified in empirical research is that, in oligopolistic markets, the powerful actors will form cartels while, in highly competitive markets, associations will play a more important role. However, in some cases, big players will use associations to exercise their powers, using cartels as purely informal mechanisms.

In the real world, even in industry-driven models, perfect coincidence between regulators and regulated is often lacking. Three examples show these divergences and their governance implications.

In the area of financial markets, accounting standards are generated by professional firms to regulate listed companies for the benefit of investors.[59] The International Accounting Standards Board (IASB) produces international financial reporting standards (IFRSs), adopted by firms to comply with requirements expressed by Stock Exchanges, the Financial Stability Board, and other entities.[60] Here, concurrence is not always at the maximum level between the regulators (a few professional firms operating in an oligopolistic market) and the regulated (their clients). The professional independence of the regulator from the regulated entities is highly disputed; pressure from public entities and, to a certain extent, market institutions has generated important transformation, and the due process handbook was meant to address some of the accountability problems arising out of the professional relationship between some of the regulators and the regulated.[61] The interests of the regulator and those of the regulated are de facto aligned, and incentives to monitor in the interest of the beneficiaries might be weak.

A second example can be found in the area of food safety when competing retail trade associations produce food safety standards to be applied along the supply chain by suppliers and retailers. This can be found only of the various private standard setting models developed in the last 15 years.[62] Trade associations' regulatory products are, for example, the codes produced by the British retail association, later endorsed also by the Dutch retail associations (BRC), or those drafted by the IFS (a Franco-German alliance). A more general example is the International Chamber of Commerce (ICC) which issues policy documents and standard contract forms in almost all relevant business sectors and hosts one of the most important arbitral institutions.[63] The difference between this and the second and the third

---

59 See T. Buthe and W. Mattli, *Private Global Regulation: The Politics of Setting Standards for International Products and Financial Markets* (2011); T. Buthe and W. Mattli, 'Global Private Governance: Lessons from a National Model of Setting Standards in Accounting' (2005) 68 *Law and Contemporary Problems* 225–62.

60 For an overview concerning SEs explicitly requiring listed firms to comply with IFRS, see at <http://www.iasplus.com/country/useias.htm>.

61 For instance, the board of IASB consists of 15 experts appointed by the IFRS board of trustees, according to either their experience in standard setting or as a member of the user, accounting, academic or preparer communities, see <http://www.ifrs.org/The+organization/Members+of+the+IASB/Members+of+the+IASB.htm>. See Buthe and Mattli, op. cit., n. 59; T. Buthe and W. Mattli, 'International Standards and Standard-setting Bodies' in *The Oxford Handbook of Business-Government Relations*, eds. D. Coen, G. Wilson, and W. Grant (2009) 440.

62 See OECD, op. cit., n. 29; see, also, GLOBALGAP, *General Regulations, Integrated Farm Assurance*, Part II 3.1(vii), available at: <http://www.globalgap.info/cms/front_content.php?idart=14>.

63 See ICC homepage: <http://www.iccwbo.org/id97/index.html>.

33

model below is not so much related to the issue of whether there is a single stakeholder or multi-stakeholders but, rather, to the lack of representation of the beneficiaries' interest in the governance body.

2. A second model, primarily organizational and led by NGOs

In this model, the regulators and regulated differ but regulators and (some) beneficiaries coincide. The regulatory body is governed by NGOs while the regulated are firms. This model is deployed in certification where NGOs define requirements to certify products and services that firms have to comply with in order to benefit the final consumers. But often these organizations contribute to the monitoring and enforcement of consumer rights.

Consumer International is an independent non-governmental organizations with members and affiliates. Its legal status is that of a not-for-profit company limited by guarantee regulated by English law. Full members are consumer organizations which must be not-for-profit and politically independent. Affiliate members can be private or government organizations.

Oxfam International is a foundation incorporated in the Netherlands. The foundation was founded in 1995 by a group of NGOs. It consists of 14 member organizations, called affiliates, each represented by a voting trustee on the board of trustees.[64] Oxfam is composed only of NGOs but its role as regulator is limited primarily to lobbying national governments. Another example is that of Amnesty International. Amnesty International started campaigning in 1961 and now has 2.2 million members in about 150 countries in the world.[65] As provided by its statute, Amnesty International 'consists of sections, structures, international networks, affiliated groups and international members'.[66] It also operates by means of the publication of reports that can raise controversial themes. Its main activity is related to monitoring rather than standard setting

3. The expert-led model

A different type of private regulation from those just described is primarily expert-led. This is generally the case for issues of technical standardization, though frequently their 'capture' by industry dilutes their neutrality and objectivity.[67] The definition of experts has changed over time and in some areas expertise has become much less hierarchical. In the field of internet

---

64 There is no governmental or industry involvement in the foundation, see constitution of Oxfam, at <http://www.oxfam.org/sites/www.oxfam.org/files/constitution_0.pdf>.
65 See <http://www.amnesty.org/en/who-we-are/history>.
66 See <http://www.amnesty.org/en/who-we-are/accountability/statute-of-amnesty-international>.
67 See H. Schepel, *Constitution of Private Governance* (2005).

34

governance, the diffusion of self-regulating epistemic communities has bloomed, giving rise to a multiplicity of non-profit organizations or informal networks. In this model the rules are mainly technical; the regulator is a private non-profit organization, supposedly independent from the industry and from the final beneficiaries but often subject to capture. The regulator differs from the regulated and from the beneficiaries and its legitimacy is based on expertise.

4. *The multi-stakeholder model*

A fourth category is the multi-stakeholder model where both the regulated and the beneficiaries are represented in the regulatory body with differences concerning interest representation. Occasionally public bodies are also part of the governance either directly or as observers. There are two variants of this model: one organizational and one contractual.

In the organizational variant, the regulatory bodies, associations, foundations, non-profit corporations, and for-profit organizations are composed of multiple constituencies. It should be pointed out that often the organizational model carries out regulatory tasks by using different types of regulatory contracts, frequently reaching outside the membership of the regulatory body. The two most recurring features are those of the federation (for example, a second-tier representative body of national organizations) or a functional multi-stakeholder model where both individuals and organizations participate. Within the governing body, different stakeholders are represented in the board and in the general assembly.

Even within multi-stakeholder organizations there are differences dependent upon the distribution of power among the constituencies. In some, there is a leading constituency, shaping the choice of regulatory regime and its enforcement mechanisms while leaving the others some degree of control by voice or exit. In others, the power is distributed symmetrically, often producing a more principle-based regulation which is later specified at the stage of implementation.[68] This model is best illustrated by ICANN in the field of internet governance. It is a non-profit public-benefit organization with the legal status of a corporation, organized under California law. ICANN is not based on membership. It is governed by a board of directors whose members are appointed by different, primarily technical, organizations on the basis of a global representation principle which should ensure wide geographical representation. The interesting features are related to the combination of technical and non-technical members of the governing board and to the nature of the regulated, which encompass international organizations, states, firms, and consumers.

68 Typically in multi-stakeholder models, regulation is incomplete at the stage of rule-making when compromises lead to vague rules. Regulatory contract completion occurs only later.

A second illustration is provided by the Forest Stewardship Council (FSC) and the Marine Stewardship Council (MSC). The former is an association, regulated by Mexican law.[69] The latter is a British-based company limited by guarantee and registered as a charity with the Charity Commission.[70] The FSC is composed of three chambers representing different interests (social and indigenous organizations, environmental organizations, and economic organizations) which are then coordinated by the general assembly and fully and equally represented on the multi-stakeholder board. Clearly the two chambers of indigenous and social organizations and environment organizations lead the FSC while the economic interests of industry are voiced by the third chamber, enjoying one third of the voting power.[71] Here, conflicts of interests between the regulator and regulated are less frequent since the regulator encompasses in its governing structure both the regulated and beneficiaries.[72] However, some conflicts might still arise and organizational responses are required.[73]

A third example is the International Swaps and Derivatives Association (ISDA).[74] This was born out of the initiatives of financial institutions and the technical advice of international law firms and has fundamentally defined the rules for the OTC (over-the-counter market).[75] The rules concerning transactions in swaps and derivatives are cast in a master agreement drafted by ISDA, and subsequently adapted and tailored to state legislation.[76] ISDA is an example of private regulation associated with soft law at international level and hard law at state level.

The organizational model also features collaboration among private and public actors. Examples including states can be found in the field of sports

---

69 See, for a good overview, E.E. Meidinger, C. Elliott, and G. Oesten, 'The Fundamentals of Forest Certification' in *Social and Political Dimensions of Forest Certification*, eds. E.E. Meidinger, C. Elliott, and G. Oesten (2003) 3; E.E. Meidinger, 'Multi-Interest Self-Governance through Global Product Certification Programs' in *Responsible Business? Self-Governance in Transnational Economic Transactions*, eds. O. Dilling, M. Herberg, and G. Winter (2008) 259–91.

70 The organizational structure consists primarily of three bodies: the Board of Trustees, the Stakeholder Council and the Technical Advisory Board.

71 See, for an overview of the organizational setup, <http://www.fsc.org/governance.html> for the FSC and <http://www.msc.org/about-us/governance/structure> for the MSC.

72 Meidinger, op. cit., n. 69.

73 See, for instance, reform of the enforcement system recently introduced in FSC. See, also, Meidinger id.

74 For a succinct description, see G. Morgan, 'Market Formation and Governance in International Financial Markets: The Case of OTC Derivatives' (2008) 61 *Human Relations* 637–60. For further information, see ISDA's homepage at <http://www.isda.org/>.

75 '*The association is composed of three categories (1) primary members (the sellers) (2) associate members (primarily law firms and expertise providers) (3) the subscribers.*' See ISDA Bylaws at <http://www.isda.org/>.

76 See ISDA Master Agreement (2002).

36

and corporate social responsibility: WADA and the UN Global Compact.[77] WADA is the world anti-doping agency in charge of regulating and monitoring rules regarding anti-doping. It is composed of private and public organizations representing different sports constituencies.[78] The UN Global Compact is a voluntary policy initiative launched by the UN in 2000 with the main goal of crystallizing ten universally accepted principles for corporate behaviour. Global Compact addresses, first and foremost, companies whose actions it intends to regulate. However, standards have been developed involving other stakeholder groups, such as governments, labour and civil society organizations, and the United Nations, as well.[79]

In the domain of expert-led organization we find multi-stakeholder organizations like ISO. It is an association incorporated in Switzerland and subject to the Swiss Civil code. Its membership is made up of national standard-setting bodies.[80] While in developed countries these bodies are primarily private, in developing countries they are mainly represented by governmental departments or agencies. ISO develops predominantly voluntary standards sold in the marketplace. This said, mandated adoption of ISO standards by international organizations is growing, featuring one instance of horizontal institutional complementarity.

The second variant is represented by the contractual model. It operates through regulatory contracts in the form of multilateral contracts, network contracts, and master agreements. Regulatory contracts are often used in the field of corporate social responsibility (CSR) but diffused also in other areas, from financial markets to environmental protection and food safety. Within CSR, the leaders are often retailers but it also includes suppliers, workers, and consumers.[81] In other circumstances, it is driven by producers but includes also distributors and consumers. This private regulatory model uses commercial contracts along the supply chain to coordinate and regulate the activity of different enterprises (that is, retailers and suppliers), and the relationships between second- or third-tier suppliers and their employees. The most powerful illustration is in the field of food safety where the specific endorsement of the supply-chain approach demonstrates the regulatory function of (bilateral and multilateral) contracts often in the network form.[82] Here, the main governance question is related to the incentives of retailers, often the most powerful players in the regulatory process, to act on

---

77 For an overview of the different models, see J.G. Ruggie, 'Business and Human Rights: The Evolving International Agenda', CSRI Working Paper no. 38 (2007).
78 WADA was founded in 1998 as an independent agency with foundation board, an executive committee, and several specialized committees, see <www.wada-ama.org/Documents/About_WADA/Statutes/WADA_Statutes_2009_EN.pdf>.
79 For a more detailed overview of the governance scheme, see <www.unglobalcompact.org/AboutTheGC/stages_of_development.html>.
80 See articles 3.1. and 3.1.1 of ISO Bylaws.
81 See Ruggie, op. cit., n. 77.
82 See CAC, op. cit., n. 44, p. 8.

37

behalf of the beneficiaries, employees of the suppliers and their final consumers. While incentives to regulate safety on behalf of the final consumers are rather powerful, even if safety is often a credence good, employment standards are often lacking or weak. In particular, the enforcement of labour and other CSR standards seems to be problematic since, unless strong pressure is exercised by consumers, significantly sized retailers might not have sufficient incentives to monitor, let alone enforce, violations.

This brief comparative account of the various models shows both the complexity of the private sphere but also the necessity to incorporate the beneficiaries into the analysis so as to engage in cross-sector analysis. The models described highlight various regulatory relationships defined by the choice of governance arrangement in each regime on the basis of the different positions occupied by regulatees and beneficiaries. They all represent a departure from traditional self-regulatory arrangements, where the regulators and regulated coincide whilst the beneficiaries are left out of the picture. The different positions of the beneficiaries, placed either inside or outside the organizations, generate different governance architectures shedding light on the overly simplistic representation of private regulation. Disentangling the private sphere permits one to reframe legitimacy questions depending on how conflicting interests are aligned or misaligned within the organizations.

Hence, these models present different legitimacy questions, associated with the different typologies of conflicts and illustrate different governance responses. A high degree of unsolved conflicts lowers both internal and external legitimacy. The different organizational options suggest that the distinctive feature is not only the internalization of the beneficiaries in the regulatory relationship but also the recognition and solution of conflicts among different interests of the regulated entities.[83] The challenges posed by the emergence of the new regimes concern the effectiveness of current organizational models in governing conflicts of interests and in providing accountability to parties who are external to the organization but internal to the regime.[84] In the next section we analyse the relationship between the private sphere and the public sphere, so as to identify how different features of institutional complementarity operate.

83 To simplify the classification we have implicitly assumed homogeneity of regulatees, while underlining that beneficiaries' interests can differ.
84 See, for a more detailed analysis of the governance dimension, Cafaggi, op. cit. (2011), n. 55.

38

III. THE PUBLIC/PRIVATE DIVIDE AND THE APPROACH OF INSTITUTIONAL COMPLEMENTARITY IN MULTILEVEL SYSTEMS

After disentangling the private sphere and providing a brief description of the different models, a new framework is needed to describe the interaction between the private and the public sphere at transnational level.[85] First, it is necessary to describe the changes in the allocation of rule-making power and then to try to infer which normative implications can be drawn.

The reallocation of rule-making power between public and private actors at state level has been taking place for at least four decades, when structural transformations of the regulatory state were initially promoted in the Anglo-American area and then spread across the Western world.[86] The change from the welfare to the regulatory model has further developed into the creation of different forms of cooperation and/or competition between public and private regulatory bodies.[87] The conventional division of tasks between global markets and nation-states has been profoundly transformed.[88] Not only have states withheld from direct intervention in the market by privatizing and regulating many activities but also the regulatory dimension has been radically transformed, giving rise to different forms of regulatory capitalism.[89] Private actors, as we have seen, have come to play new roles, engaging in different forms of private regulation. This phenomenon might imply various characterizations depending on (i) who is considered to be part of the private sphere (industry, experts, NGOs), (ii) what is the scope of the regulatory activity, and (iii) which sectors are examined (market regulation or fundamental rights).

Different forms have been employed, from express transfer of rule-making power to private actors to informal delegation, from co-regulatory arrangements with different allocation of tasks to shifts between *ex ante* regulation to *ex post* liability, triggering bargaining among litigants poten-

---

85 id.
86 See R. Baldwin and M. Cave, *Understanding Regulation* (1999); W. Streeck, *Reforming Capitalism* (2008); L. Bruszt and R. Holzhacker, *The Transnationalization of Economies, States, and Civil Societies* (2009); C. Scott, 'Regulatory Governance and the Challenge of Constitutionalism' in *Regulation After the Regulatory State*, eds. D. Oliver, T. Prosser, and R. Rawlings (2010); T. Prosser, *The Regulatory Enterprise* (2010).
87 See J. Black, 'Constructing and Contesting Legitimacy and Accountability in Polycentric Regulatory Regimes' (2008) 2 *Regulation & Governance* 137–64; C. Scott, 'Regulating Private Legislation', and T. Prosser, 'Regulatory Agencies, Regulatory Legitimacy and European Private Law' in *Making European Private Law*, eds. F. Cafaggi and H. Muir Watt (2008) at pp. 235 and 254 respectively. For a comparative analysis, see G. de Búrca and C. Scott (eds.), *Law and New Governance in the EU and the US* (2006); C.F. Sabel and J. Zeitlin, *Experimentalist Governance in the European Union: Towards a New Architecture* (2010).
88 See Abbot and Snidal, op. cit., n. 7.
89 Levi-Faur and Jordana, op. cit., n. 9.

tially translating into private regulation.[90] At the state level, these modes are constrained by constitutional limitations.[91] Delegation of law-making power is limited in many legal systems by 'state action' doctrines or functional equivalents; the limits are partly due to the general principles of the non-delegation doctrines, partly due to specific, often constitutional constraints, that states face when divesting themselves of their powers in favour of private actors.[92] These transfers are often interpreted as the consequence of decreased state capacities to regulate, either because of capture or because of a lack of technical expertise.

The search for legitimacy for these different regulatory forms requires different answers depending upon the origins and effects of the rule-making power.[93] Regimes based on freedom of contract and association have different legitimacy responses from those based on the protection of fundamental rights or the environment.

The transfer of rule-making power, however, is not the only form affecting its redistribution. In many contexts the newly globalized fields (like the internet or CSR) generate innovative modes of governance which translate into different forms of power sharing between public and private. What is the nature of the relationship existing between the reallocation of regulatory power at state and that at the international level between public and private actors?

Three distinctive features of the public sphere are modifying the relationship with the private sphere: the significantly increased use of soft law; the limited delegability of law-making power by IO and IGO to private regulators; the limited, although increasing, direct effects on private parties of public regulatory regimes. For reasons of space I will focus on the first dimension.

Soft law can be used either as an alternative or as a complement to private regulation. At transnational level, soft law may increase competition between public and private regulation and decrease cooperation when deployed as an alternative to private regulation. When used as a complement, it reinforces coordination since it needs private law to render its principles binding at domestic level. The expansion of soft law at the transnational level may reduce the number of 'formal' co-regulatory arrangements based on the combined use of public and private regulation and an increased retrospective

---

90 See G.D. Majone, 'International Regulatory Cooperation. A Neo-institutional Approach' in *Transatlantic Regulatory Cooperation*, eds. G.A. Bermann, M. Herdengen, and P. Lindseth (2001) 109; F. Cafaggi, 'Rethinking self-regulation in European Private Law' in Cafaggi, op. cit. (2006), n. 55.

91 See F. Cafaggi, 'Private Law Making and European Integration' in Oliver et al., op. cit., n. 86.

92 For a detailed analysis concerning the United States, see G.E. Metzger, 'Private Delegation, Due Process and the Duty to Supervise' in *Government by Contract*, eds. J. Freeman and M. Minow (2009) 291. For an overview, see Cafaggi, id.

93 Black, op. cit., n. 87.

40

recognition of privately designed standards by international organizations. Private law, especially at national level, may become an instrument to harden international soft law, albeit with limited reach, giving rise to vertical institutional complementarity.

While the preferences of private actors for international organizations choosing hard or soft law have been analysed to a limited extent, little work has been done on the influence of (and choice of) soft law on the forms and substance of transnational private regulation. Soft law is often coupled with self-regulation in a single category, unified by the assumed non-binding nature of both. I have shown in previous work that this is not an accurate account since private regulation is voluntary but binding and should not be identified with soft law.[94]

So far in this essay, the use of soft law has been associated with recourse to private regulation, emphasizing their complementarity. These regimes have been distinguished from those, dominant in domestic orders, combining hard law and private regulation. However, in certain conditions soft law may constitute an alternative rather than a complement to private regulation. It preserves the rule-making power held in public hands while providing a higher degree of flexibility and adaptability.

1. *Refining institutional complementarity*

Institutional complementarity may take different forms: horizontal complementarity when public and private regimes coexist at the transnational level; vertical complementarity when a transnational private regime is complemented by public legislation at the national level or vice versa. The two forms give rise to different forms of coordination and, consequently, different governance issues.

The institutional complementarity approach, developed in earlier work, suggests that at the transnational level the effectiveness of private regulation strongly depends on the credibility and legitimacy of public institutions, including that of the judiciary both at domestic and international level. But perhaps surprisingly, TPR contributes to a strengthening of the legitimacy of public regimes as well. The conventional view that ascribes legitimacy to the public sphere and effectiveness to the private is deeply unsatisfactory. It is the nature of complementarity between the spheres and the relationship between legitimacy and effectiveness which varies at the transnational level.[95]

In many circumstances, TPR regimes are functionally correlated to (i) the existence and (ii) the nature of public regimes. Institutional complementarity

---

94 See Cafaggi, op. cit. (2006), n. 55.
95 Such complementarity becomes particularly relevant when conflicting regimes attempt to externalize costs on the each other because the typical states' institutions that govern these processes are missing. Private macro-governance acquires greater importance.

between international public organizations and transnational private regulation may materialize in different ways depending on the specific regulatory function.[96] Within rule making there is a wide spectrum, from delegation to endorsement, from regulatory agreements with mutual obligations to public-private partnerships, including organizational integration with the creation of networks or other kinds of collaborative ventures. Each regulatory mode poses different problems of legitimacy, effectiveness, and their correlation.[97]

Transnational private rule making may complement international treaties or soft law or may be complemented by public enforcement through domestic courts. Complementarity may take place through forms of endorsement or recognition similar to that occurring at the national level, where the state recognizes self-regulatory arrangements of professionals or collective agreements between trade and consumer organizations. Often, private regulatory regimes are endorsed by international organizations and become binding, at least within the jurisdictions of those organizations.[98] For instance, CSR standards may be recognized by the ILO, and private standards produced by ISO may be endorsed by WTO when complying with SPS or TBT agreements.[99]

The claim in this article is that the public and the private spheres influence each other: the distribution between hard and soft law within the public domain affects the functions of TPR, while the choice among different regulatory models, implying different regulatory relationships, reflects but also affects the nature of the public international regime. When hard law, including international treaties, is in place, private regulation acts as a complement to specify rules and it tailors them to specific markets and,

---

96 It should be underlined that unlike law making by international organizations, in the field of transnational private regulation we are far away from the identification of common rules for all the regimes. The gap filler function is primarily played by different private domestic laws. Given their strong differences, the construction of a set of common principles is a very delicate and challenging task.

97 This is the key issue addressed by GAL. See Kingsbury et al., op. cit., n. 17, pp. 19 ff.; B. Kingsbury and R.B. Stewart, 'Legitimacy and Accountability in Global Regulatory Governance: The Emerging Global Administrative Law and the Design and Operation of Administrative Tribunals of International Organizations', at <www.iilj.org/aboutus/documents/LegitimacyAccountabilityandGAL.UNAT volumefinalAug82008.pdf>.

98 See, for example, the explicit recognition of the ISO/IEC system as internationally accepted standards by the TBT Agreement. See, on the financial markets sector, J. Black and D. Rouch, 'The Development of the Global Markets as Rule-Makers: Engagement and Legitimacy (2008) 2 Law and Financial Markets Rev. 218–33, at 223.

99 See Ruggie, op. cit., n. 77; J. Ruggie, 'Promotion and protection of all human rights, civil, political, economic, social and cultural rights, including the right to development' A/HRC/8/5 (2008); J. Stiglitz, 'Regulating Multinational Corporations: Towards Principles of Cross-border Legal Frameworks in a Globalized World Balancing Rights with Responsibilities' (2008) 23 Am. University International Law Rev. 451–558.

42

frequently, formal or informal delegation takes place. When soft law is chosen, private regulation mainly operates as a vehicle to harden soft law, providing binding force. In the former case, it increases effectiveness, in the latter, it confers higher legitimacy. Obviously there are TPR regimes that operate independently from any public regime and they seek legitimacy on different grounds.

IV. THE PUBLIC/PRIVATE DIVIDE AT TRANSNATIONAL LEVEL: PATTERNS AND INSTITUTIONS

This section provides a preliminary answer to the following questions: are the patterns of relationship between public and private regulation at the transnational level similar to or different from those occurring at national level? Do public and private regulators present similar or different governance features at domestic and transnational level? What are the features of the redistribution of rule-making power between public and private actors? What are the main determinants when this redistribution occurs?

It should be stated at the outset that the private-public distinction exists also at the transnational level but it displays very different features from those developed at state level. The modes of allocation of rule-making power between public and private actors at state level cannot simply be transposed at the transnational level.[100]

Differences between the public and private sphere concern, in particular, the legal framework. While international public law is composed of a general part, applicable to all states and international organizations, and a specific part binding only on the signatory states, TPR so far lacks a common legal framework and tends to be sector specific and influenced by domestic private law regimes. Furthermore, rules of interpretation differ. While in the public domain the rules are those of the Vienna Convention on the law of Treaties (articles 31, 32) in addition to the specific rules stated by each legislative instrument and the practice of institutions, in the field of TPR interpretation rules are those related to the instrument deployed to constitute the regime (contract, association, corporate law). They depend on the domestic system chosen to incorporate when the regulatory body takes on an organizational form and on the private international rule if a regulatory contract has been used to set up the system.

The shift from the national to the transnational level produces remarkable phenomena concerning the reallocation of rule-making power from the public to the private. Private power and authority has grown in the past years acquiring a larger regulatory share.[101] The apparent paradox is that the

---

100 See Cassese, op. cit., n. 37, pp. 670 ff.
101 See Cutler et al., op. cit., n. 19; J. Braithwaite and P. Drahos, *Global Business Regulation* (2000); Cutler, op. cit., n. 7.

transfer of regulatory power from public to private at transnational level occurs within the framework of the legalization of international relations, historically associated with the emergence of state and the public sphere.[102] This 'apparent' paradox explains the differences with other patterns of the growth of the private sphere which have coincided with de-juridification and de-legalization.[103] Strategic considerations entice private players to choose the transnational level. (Some) industries promote this evolution not only to respond to trade integration and international competition, but also to improve their relative position by enhancing their influence and effectiveness at transnational level hoping to have greater impact on domestic policy.

There are four different forms of transformation of the relationship between the public and private dimension: (i) hybridization; (ii) collaborative rule making; (iii) coordination; (iv) competition.[104]

(i)   *Hybridization* between private and public law tools occurs in both directions: administrative law principles are applied to private organizations exercising rule-making power at transnational level;[105] contract and organizational law rules and principles are applied to the activity of IO and IGO to regulate firms and other entities.

(ii) *Collaborative rule making* occurs when private and public actors engage in a process by which rules are jointly drafted.[106] A variant is when private actors draft rules and the public actors subsequently approve or endorse them.[107] Clearly, when the latter occurs, the private actor internalizes the principles upon which the public actor will endorse the private rules.[108] Collaborative rule making can take place within multi-stakeholder organizations encompassing both private and public actors or through regulatory contracts in the form of agreement or MoU.

---

102 There is a general phenomenon of the legalization of international relations. This is partly the consequence of increased interdependences, associated with systemic risks, which demand greater coordination and a global governance response. But it takes different forms and organizational models. On the issue of the legalization of international relations, see J. Goldstein, M. Kahler, R.O. Keohane, and A.-M. Slaughter, *Legalization and World Politics* (2001).

103 See G. Teubner (ed.), *Global Law Without a State* (1997).

104 For different perspectives see Kingsbury, op. cit., n. 30 and von Bogdandy et al., op. cit., n. 11.

105 See Kingsbury et al., op. cit., n. 17.

106 Often cited examples are the code of good practice for setting social and environmental standards by ISEAL and the UN Global Compact.

107 Such collaborative rule making occurs within a multi-stakeholder organization: for example, the Anti Doping Code drafted by the WADA.

108 One increasing phenomenon is the negotiation of standards between big MNCs and strong individual developing countries or clusters of them. On these phenomena in relation to financial markets, see K. Pistor, 'Global Network Finance: Institutional Innovation in the Global Financial Market Place' (2009) 37 *J. of Comparative Economics* 552–67.

(iii) *Coordination* implies interdependence between independent private and public regimes. Unlike collaborative rule-making, here the two regimes are autonomous but their regulatory activities are mutually influenced. Coordination has different goals. In some cases, coordination serves to improve deterrence. A typical example is that of a public regime defining due diligence in relation to compliance with private standards. In other instances, it increases effectiveness by using targeted monitoring of transnational rules. Coordination favours legal transplants; it promotes transfer of regulatory strategies and enforcement from private to public and vice versa, as is the case for the 'supply-chain approach' adopted in many public safety regimes.[109] Often private regulators design rules to be later endorsed by the public regulator, either through judicial or administrative recognition.

(iv) *Competition* between public and private regimes at transnational level occurs when private actors raise the standards defined by the public actor, thereby decreasing the legitimacy of public regulation and taking leadership without being subject to the procedural requirements applied to international public law regimes. To some extent, even competition can produce legal transplants when those who are winning the competition are imitated by newcomers. Competition takes place both in vertical complementarity between transnational regulators and states and in horizontal complementarity between IO and IGO and private regulators.

The four modes suggest that institutional complementarity may take different forms depending on: the identity of the participants and, in particular, which private actors play a dominant role; the instruments adopted, contractual or organizational; the objectives of the regulatory regimes – increasing legitimacy and/or improving effectiveness. The incentives for parties to adopt one or the other may vary depending on the sector, the level of market integration, and its structure. While it was emphasized that changes in the public sphere had been an important factor in determining whether and how private regulation developed, the forms of complementarity depend significantly upon the model of private regulators.

In relation to private parties, the different combinations of governance models between regulatees and beneficiaries may affect the choice. Empirical research is needed to clarify whether general patterns exist to distinguish between forms of complementarity selected by NGO-led regulators versus forms of complementarity chosen by industry-led private regulators. Linking the four models of TPR described earlier with the four modes of complementarity outlined here will provide new insights into how the transnational regulatory space is defined.

---

109 See F. Cafaggi, 'Legal transplants in TPR: New challenges for Comparative Law', on file with the author.

CONCLUSIONS

In this article, I have looked at the different models of TPR: (i) from pure self-regulatory regimes, characterized by the coincidence between regulators and regulated, to multi-stakeholders including business, NGOs, and public entities, encompassing both regulated and beneficiaries in their governance structure; (ii) from integrated forms of cooperation between public and private through regulatory contracts to formal or informal delegation beforehand, when the regulatory power is conferred on private regulators by IOs, IGOs or directly by international law; (iii) private regulation, endorsed after the event by public entities, through judicial or administrative recognition; (iv) guidelines and principles directing private parties with the threat of introducing hard-law legislation. Two distinguishing conceptual features characterize the approach taken here: the link between governance of the private regulator and regulatory activity, and the shift of focus from single organizations to regimes.

The link between governance and activity is built around the regulatory relationship. As has become clear when exploring the different models of regulatory relationship, the boundary of a private organization, exercising regulatory functions may be legally defined by membership. But often, the beneficiaries are outside the legal boundaries of the organization, albeit within the regime. Incorporating the beneficiaries in the regulatory relationship contributes to shifting from self- to private regulation while changing the nature of regulation as a collective good from a club to a semi-public one.[110] On the one hand, contemporary private regulation reduces the degree of excludability, typically a feature of club goods. On the other, it limits the degree of negative externalities by internalizing, within the regulatory process, the product and the interests of the final beneficiaries.

The shift from organizations to regimes permits the capture of both inter-organizational and intra-organizational dynamics in private regulation. The notion of regime in this context is not primarily based on who the members are but, rather, on what the effects of regulation might be. In the adopted framework, organization is an actor-based definition, whilst regime is an effect-based definition. Regimes as units of analysis allow a functional rather than a structural definition of regulation, fitting better with the purpose of analysing the scope of TPR. They define common rules to regulate the activities of regulated entities, often on behalf of third parties, the final beneficiaries of the regulatory process.

The global regulatory space is fast changing; new players have acquired powers and influence, partly at the expense of old and conventional players, partly occupying new fields, thereby posing challenges to the conventional

---

110 See Cafaggi, op. cit., n. 91, and A. Katz, 'Taking Private Ordering Seriously' (1996) 114 *University of Pennsylavania Law Rev.* 1745–63.

concepts of democracy, representation, and sovereignty. The growth of TPR reflects a redistribution of regulatory power from domestic to transnational levels and from public to private entities. This redistribution is, however, neither uniform nor uni-directional. In some circumstances, even the opposite pattern is observed shifting from private to public, with an increasing role for international public regulation, especially in terms of oversight of private regimes and a stronger role for regional institutions ranging from new political entities to trade agreements (EU, NAFTA, Mercosur).

The private sphere at the transnational level includes different components, often holding conflicting views on both the model of regulation and its enforcement. Changes in the private sphere have occurred over time both in the allocation of power between industry and NGOs but also within the same industry, where MNCs, located in developed economies, have different regulatory preferences from those of small and medium enterprises in developing countries. In this context, allocation of market power translates into the distribution of rule-making power among market players. Hence, market regulatory shares become slices of global sovereignty.

Conventional wisdom claims that private regulation provides the regulator with greater flexibility, both in terms of regulatory design and sanctions, while public hard law is more rigid but provides higher legal certainty and stability. In fact, TPR allows a much broader spectrum of sanctions, especially when one considers a combination of legal and non-legal measures. This picture, if at all convincing, has been seriously challenged by the increasing use of soft law which also provides greater flexibility as opposed to hard-law treaty-based regimes. The relationship between the private and public sphere has profoundly changed, giving rise to new combinations not yet fully explored.

Significant differences exist between the domestic and transnational levels. These differences are caused more by the transformation of the public sphere than the private one. The sweeping use of soft law as an instrument of international regimes modifies the functions of private law instruments to regulate firms' behaviour in the international arena. Often contract and tort are deployed to harden soft law at domestic level and make binding rules that would not otherwise have been enforceable. From this perspective, private law instruments lend strength and legitimacy to international soft-law regimes reversing the conventional view that private regulation is more effective but less legitimate than public regulation. From a broader institutional perspective, the general conclusion that effective private regulatory regimes arise when strong public institutions are in place holds for transnational regulation as well.

Soft law may operate either as an alternative or as a complement to private regulation. At the transnational level, it may increase competition between public and private regulation and decrease cooperation when deployed as an alternative to private regulation. When used as a complement, it requires private law to make its principles binding at domestic level.

47

But it can also affect the choice of private regulatory strategy, for example, between command and control and responsive regulation. In fact the increased expansion of soft law at the transnational level may reduce the number of 'formal' co-regulatory arrangements based on the combined use of public and private regulation and increase later recognition of privately designed standards by international organizations. Private law, especially at national level, may become an instrument used to harden international soft law, albeit with limited reach, giving rise to vertical institutional complementarity.

Unlike the conventional view that sees public and private regulation primarily as alternatives and suggests that public regulation should be chosen when private regulation fails, and vice versa, I have argued that strong public institutions are needed for private regulation to operate effectively and credibly. This is the institutional complementarity approach. Effective and legitimate private regulation requires both at the national and transnational levels, a very strong set of institutions operating within a solid constitutional framework.

It should, however, be recognized that private regulation does often, in practice, operate as a substitute for public regulation. This occurs because public regulation is slower, more costly, and less effective. When private regulation precedes, public regulation often follows and subsequently internalizes private rules and even practices by way of recognition after the fact in legislative or administrative acts or different forms of endorsement. Thus, descriptively, private regulation is both a complement and a supplement; normatively, it should primarily operate as a complement.

Complementarity operates not only within one stage of regulatory process (that is, standard setting) but also along the different phases. Recently public-private partnerships, engaging in cooperative rule making, have been complemented by a more complex architecture, where rule making is mainly carried out by one actor (for instance, the public as it is the case for UN) monitored by private actors at transnational level (jointly by firms and NGOs) and enforced at the national level by courts. These regimes imply the existence of both horizontal and vertical complementarities.

Horizontal complementarities occur when at the transnational level public and private regulatory regimes interact (this is the case for many food-safety regulatory regimes but it is also common in environmental law). This complementarity is reflected in the use of different regulatory instruments. However, TPR lacks a common legal framework, similar to that provided by international general law and develops specific tools to coordinate and solve conflicts.[111] TPR does not yet have a common set of principles to fill gaps for each regime. Domestic private law is primarily deployed to perform this function. However, given the differences among state private laws, this gap-

---

111 See Cafaggi, op. cit., n. 55.

filling method generates fragmentation and inconsistencies within the same regime.

Vertical complementarities occur when there is a multilevel hybrid regime: one activity (rule making) operates at transnational level and the other(s) at national level (for example, monitoring or enforcement or both). Sometimes the private regime is transnational and is implemented by public legislation at the state level (for example, accounting standards);[112] sometimes a public regime is defined by hard or soft law at the international level and implemented primarily by private regulation at the national level. Multi-level regimes imply coordination between both the transnational and the national level, but also among the different national levels. For example, in the case of decentralized enforcement, a multi-level regime needs coordination among national courts, enforcing the same regime in order to avoid too high a degree of differentiation. Incentives for judicial coordination may be fostered by legal provisions applying a duty of loyal cooperation which exists in the domain of public institutions and can be inferred from the principle of good faith in the domain of private institutions. Clearly, the judicial power to enforce such a duty is limited in relation to private-public multi-level system.

Within the private sphere, trans-nationalization produces significant rule-making transfers from developing to developed countries. These transformations take place in a context where public international hard law suffers from limitations concerning its scope and instruments, giving rise to soft law on the one hand, and transnational private regulation on the other. Private Western actors, including both firms and NGOs, have acquired more rule-making power.

The regulatory regimes discussed here are sector-specific and often represent conflicting interests at the global level. These include conflicts between industry and NGOs and trade unions, between large multinational corporations and small suppliers that require coordination and rules. Often domestic courts have provided techniques to define the boundaries and the jurisdiction over regulated entities and to secure compliance with democratic principles. Still these regimes – whose regulatory effects go well beyond the sphere of the regulator, encompassing regulated entities and beneficiaries that did not voluntarily opt in at the time of drafting – pose serious accountability challenges. They challenge states' sovereignty when regulating matters traditionally subject to domestic legislation. Their private nature limits the scope for judicial review by domestic courts and often allows escape from accountability mechanisms deployed in the domestic arena. Those challenges require normative responses that call for changes in the governance of private regulators and in the regulatory process to enhance voice and exit options for regulatory beneficiaries.

112 Advertising provides a good illustration of multi-level complementarity between transnational private law and 'regional' or state legislation.

JOURNAL OF LAW AND SOCIETY
VOLUME 38, NUMBER 1, MARCH 2011
ISSN: 0263-323X, pp. 50-75

Neither 'Public' nor 'Private', 'National' nor 'International': Transnational Corporate Governance from a Legal Pluralist Perspective

Peer Zumbansen*

This paper contends that the challenging nature of the regulation of global corporate conduct requires an adequately differentiated approach towards the identification and analysis of the norms in question. In part I, I review the context of 'state intervention' and 'market self-regulation', in which the current discussion of regulatory responses to the economic/financial crisis and the role of self-regulation occurs, before laying out the concept of 'transnational legal pluralism' in part II. In part III, I argue that an exemplary area such as corporate governance can best be understood as an instance of transnational legal pluralism, a field that becomes visible through a particular methodological lens. In part IV, I conclude by suggesting how the lessons of such a case study can contribute to an ongoing theoretical investigation into the nature of global regulatory governance, using the concept of 'rough consensus and running code'.

INTRODUCTION

Much of today's writing on 'global governance' presumes a fundamental gap between the domestic forms, institutions, and instruments of legal regulation on the one hand and what is perceived as a dramatic regulatory void on the

* Osgoode Hall Law School, York University, 4700 Keele St., Toronto, Canada M3J 1P3
pzumbansen@osgoode.yorku.ca

This paper was presented at the first annual conference on 'Transnational Private Regulation: Constitutional Foundations and Governance Design', University College Dublin, Ireland. Financial support from the Hague Institute for the Internationalisation of Law, at <www.hiil.org>, and from the Social Sciences and Humanities Research Council of Canada (grant no. 864-2007-0265) is gratefully acknowledged. Helpful feedback was provided by Fabrizio Cafaggi and Colin Scott and an anonymous reviewer. This paper partially draws on work developed in greater detail in G.-P. Calliess and P. Zumbansen, *Rough Consensus and Running Code: A Theory of Transnational Private Law* (2010).

global scale on the other. This anxiety is particularly accentuated with regard to border-crossing, global corporate activity, which is seen as having over time successfully escaped the reach of traditional, nation-state-based forms of regulation. As the literature on the challenges of regulating the conduct of multinational business corporations (MNCs) has been growing exponentially, the question remains, however, whether or not an answer to this alleged exhaustion of the regulatory state in the face of global corporate (mis-)conduct is likely to be found in the *extension* of the regulatory grasp of the nation state – or of international state bodies – in a kind of 'expanded jurisdiction' sense. By contrast, what appears to emerge from a continuing assessment by lawyers,[1] political scientists,[2] and economists[3] of the corporate, labour law, and human rights dimensions of MNC is a growing awareness of the need to approach the problem from what has fruitfully been referred to as a 'regulatory governance' perspective.[4] From this vantage point the challenge presents itself as no longer one of law's limits (or as the 'end of the state'), but as one which is foremost concerned with the way in which law operates, is created and enforced in the global arena. And from this perspective, then, we can begin to take into view the actually *existing* forms of corporate regulation. In other words, a theory of norm creation in the context of global market activities might not be found through a mere extension or *translation* of nation-state-based doctrine onto a rudimentarily defined sphere 'beyond' or 'outside' the nation state. What is needed, instead, is a theory that allows for reflection on the manifold ways in which norms have been emerging in the space between what we refer to as the 'domestic' on the one hand and the 'global' on the other. As elaborated in this paper, for a legal theory of global regulation, 'space' is not meant to depict a geographical realm, but instead a *methodological* one in which the meanings – and limitations – of our distinction between the 'national' and the 'global' can be addressed.

Such reflection must incorporate a high degree of empirical evidence of existing forms of self-regulation such as codes of conduct,[5] of best practices,

---

1 P. Muchlinski, *Multinational Enterprises and the Law* (2007, 2nd edn.); see, previously, D.F. Vagts, 'The Multinational Enterprise: A New Challenge for Transnational Law' (1969) 83 *Harvard Law Rev.* 739–92.

2 J. Ruggie, 'Business and Human Rights: Further steps toward the operationalization of the "protect, respect and remedy" framework'. *Report of the Special Representative of the Secretary General on the Issue of Human Rights and Transnational Corporations and Other Business Enterprises A/HRC/14/27* (2010), at <http://baseswiki.org/w/images/en/0/04/2010_Advance_Edited_Report.pdf>.

3 J.H. Dunning and S.M. Lundan, *Multinational Enterprises and the Global Economy* (2008, 2nd edn.).

4 C. Scott, 'Regulatory Governance and the Challenge of Constitutionalism' in *The Regulatory State: Constitutional Implications*, eds. D. Oliver, T. Prosser, and R. Rawlings (2010).

5 D. Vogel, 'The Private Regulation of Global Corporate Conduct' in *The Politics of Global Regulation*, eds. W. Mattli and N. Woods (2009) 151–88.

recommendations, and 'social norms'[6] or 'governing contracts',[7] but it must do so against the background of a theoretical investigation into the concept of law, which underlies and informs the almost habitual, routine distinction between 'law' on the one hand and these myriad 'alternative forms of regulation' on the other. The lawyer (as any other scientist) cannot simply 'go out and see', but must account for the conceptual bias with which this confrontation with 'reality' occurs. In this process, the study of the fast-proliferating forms of public-private, hybrid norms that apply to market activity turns into self-reflection on the theoretical starting points of the larger legal theory from the vantage point at which this incorporation of empirical evidence takes place.[8] It is, thus, not simply an option to build a theory on, say, the 'fact' of ubiquitous forms of market self-regulation but, instead, a necessary reflection on how one or more existing theories of how legal norms are in fact incorporated *into* and account *for* this particular empirical evidence.[9]

The core contention of this paper is that the challenging nature of the regulation of global corporate conduct requires an adequately differentiated approach towards the identification and analysis of the norms in question. The central question is: *'What is the concept of law that underlies the regulation of global corporate conduct?'* which I will try to answer by proceeding in three steps. In part I, I briefly review the context of 'state intervention' and 'market self-regulation', in which the current discussion of regulatory responses to the economic/financial crisis and the role of self-regulation occurs before laying out the concept of 'transnational legal pluralism' in part II. In part III, I argue that an exemplary area such as corporate governance can best be understood as an instance of transnational legal pluralism, that is, as a field that becomes visible through a particular methodological lens, which revisits the long-standing legal sociological analysis of norm creation in the transnational arena. A brief introduction follows into the place and relevance of corporate governance codes in the present evolution of this regulatory area, emphasizing the particular nature

6 L. Bernstein, 'Opting out of the Legal System: Extralegal Contractual Relations in the Diamond Industry' (1992) 21 *J. of Legal Studies* 115–57.

7 See the contributions to the Symposium: 'Governing Contracts: Public and Private Perspectives' (2007) 14 *Indiana J. of Global Legal Studies* 183–483.

8 S. Macaulay, 'Relational Contracts Floating on a Sea of Custom? Thoughts about the Ideas of Ian Macneil and Lisa Bernstein' (2000) 94 *Northwestern University Law Rev.* 775–804; V. Nourse and G. Shaffer, 'Varieties of New Legal Realism: Can a New World Order Prompt a New Legal Theory?' (2009) 61 *Cornell Law Rev.* 61–137.

9 See, in this context, P. Zumbansen, 'The Conundrum of Order: Governance from an Interdisciplinary Perspective' in the *Oxford Handbook of Governance*, ed. D. Levi-Faur (2011), available at: <http://ssrn.com/abstract=1671673>; P. Zumbansen, 'The Future of Legal Theory' (2010), contribution to the Hague Institute of the Internationalisation of Law (HiiL) Project on 'The Future of Law', at <http://ssrn.com/abstract=1688455>.

52

and dynamics of overlapping forms of state and non-state, hard and soft regulation. The central insight from this section is concerned with refuting the common view that transnational governance unfolds in considerable distance from state-based law, making it an allegedly autonomous realm. In fact, a close study of a new governance form such as corporate governance codes written by mostly private, occasionally mixed, public-private expert committees, reveals the 'close ties' between state and market in initiating, formulating, and implementing this type of regulation. In part IV, I conclude by suggesting how the lessons of such a case study can contribute to an ongoing theoretical investigation into the nature of global regulatory governance, using the concept of 'rough consensus and running code'.

I. MARKETS AND STATES AS REFERENCE POINTS IN THE REGULATION DEBATE

The ongoing investigations among administrative and constitutional lawyers, political scientists, sociologists, and regulatory theorists give ample evidence of how the state has long become involved in complex collaborations, delegations, trade-offs, and a myriad other divisions of labour with civil society or 'market' actors.[10] At the same time, there is a rich repository of studies related to the creation and nature of norms in the context of market self-regulation, that point not to the end of the state but, rather, suggest a highly complex relationship between state and non-state actors in the production and administration of these norms.[11] In light of this evidence, the oft-painted picture of law's limits, or even exhaustion, under the impact of globalization begins to fade. Instead of a futile struggle, where nation states play a regulatory and policy catch-up game with de-territorialized corporate and commercial actors or other amorphous crystallizations of globalization forces, an image has long begun to form, which depicts a rising number of actors with the capacity to expand on a vast territorial and operational scale.[12] Central to this depiction is an intricate overlapping of 'hard' and

10 See, for example, M. Loughlin, 'The Functionalist Style in Public Law' (2005) 55 *University of Toronto Law J.* 361–403.

11 L. Bernstein, 'Merchant Law in a Merchant Court: Rethinking the Code's Search for Immanent Business Norms' (1996) 144 *University of Pennsylvania Law Rev.* 1765–821; G. Hadfield, 'The Public and the Private in the Provision of Law for Global Services' in *Contractual Certainty in International Trade. Empirical Studies and Theoretical Debates on Institutional Support for Global Economic Exchanges,* ed. V. Gessner (2009) 239–56; for a discussion, see, for example, G.-P. Calliess and P. Zumbansen, *Rough Consensus and Running Code: A Theory of Transnational Private Law* (2010) ch. 2.

12 See, for example, W. Mattli and N. Woods, 'In Whose Benefit? Explaining Regulatory Change in Global Politics' in *The Politics of Global Regulation,* eds. W. Mattli and N. Woods (2009) 1–43; For earlier investigations, see the contributions to A.C. Cutler, V. Haufler, and T. Porter, *Private Authority and International*

'soft' norms, which are being produced by both state and non-state actors in the regulation of these activities, an overlapping which in itself still remains in need of much greater explanation as to the transition as well as the relations and linkages between hard and soft norms. Overshadowing this ongoing investigation are too often cliché-like associations of hard norms with the state, while soft norms are relegated to an allegedly separated, quasi self-regulatory sphere of the market. Especially in times of perceived 'regulatory' and 'market' failures'[13] the strained nature of such categorizations becomes strikingly apparent, and our analysis is redirected to long-standing findings regarding the regulated and constituted nature of markets[14] and to the long-grown web of institutions and practices of public-private interaction between the state and the market.[15] Thus, despite the exaggerated news of its decline, the state continues to be deeply involved in the production and administration of the norms that govern the global market-place[16], even if it is far from the sole author of governing regulations.[17]

This constellation invites analysis from a host of perspectives, and the intriguing emphasis placed by legal scholars in the recent past on the importance of 'regulation' and 'governance' is an important and crucial element in this regard.[18] It is becoming increasingly clear that a legal theory of these forms of regulation 'within' and 'beyond' the nation state cannot be

Affairs (1999) and the important study by A.C. Cutler, *Private Power and Global Authority: Transnational Merchant Law in the Global Economy* (2003).

13 See the astute observations by K.W. Dam, 'The Subprime Crisis and Financial Regulation: International and Comparative Perspectives' (2010) 10 *Chicago J. of International Law* 581–638.

14 R.L. Hale, 'Coercion and Distribution in a Supposedly Non-Coercive State' (1923) 38 *Political Science Q.* 470–94; M.R. Cohen, 'Property and Sovereignty' (1927) 13 *Cornell Law Q.* 8–30.

15 P.P. Craig, 'Constitutions, Property and Regulation' (1991) *Public Law* 538–54, reprinted in *Regulation,* ed. C. Scott (2003) 145–62; C. Harlow, 'The "Hidden Paw" of the State and the Publicisation of Private Law' in *A Simple Common Lawyer. Essays in Honour of Michael Taggart,* eds. D. Dyzenhaus, M. Hunt, and G. Huscroft (2009) 75–97.

16 See, for example, S. Sassen, 'The State and Globalization' in *Governance in a Globalizing World,* eds. J.S. Nye and J.D. Donahue (2000) 91.

17 K.W. Abbott and D. Snidal, 'Strengthening International Regulation Through Transnational New Governance: Overcoming the Orchestration Deficit' (2009) 42 *Vanderbilt J. of Transnational Law* 501–78; R.B. Hall and T.J. Biersteker, 'The Emergence of Private Authority in the International System' in *The Emergence of Private Authority in Global Governance,* eds. R.B. Hall and T.J. Biersteker (2002) 3–20; Cutler, op. cit., n. 12.

18 See the introduction to this volume by C. Scott, F. Cafaggi, and L. Senden, pp. 1–19. See, also, C. Scott, 'Regulation in the Age of Governance: The Rise of the Post-regulatory State' in *The Politics of Regulation: Institutions and Regulatory Reforms for the Age of Governance,* eds. J. Jordan and D. Levi-Faur (2004) 145–74; B. Morgan and K. Yeung, *An Introduction to Law and Regulation. Texts and Materials* (2007); F. Cafaggi, 'New Foundations of Transnational Private Regulation' in this volume, pp. 20–49.

adequately developed *from within*, but must instead take into account how existing forms of regulation testify to an intricate overlap of different forms and concepts of regulation. The impressive rise in importance of *new institutional economics* in the idea of competition over a pervasive theory or concept of 'governance' is of eminent importance in this regard.[19] As a result, 'economic governance'[20] has developed into a sophisticated regulatory theory that must be taken seriously by anyone interested in the evolution of regulatory governance – which certainly should include lawyers.[21] As this short paper cannot do justice to the rich and wide-ranging exchanges between lawyers and economists on the respective boundaries and overlaps between their fields,[22] it must suffice at this point to note that the general contention regarding a *choice* between state 'intervention' and 'self-regulating markets' regularly renders invisible and de-politicizes the de facto applied theories of political and legal order. Long before scholars (and policy-makers) began recently to unveil the regulatory 'reality' of what had until now been portrayed as an overwhelming 'retreat of the state' in the face of economic and financial globalization over the past thirty years,[23] there has existed a great body of work addressing and describing the complex regulatory constitution of market activity.[24] Central to this line of argument had always been a scrutiny of the role of *legal rights* in furnishing market actors with legally sanctioned freedoms to engage in binding activities. In other words, markets did not simply evolve according to 'natural' laws, but were instead subject to and the result of regulation, at the centre of which existed a fragile if crucial tension between 'negative' and 'positive' rights.[25]

---

19 See D.C. North, *Institutions, Institutional Change and Economic Performance* (1990); O.E. Williamson, 'The New Institutional Economics: Taking Stock, Looking Ahead' (2000) 38 *J. of Economic Literature* 595–613.

20 O.E. Williamson, 'The Economics of Governance' (2005) 95 *Am. Economic Rev.* 1–18.

21 P. Zumbansen and G.P. Calliess, 'Law, Economics and Evolutionary Theory: State of the Art and Interdisciplinary Perspectives' in *Law, Economics and Evolutionary Theory*, eds. P. Zumbansen and G.P. Calliess (2011).)

22 For the area of corporate law, see, for example, G.K. Hadfield and E. Talley, 'On Public versus Private Provision of Corporate Law' (2006) 22 *J. of Law, Economics and Organization* 414–41.

23 See D. Campbell, 'The End of Posnerian Law and Economics' (2010) 73 *Modern Law Rev.* 305–30; L.E. Mitchell, 'Financialism – A (Very) Brief History' in *The Embedded Firm: Corporate Governance, Labour and Financial Capitalism*, eds. C.A. Williams and P. Zumbansen (2011, forthcoming).

24 See the references in n. 14 above and see, further, B.H. Fried, *The Progressive Assault in Laissez Faire: Robert Hale and the First Law and Economics Movement* (1998).

25 R. Wiethölter, 'Die Position des Wirtschaftsrechts im sozialen Rechtsstaat' in *Wirtschaftsordnung und Rechtsordnung, Festschrift für Franz Böhm zum 70. Geburtstag,* eds. H. Coing, H. Kronstein, and E.-J. Mestmäcker (1965) 41–62; P. Zumbansen, 'Law After the Welfare State: Formalism, Functionalism and the Ironic Turn of Reflexive Law' (2008) 56 *Am. J. of Comparative Law* 769–805.

The 'mindset' described above regarding 'free' markets and 'enabling' states[26] provides a pertinent background and context for an analysis of a form of regulation that has attained considerable prominence in recent decades – that of market self-regulation through 'private' standard setting and best practice 'in the shadow', as it were, of an allegedly 'formal' framework, offering safeguards and an effective institutional foundation associated with the state and its authority to make law. The following section will illustrate the problematic consequences of such categorizations and distinctions for an adequate understanding and theorizing of the widely proliferating forms of transnational law making.

II. TRANSNATIONAL LEGAL PLURALISM: NEITHER NATIONAL NOR INTERNATIONAL, NEITHER PUBLIC NOR PRIVATE

The following observations are limited to what can at best be a cursory study of the institutional and conceptual dimensions of a particular form of market regulation illustrated by the example of corporate governance codes. Such an investigation offers a host of insights into the particular way in which market regulation has been evolving in a framework that cannot be adequately depicted as either national or international, public or private. Instead, the particular relation between state and non-state actors in the initiation and execution of the norm-creation process and the ensuing implementation, dissemination, and administration of the norms in question defy categorization that would allow one neatly to assign authority for such a particular regulatory regime to one side or the other. The chosen field, corporate governance, is a case in point in the study of transnational law making, as I will try to argue by scrutinizing both the underlying meaning of transnational and the concept of law informing this approach. I will argue, that areas such as corporate governance regulation must today be understood as instances of 'global assemblages',[27] or, from a legal theoretical viewpoint, as examples

26 For a succinct analysis and critique, see S. Deakin, 'Corporate Governance and Financial Crisis in the Long Run' in Zumbansen and Williams, op. cit., n. 23. See, also, K. Rittich, 'Functionalism and Formalism: Their Latest Incarnations in Contemporary Development and Governance Debates' (2005) 55 *University of Toronto Law J.* 853–68.

27 For this concept, see S. Sassen, *Territory – Authority – Rights. From Medieval to Global Assemblages* (2006). For earlier elaborations, see S. Sassen, *The Global City* (1991); J. Stiglitz, *Globalization and Its Discontents. Essays on the New Mobility of People and Money* (1998). See, also, M. Amstutz and V. Karavas, 'Weltrecht: Ein Derridasches Monster' in *Soziologische Jurisprudenz. Liber Amicorum für Gunther Teubner zum 65. Geburtstag*, eds. G.-P. Calliess, A. Fischer-Lescano, D. Wielsch, and P. Zumbansen (2009) 647–74; M. Amstutz, 'Métissage. Zur Rechtsform in der Weltgesellschaft' in *Europäische Gesellschaftsverfassung. Zur Konstitutionalisierung sozialer Demokratie in Europa*, eds. A. Fischer-Lescano, F. Rödl, and C. Schmid (2009) 333–51.

of transnational legal pluralism.[28] As such, a regulatory field such as corporate governance is, on the one hand, neither exclusively national (domestic) nor international, while, on the other, this does not imply the elimination or the overcoming of the nation state.[29] In addition, such an area cannot adequately be grasped through a separation of public and private as long as that distinction seeks to demarcate two distinct and autonomous norm-creating actors.[30] Instead, the evolving regulatory regimes or, 'assemblages', as coined by Sassen, are constituted through persistent local activity and interpretation, comprised of human, institutional, and techno-logical elements, the latter resulting predominantly from the breathtaking advances in information technology ('digitalizations').[31] By comparison, as will be laid out in more detail below, the concept of transnational legal pluralism illustrates a continuing need for a specifically legal perspective on the reconfiguration of an increasingly cross-jurisdictional, transnational regulatory landscape. Such a perspective incorporates long-standing legal sociological insights into pluralistic normative orders[32] and a renewed analysis of Polanyi's assessment of market dis/embeddedness.[33]

III. TRANSNATIONAL CORPORATE GOVERNANCE

1. The transnational regulatory landscape

Corporate governance has to be seen in the context of a highly diversified series of transnational norm-setting processes resulting in a veritable explo-sion of corporate governance codes in Europe and elsewhere. With the proliferation of corporate governance codes, influenced and pushed by international[34] and transnational activities of norm setting, discussion, and

---

28 P. Zumbansen, '"New Governance" in European Corporate Governance Regulation as Transnational Legal Pluralism' (2008) 15 *European Law J.* 246–76, at <http://ssrn.com/abstract=1128145>; P. Zumbansen, 'Transnational Legal Pluralism' (2010) 1 *Transnational Legal Theory* 141–89, at <http://ssrn.com/abstract=1542907>.

29 Sassen, op. cit. (2006), n. 27, p. 325.

30 C. Harlow, '"Public" and "Private" Law: Definition without Distinction' (1980) 43 *Modern Law Rev.* 241–65.

31 Sassen, op. cit. (2006), n. 27, p. 349 (noting the importance of focusing on financial centres, not 'markets', 'as key nested communities enabling the construction and functioning of such cultures of interpretation'.

32 E. Ehrlich, *Fundamental Principles of the Sociology of Law* (1913/1962); G. Teubner, 'The Two Faces of Janus: Rethinking Legal Pluralism' (1992) 13 *Cardozo Law Rev.* 1443–462.

33 K. Polanyi, *The Great Transformation. The Political and Economic Origins of our Time* (1944); J. Beckert, *The Great Transformation of Embeddedness. Karl Polanyi and the New Economic Sociology*, Max-Planck-Institute for the Study of Societies, Discussion Paper 07/1 (2007).

34 OECD; WCFCG; IVCGN.

thought exchange,[35] it has become increasingly difficult to identify a single institution or author of a set of norms. Instead, much of the production and dissemination of corporate governance rules operates through the migration of standards[36] and a cross-fertilization of norms. A distinct feature of this de-territorialized production of norms is the radical challenge these processes pose for our understanding of what we call *law proper*. The dissemination of corporate governance codes, disclosure standards and rules, best practices and codes of conduct, affects the entire juridical 'nexus of corporate govern-ance' as comprised of norms pertaining to company law, labour law, and securities regulation,[37] as the decentralization of norm producers is repeated, mirrored, and reflected in the hybridization of the norms themselves. It is in this sense, that the study of the proliferation of corporate governance codes and company law production in general, and of the rules of remuneration disclosure in particular, feeds into a broader research inquiry into the changing face of legal regulation in globally integrated marketplaces. A more serious engagement between political economists and economic sociologists on the one hand and corporate law scholars on the other about the distinct institutions and dynamics of regulatory change, which constitute the direly neglected groundwork, as it were, of what has for nearly two decades now been discussed under the umbrella of the 'convergence v. divergence' of corporate governance standards,[38] would complement and challenge the apparently exclusionary choices between harmonization and regulatory competition with a considerably deeper and more differentiated assessment of present market-'disembeddedness'.[39]

Against this background, corporate governance emerges today as a telling illustration of the fundamental transformations informing the regulatory instruments and institutions of market governance. As corporate law is being shaped by a complex mixture of public, private, state- and non-state-based norms, principles, and rules which are generated, disseminated, and monitored by a diverse set of actors, a closer look at this field can serve

---

35 ECGI, INSEAD, Euroshareholders.
36 See, for a comparable analysis of 'migrating' human rights standards, C. Scott and R. Wai, 'Transnational Governance of Corporate Conduct through the Migration of Human Rights Norms: The Potential of Transnational "Private" Litigation' in *Transnational Governance and Constitutionalism*, eds. C. Joerges, I.-J. Sand, and G. Teubner (2004) 287–319.
37 See J.W. Cioffi, *Public Law and Private Power: Corporate Governance Reform in the United States and Germany in an Age of Finance Capitalism* (2010).
38 H. Hansmann and R. Kraakman, 'Toward a Single Model of Corporate Law?' in *Corporate Governance Regimes. Convergence and Diversity*, eds. J. A. McCahery, P. Moerland, T. Raaijmakers, and L. Renneborg (2002) 56–82.
39 See, for example, S.M. Jacoby, 'Corporate Governance in Comparative Perspective: Prospects for Convergence' (2002) 22 *Comparative Labor Law & Policy J.* 5–32; C. Crouch and W. Streeck, 'Introduction: The Future of Capitalist Diversity' in *Political Economy of Modern Capitalism. Mapping Convergence and Diversity*, eds. C. Crouch and W. Streeck (1997) 1–18.

two purposes, both of which this paper briefly addresses. One is the way in which the analysis of contemporary corporate governance regulation can help us to assess the emerging, new framework within which corporate governance, but also other rules of market regulation, are evolving. Secondly, through the way in which we begin to understand this emerging transnational regulatory framework as an illustration of contemporary rule-making in spatial regimes not confined to nation states' jurisdictional boundaries, these regimes can be seen as new instantiations of the legal pluralist order that legal sociologists have long been concerned with and in the context of which they asked how 'to investigate the correlations between law and other spheres of culture'.[40] On this basis, the *transnational* emergence of regulatory regimes raises similar questions. The transnational lens allows us to study such regimes not as being entirely detached from national political and legal orders, but as emerging out of them, and reaching beyond them. The transnational dimension of the new actors and the newly emerging forms of norms radicalizes their 'semi-autonomous' nature, represented in the tension between a 'formal' law and policy-making apparatus on the one hand and spontaneously evolving 'informal' norms in particular social contexts on the other.[41]

2. Corporate governance codes

The development of corporate governance codes is thus an example of intricate, domestic and transnational, multi-level processes of norm genera-tion and norm enforcement. Starting from mere factual evidence, the emergence of corporate governance codes in recent years has begun to alter fundamentally the legal landscape of corporate law.[42] Despite their recognition as an essential element of corporate law,[43] these codes constitute a particular challenge to other, statutory approaches to law making, as they are regularly drafted by non-state actors such as non-governmental associa-tions, private industry institutes or corporate actors.[44] In general, corporate

40 Ehrlich, op. cit., n. 32, pp. 486–506; see, also, G. Gurvitch, *Sociology of Law* (1947); M. Rheinstein, 'Review: Two Recent Books on Sociology of Law [reviewing Timasheff's 'Introduction' and Gurvitch's 'Elements']' (1941) 51 *Ethics* 220–31, at 221–2.

41 S.F. Moore, 'Law and Social Change: the semi-autonomous field as an appropriate subject of study' (1973) 7 *Law & Society Rev.* 719–46.

42 For an overview of existing corporate governance codes in various countries, see <http://www.ecgi.org/codes/all_codes.php>.

43 See M. Eisenberg, 'The Architecture of American Corporate Law: Facilitation and Regulation' (2005) 2 *Berkeley Business Law J.* 167–84, at 176, 182.

44 For one of the first examples, the German Corporate Governance Code, see the interview with Professor Theodor Baums, who chaired the commission that preceded the drafting commission: T. Baums, 'Interview: Reforming German Corporate Governance: Inside a Law Making Process of a Very New Nature' (2001) 2 *German Law J.*, at <http://www.germanlawJ..com/past_issues.php?id=43>.

59

governance codes are relatively short collections of, on the one hand, legal regulations that are already in force in a particular jurisdiction, and recommendations and suggestions, directed either to private corporations or, in some cases,[45] the law maker, concerning a company's organization, its governance rules and disclosure regime not included in statutory law, on the other.[46] In the case of the German Corporate Governance Code, for example, *recommendations* are marked by the word 'shall'. While companies are free to deviate from them, they are under an obligation to disclose this devia-tion.[47] By contrast, *suggestions* can be deviated from without disclosure.[48] We shall see below how the German legislator has chosen to transpose this disclosure obligation into statutory law. These hybrid norms of corporate regulation,[49] which are neither exclusively public nor private, pose a formidable challenge to traditional thinking about law-making authority, non-legal rules, and their enforcement.

Corporate governance relates to the exercise of powers inside the firm: the analytical focus can, for one, be directed to the relationship between the owner (shareholder; principal) and the management (agent). Alternatively, one may focus on the overall organizational structure of the firm. While this also includes the principal-agent ties, it also encompasses the other 'stake-holders' in the firm, such as employees and creditors. The first, control-oriented approach centres on shareholders as the prime residual claimants of the firm: therefore, the firm's organization is governed by the overriding principle of maximizing 'shareholder value'.[50] The other, stakeholder-oriented, approach considers the actors in and around the firm and its business with regard to their vested interests in the firm. It sees the firm as

---

45 See U. Noack and D. Zetzsche, 'Corporate Governance Reform in Germany: The Second Decade', CBCWP No. 0010 (2005) 6–7, at <http://ssrn.com/abstract=646761>.

46 C. Mallin, *Corporate Governance* (2005) 19–40; J. Hill, 'Regulatory Responses to Global Corporate Scandals' (2005) 23 *Wisconsin International Law J.* 367–416, at 376 (highlighting how CGC have tended to be either a response to the absence of governmental regulation or a justification of such absence); Eisenberg, op. cit., n. 43, p. 182: 'bodies of standards, principles, or rules that are promulgated by private institutions, and that have force of some sort although they are not directly backed by state sanctions'.

47 'Preface', *German Corporate Governance Code* (2002) 2, at: <www.bmj.bund.de/ enid/Corporate_Governance/German_Corporate_Governance_Code_1gj.html>.

48 id.

49 R.C. Nolan, 'The Legal Control of Directors' Conflicts of Interest in the United Kingdom: Non-Executive Directors Following the Higgs Report' (2005) 6 *Theoretical Inquiries in Law* 413–62, at 418: 'complex mixtures of private and public action'; R. Mitchell, A. O'Donnell, and I. Ramsay, 'Shareholder Value and Employee Interests: Intersections between Corporate Governance, Corporate Law and Labor Law' (2005) 23 *Wisconsin International Law J.* 417–75, at 451 (clearly distinguishing CGC from law as '"self-regulation" or "soft law" provisions').

50 M.C. Jensen, *A Theory of the Firm. Governance, Residual Claims, and Organizational Forms* (2000).

embedded in a specific legal, economic and political culture, herein playing a role as societal actor.[51] In contrast to the shareholder approach, this perspective takes into account the public services rendered by a large firm in view of employment capacities and overall socio-economic spin-off.[52]

These two definitions lie at the base of a debate over different patterns of corporate organization, which was for the longest time driven by an almost overwhelming belief in what some recognized as nothing less than the 'end of history in corporate law',[53] namely, the eventual triumph of the share-holder value theory. The present crisis appears to have seriously undermined this credo. However, it is important to emphasize that what might have been perceived as a dispute merely among corporate law scholars (and policy makers) had instead long become a forum of much wider impact, as participants acknowledged the exemplary role of corporate governance for a timely and much needed scrutiny and critique of market regulation.[54]

Corporate governance codes such as those developed in countries around the world illuminate the significant characteristics of law-making processes that have been undergoing dramatic changes with regard to the *actors* involved and the *nature of the norms* generated in these processes. These developments have to be placed in the wider context of law-making reform. In this respect, reform does not concern only company law but, more generally, involves national, European, and international attempts to improve law-making procedures by allowing for a wider inclusion of private actors in rule-making procedures.[55] What is involved, from the point of view of democratic theory, is a tension that has long been growing between a functionally reduced, rubber-stamping parliament on the one hand and a fast-moving, hardly controllable administration which is in close contact and interaction with private actors, on the other.[56] At the same time, the currently

---

51 J. Parkinson, 'Models of the Company and the Employment Relationship' (2003) 41 *British J. of Industrial Relations* 481–509.

52 S. Jacoby, 'Corporate Governance and Society' (2005) 48 *Challenge* 69–87.

53 H. Hansmann and R. Kraakman, 'The End of History for Corporate Law' (2001) 89 *Georgetown Law J.* 439–68.

54 See, for example, P.A. Gourevitch and J. Shinn, *Political Power and Corporate Control. The New Global Politics of Corporate Governance* (2005); P.A. Hall and D. Soskice, *Varieties of Capitalism. The Institutional Foundations of Comparative Advantage* (2001).

55 See, for example, for the current endeavours on the European level, K.A. Armstrong, 'Civil Society and the White Paper – Bridging or Jumping the Gaps?' in *Mountain or Molehill? A Critical Appraisal on the Commission White Paper on Governance*, eds. C. Joerges, Y. Meny, and J.H.H. Weiler, Harvard Law School Jean Monnet Working Paper No.6/01 (2001) 95–102, 99–100: 'The normative case for a more autonomised transnational civil society [...] lies in the inclusion of a new constituency of voices, interests and expertise within élite transnational governance.'

56 For a powerful reconstruction of the pertinent role of the administration in designing rules 'close to the ground', see the landmark assessment by J.W. Landis, *The Administrative Process* (1938).

widespread attempts at improving respective national laws on corporate governance and firm organization[57] must be seen against the background of what was until just a couple of years ago an overwhelming pressure for international convergence towards a set of corporate governance principles, most notably established in the United States and the United Kingdom,[58] an effort that was for years informed by a sense of urgency with regard to adapting stakeholder-oriented, close-knit, bank-financed corporate governance systems to an extremely volatile competition for globally available investments. This understanding is currently, at the time of writing, shaped anew by widespread concerns with the consequences and externalities of the finance capitalism of the last twenty years.[59]

These developments can no longer solely be studied within contained, embedded systems of national political economies. Instead, there is a growing awareness of the fact that the adaptations of historically evolved governance systems display a particular *transnational* dimension. In light of the globally intertwined business and interaction among firms created under different legal rules, corporate governance rules have increasingly become a competitive asset in a 'law market',[60] a market, however, that is not only constituted by sovereign sellers with vested authority in the creation of binding legal norms, but by an amalgamation of national governments and through supranational norm setting such as by the OECD or in form of the UN Global Compact, by private parties such as multinational corporations and interest group representations. This particularly global regulatory landscape has not failed to capture the imagination of scholars of comparative law,[61] regulatory theory,[62] and institutional analysis.[63] The corporate governance landscape is not only populated by national governments eagerly engaged in a headstrong pursuit of regulatory reform: complementing such efforts is a vast proliferation of private and mixed public/private, hybrid processes of rule making, cutting across jurisdictional boundaries and con-

---

57 See the contributions in K.J. Hopt and E. Wymeersch, *Comparative Corporate Governance – Essays and Materials* (1997); T. Baums, introduction to *Bericht der Regierungskommission Corporate Governance. Unternehmensführung, Unternehmenskontrolle, Modernisierung des Aktienrechts* (2001).

58 See H. Hansmann and R. Kraakman, 'The End of History for Corporate Law' (2001) 89 *Georgetown Law J.* 439–68; critically, D.M. Branson, 'The Very Uncertain Prospect of "Global" Convergence in Corporate Governance' (2001) 34 *Cornell International Law J.* 321–62.

59 See Deakin, op. cit., n. 26.

60 E.A. O'Hara and L.E. Ribstein, *The Law Market* (2009).

61 J. Hill, 'Regulatory Show and Tell: Lessons from International Statutory Regimes' (2008) 33 *Delaware J. of Corporate Law* 819–43.

62 J. Black and D. Rouch, 'The development of global markets as rule-makers: engagement and legitimacy' (2008) *Law and Financial Markets Rev.* 218–33.

63 See, for example, the recent monograph study by A. Busch, *Banking Regulation and Globalization* (2009) with case studies on the United States, Germany, the United Kingdom, and Switzerland.

tributing to an increasingly densely woven net of guidelines, best practices, and standards. The defining feature of the emerging transnational body of corporate governance norms is the intricate resurfacing of a series of para-doxes pertaining to the inseparability of substantive/procedural, coordinative/regulatory and authority/affectedness aspects of the norms in question.[64] In order to illustrate the theoretical challenge facing any legal theory that wishes to explain the norm creation dynamics in this area, our analysis cannot be confined to the *substantive* law governing specific forms of societal activity, which has long remained the hallmark of comparative work in the law of corporate governance;[65] rather, our attention has to turn as well to the dynamics that are unfolding between different levels and sites of rule making from a *regulatory* perspective. From this combined perspective, the law of corporate governance becomes a prime example of a *transnational law regime*. The intricate embeddedness of regulatory innovation in locally defined governance structures on the one hand, and their integration in transnationally unfolding rule-making processes is characteristic of the current regulatory landscape in corporate governance, as illustrated by the particular dynamics of corporate governance codes. From this perspective, codes are a powerful example of the way in which private ordering maintains an intricately challenging tension with the institutional frameworks for official law making.

3. Hybrid law making: the example of the German Corporate Governance Code

For an adequate understanding of the drafting of the German Corporate Governance Code as an illustration of transnational regulatory processes, it is important to acknowledge the particular interplay between 'hard' and 'soft' law in this fast-moving regulatory area against the background of the global convergence debate regarding corporate governance standards. The 'hard' law, that is of eminent interest in this context, is a 2002 Act which had prior to that passed the national parliament (*Bundestag*), and which introduced a number of substantial changes to the German *Aktiengesetz* (Stock Corpora-tion Act).[66] This particular statute had to a large degree been contemplated

---

64 For a detailed discussion, see G. Hadfield, 'The Public and the Private in the Provision of Law for Global Services' in Gessner, op. cit., n. 11, pp. 239–56; Calliess and Zumbansen, op. cit., n. 11, ch. 2.

65 See the excellent study by D. Vagts, 'Reforming the "Modern Corporation": Perspectives from the German' (1966) 80 *Harvard Law Rev.* 23–89.

66 See *Gesetz zur weiteren Reform des Aktien- und Bilanzrechts, zu Transparenz und Publizität (Transparenz- und Publizitätsgesetz – abbr. TraPuG)* [Transparency and Disclosure Act], adopted by the German Bundestag on 17 May 2002. See, also, the documentation in (2002) *Neue Zeitschrift für Gesellschaftsrecht [NZG]* 78–81, and the comprehensive presentation of the TraPuG's main elements by H. Hirte, *Das Transparenz- und Publizitätsgesetz* (2003).

and prepared under the auspices of two specially formed governmental commissions concerned with a reform of German corporate governance. The second of these commissions, the so-called 'Corporate Governance Code-Commission', had been convened with the mandate of taking up the suggestions of the first commission, central to which was the drafting of a voluntary Code of Corporate Governance Rules.[67] Among the many interesting features of the German Corporate Governance Code, by some seen as a 'novum' in the system of German legal sources[68], was an initially vivid but meanwhile relatively subsided debate regarding the Code's legal nature.[69]

The Code itself includes those *norms* and *regulations* that are mandatory corporate law rules which are already set out in the German Stock Corporation Law. The Code's purpose, according to its drafters, in reiterating these norms here is to provide foreign investors with a transparent and simple introduction to central rules pertinent to the corporate governance rules existing in Germany.[70] Furthermore, the Code includes *recommendations*, which are expressed by the word '*sollen*' (shall) and the observation of which is to be made transparent in an annual statement by the firm's management.[71] Lastly, the Code contains *suggestions* as to corporate conduct, the observation of which is merely 'suggested', but there is no obligation to disclose whether a company has followed these suggestions.[72] The '*comply or disclose*' principle which is endorsed in the Code with regard to 'recommendations' has been seen as an indirect enforceability anchor in the Code, whereby it could be seen to lose its genuinely voluntary

---

67 See press release at: <http://www.corporate-governance-code.de/eng/news/presse-20020226.html>.

68 P. Ulmer, 'Der deutsche Corporate Governance Kodex – ein neues Regulierungs-instrument für börsennotierte Aktiengesellschaften' (2002) 166 *ZHR* 150–81, at 152.

69 E. Vetter, 'Der Deutsche Corporate Governance Kodex nur ein zahnloser Tiger? Zur Bedeutung von § 161 AktG für Beschlüsse der Hauptversammlung' (2008) *Neue Zeitschrift für Gesellschaftsrecht [NZG]* 121–5, at 121: still not resolved satisfactorily.

70 Foreword, *German Corporate Governance Code*, at <http://www.corporate-governance-code.de/eng/kodex/1.html>:

> This German Corporate Governance Code (the 'Code') presents essential statutory regulations for the management and supervision (governance) of German listed companies and contains internationally and nationally recognized standards for good and responsible governance. The Code aims at making the German Corporate Governance system transparent and understandable. Its purpose is to promote the trust of international and national investors, customers, employees and the general public in the management and supervision of listed German stock corporations.

71 See Preface, *German Corporate Governance Code* 2, at <http://www.corporate-governance-code.de/index-e.html>.

72 id.

character.[73] That the Code in fact attains an at least indirect mandatory character, is strengthened by the enactment of a provision in the German Stock Corporation Act (AktG), whereby the disclosure duty is codified into law.[74] But does this suffice to make the Code a piece of enforceable legislation? Others have argued that, even if there is a disclosure obligation with regard to the company's compliance with the Code's recommendations, it would be wrong to perceive the Code itself as 'law'. The latter, so it was argued,[75] would only then be the case if the recommendations themselves were being made obligatory which, arguably, they are not.[76] It appears that the Code's practical relevance is to be seen in its effect on the actual *behaviour* of firms,[77] something which appears to have continuously accrued with each passing year.[78] Whether or not firms do comply with the code's dispositions relating, for example, to transparency and disclosure of executive compensation[79] (a part of the *Kodex* that spurred concrete legislative action leading up to the entering into force of a federal statute on the adequacy of executive compensation in August 2009[80]), the publication

---

73 W. Seidel, 'Der Deutsche Corporate Governance Kodex – eine private oder doch eine staatliche Regelung?' (2004) 25 *Zeitschrift für Wirtschaftsrecht [ZIP]* 285–94; W. Seidel, 'Kodex ohne Rechtsgrundlage' (2004) *Neue Zeitschrift für Gesellschaftsrecht [NZG]* 1095–6; M. Heintzen, 'Der Deutsche Corporate Governance Kodex aus der Sicht des deutschen Verfassungsrechts' (2004) 25 *Zeitschrift für Wirtschaftsrecht [ZIP]* 1933–8.

74 The quality and assessment of this obligatory annual 'explanation' must certainly be disputed, see, for example, M. Peltzer, 'Handlungsbedarf in Sachen Corporate Governance' (2002) *Neue Zeitschrift für Gesellschaftsrecht [NZG]* 593–9, at 594; regrettably, the newly published, leading commentary on German stock corporation law remains silent on this new codification, see U. Hüffer, *Aktiengesetz* (2002) s. 161 AktG.

75 H.-M. Ringleb, Introduction to *Kommentar zum Deutschen Corporate Governance Kodex [Kodex-Kommentar]*, eds. H.-M. Ringleb, T. Kremer, M. Lutter, and A. von Werder (2008, 3rd edn.); A. von Werder, 'Der Deutsche Corporate Governance-Kodex – Grundlagen und Einzelbestimmungen' (2002) 55 *Der Betrieb* 801–10; C.H. Seibt, 'Deutscher Corporate Governance Kodex und Entsprechenserklärung (s. 161 AktG-E)' (2002) 47 *Die Aktiengesellschaft (AG)* 249–59.

76 M. Lutter, 'Die Kontrolle der gesellschaftsrechtlichen Organe: Corporate Governance – ein internationales Thema' (2002) 24 *Jura* 83–8, 86, with regard to informations and suggestions.

77 C.H. Seibt, 'Deutscher Corporate Governance Kodex: Antworten auf Zweifelsfragen der Praxis' (2003) 48 *Die Aktiengesellschaft (AG)* 465–77.

78 J. van Kann and M. Eigler, 'Aktuelle Neuerungen des Corporate Governance Kodex' (2007) *Deutsche Zeitschrift für Steuerrecht* 1730–6, at 1733.

79 M. Wolf, 'Corporate Governance. Der Import angelsächsicher "Self-Regulation" im Widerstreit zum deutschen Parlamentsvorbehalt' (2002) 35 *Zeitschrift für Rechtspolitik (ZRP)* 59–60, at 60.

80 See *Gesetz zur Angemessenheit der Vorstandsvergütung – VorstAG*; full text at: <http://www.bmj.de/files/7db813ef5ce3522d02ef3547a4c2f341/3836/gesetz_vorstandsverguetung_VorstAG.pdf>.

of the firm's reports on the Internet,[81] or the facilitating of personal exercise of shareholders' voting rights[82] will, according to the rules established by the Code, remain within the discretion of the company.[83] Again, the Code explicitly foresees that companies do not have to comply with 'recommendations'. And yet they are now *obliged* to issue an annual explanation, regardless of whether or not they did comply.[84] The annual monitoring of the Code's 'acceptance' has revealed consistently growing numbers of German major corporations observing the Code.[85]

Much suggests, however, that this perspective on 'hard' versus 'soft' law is inadequate to capture the particular combination of coordinative/regulatory dimensions reflected in the Code. The preceding discussion highlights how our conceptualization of the enforcement qualities of the Corporate Governance Code is informed by our understanding of the distinction between a statutory norm of law set by the state, on the one hand, and a non-binding norm of non-law on the other. This distinction, however, is a result of a continuing association of law-making power with state organs, long after the generation of norms has become characterized by a complex interplay between public and private actors – as illustrated in the case of the German Code.

Questions of authorship and legitimacy in the area of law making become elusive in light of the fact that the state is highly dependent on expert input from societal actors in carrying out its legislative and administrative functions.[86] Furthermore, it is clear that with the growing complexity of societal relations and, correspondingly, a growing demand for sophisticated and context-sensitive public governance forms,[87] any form of norm-production and implementation has become an extremely fragile process of risk taking and of trial and error. In the light of the particular governance challenges arising in modern societies,[88] an allegedly clear-cut distinction between

---

81 See, for example, s. 2.3.1 of the Cromme commission's German Corporate Governance Code.
82 id., s. 2.3.3.
83 id., s. 1: 'Foreword', differentiating between voluntary recommendations ('shall'), suggestions ('should', 'can'), and legally compelling provisions, according to existing law.
84 See Transparency and Disclosure Act, s. 16.
85 Van Kann and Eigler, op. cit., n. 78, p. 1733.
86 See R.B. Stewart, 'The Reformation of American Administrative Law' (1975) 88 *Harvard Law Rev.* 1669; J. Freeman, 'Collaborative Governance in the Administrative State' (1997) 45 *UCLA Law Rev.* 1–98.
87 G. Teubner, 'Juridification – Concepts, Aspects, Limits, Solutions' in *Juridification of Social Spheres*, ed. G. Teubner (1987) 3–48; K.-H. Ladeur, *The Theory of Autopoiesis as an Approach to a Better Understanding of Postmodern Law*, EUI Working Paper (1999).
88 See U. Beck, 'From Industrial Society to Risk Society: Questions of Survival, Social Structure and Ecological Enlightenment' (1992) 9 *Theory, Culture & Society* 97–123.

public and private governance schemes, built on the image of a sovereign, knowledgable state presiding over a fragmented market society, would fail to grasp the intricate forms of intertwined public-private governance mechanisms, of knowledge sharing and experimental politics that characterize contemporary law making.[89]

The discussion of the *rise of governance* in contemporary law making reflects a wide-ranging interest, but also a high level of concern with what is being perceived as a 'privatization of law'.[90] As Colin Scott noted:

> ... recognition of private legislation reflects both a desire to better understand the diffuse nature of capacities underpinning regulatory and wider governance practices and a concern respecting the legitimacy of such non-governmental rule making.[91]

This combination of 'desire' and 'concern' originates from a persisting association of law and its creation with the (public) state sphere, while informal and private ordering remains relegated to the (private) market realm. Central to our analysis up to this point was an argument against this dualistic distinction, which is inadequate to grasp the ways in which both hybrid and private forms of norm generation can produce norms with regulatory functions. In concluding this section on corporate governance codes, it is time to draw out the context in which this hybrid law making occurs, a context which is both 'real', that is, consisting of actors, and conceptual, meaning that it is, at the same time, a particular, methdological reflection on the way that norms are being created in such areas today.

IV. CORPORATE GOVERNANCE AND THE INTRICACIES OF *ROUGH CONSENSUS AND RUNNING CODE*

The example of the German Corporate Governance Code can be taken to illustrate a theoretical concept, which Gralf Calliess and I, drawing on previous work in Internet governance[92] have been developing further as *Rough Consensus and Running Code* [RCRC],[93] in the following way. The German government, facing immense domestic and international pressure to

89 See, for example, M. Power, *The Audit Society: Rituals of Verification* (1997); M. Power, 'Enterprise Risk Management and the Organization of Uncertainty in Financial Institutions' in *The Sociology of Financial Markets*, eds. K.K. Cetina and A. Preda (2005) 250–68.

90 See the survey by J. Köndgen, 'Privatisierung des Rechts. *Private Governance* zwischen Deregulierung und Rekonstitutionalisierung' (2006) 206 *Archiv für die cililistische Praxis [AcP]* 477–525.

91 C. Scott, 'Regulating private legislation' in *Making European Law: Governance Design*, eds. F. Cafaggi and H. Muir-Watt (2008) 254–86, at 254.

92 A.L. Russell, '"Rough Consensus and Running Code" and the Internet-OSI Standards War' (2006) 28 *IEEE Annals of the History of Computing* 48–61.

93 Calliess and Zumbansen, op. cit., n. 11.

67

reform its corporate law regime so as to make German companies more attractive for global investors, was aware of the reform obstacles existing in the contemporary German political economy. At the same time, the government considered the potential of societal ('market') self-regulation, as highlighted by the Ministry of Justice. Furthermore, the German government was hardly taking a revolutionary step when inviting a Commission to draft this instrument. Even if the legislative project of drafting a national civil code in the latter part of the nineteenth century was, of course, in many ways different from the drafting of the Corporate Governance Code in 2002, the Schröder government's initiation of the Commission, which was markedly referred to as a 'Government Commission', also bears some important resemblances to its historical forerunner. In both instances, the government drew on private expert knowledge in preparing a comprehensive legislative instrument, the regulatory impact of which was perceived as being so large that its delegation to a commission of experts promised to channel otherwise conflicting and perhaps irresolvable positions through a discursive, outcome-oriented process. Certainly, the government's initiation of this norm-generation process remained ambivalent at best with regard to the legal nature of the Code growing out of the commission's work. The striking characteristic of both the process of the Code's drafting and of the Code itself remains, it seems, its *hybrid* nature between a non-binding, voluntary, 'private' regulatory instrument on the one hand and a document, linked to a statutory disclosure obligation by a federal law, on the other. Yet, neither dimension adequately depicts the dynamics that shape the emergence of the idea of a Code, the evolution of its drafting, and the intriguingly open-ended nature of the discussion around the legal nature of both the norms of the Code as of the Code itself. Instead, the discussion has made it clear that the repeated attempts to solve this dilemma by effectively avoiding the 'public' or 'private' question through designating the Code as *hybrid*, and by referring to its norms as 'soft law', achieves just that, namely, avoiding the underlying conundrum of how to integrate such governance processes into our legal theoretical methodology and doctrine. This, then, makes the example of the German Code particularly intriguing because its coming into being is reflective of both its embeddedness in a complex, historically evolved political economy that was historically sceptical with regard to private law making and market ordering,[94] and of a fast-evolving trans-national regulatory landscape in which public and private actors – as 'norm entrepreneurs' – not only compete in striving to make 'better rules' but in a much richer fashion overlap, intertwine, collaborate, and antagonize, and

94 See H. Großmann-Doerth, 'Selbstgeschaffenes Recht der Wirtschaft und staatliches Recht [1933]' in *Das selbstgeschaffene Recht der Wirtschaft. Zum Gedenken an Hans Großmann-Doerth (1894–1944)*, eds. U. Blaurock, N. Goldschmidt, and A. Hollerbach (2005) 77–96; D. Hart, 'Zur konzeptionellen Entwicklung des Vertragsrechts' (1984) 29 *Die Aktiengesellschaft (AG)* 66–80.

thereby contribute to a constantly changing *space* that Saskia Sassen has referred to as both institutional *and* normative.

The concept of *Rough Consensus and Running Code* combines a deliberative perspective with an experimental, law-making one. Drawing on expert and stakeholder knowledge, the regulating body, which can be public, private or hybrid, will seek to identify an evolving – *rough* – consensus in light of which it will put forward an experimental draft body of norms. These, in turn, will receive feedback and remain open to adaptation and change, constituting a *running code*. RCRC seeks to capture the particular tension between multipolar, formal/informal processes of deliberation and consensus-seeking, on the one hand, and the emergence of regulatory instruments with experimental and adaptable character on the other. Central to this approach is the emphasis on the inseparability of elementary features in theories of social order, which are traditionally defined through distinctions. Examples include, foremost, the distinction between public and private or between state and market, but also – as regards the 'function' of a norm – the distinction between coordination and regulation.[95] The RCRC model seeks to capture the particular tension inherent to norm-generating processes where the nature of the particular issue does not easily lend itself to an association with only one of these elements. The evolving norms and the processes of their generation in sensitive regulatory areas defy a categorization of either public or private, coordinative or regulative. As a result, their classification as either 'law' or 'non-law' depending on their origin in a recognized, competent law-making authority is as problematic as is the declaration that a norm constitutes a merely 'private' arrangement or, 'social norm'. RCRC, thus, problematizes the tension between the definition of a norm's legitimacy as law or non-law with reference to whether or not it emanated from an 'official' law-making authority, on the one hand, and as to whether the legitimacy of norms should be measured in light of the input into their creation by those 'affected' by the norm, on the other. As we have tried to show with regard to the fast-evolving regulatory fields of transnational contract and corporate law, the particular dynamics of norm creation in sensitive societal areas characterized by a hybrid combination of official and unofficial actors and a high degree of experimental, tentative, reflexive regulation, suggest the impossibility of associating such processes with only one of the identified sides.

From this perspective, the transnational regulatory landscape of corporate governance is marked by the intricate collision of public, private, and hybrid ceaselessly evolving norm-making processes that arise between regulatory arenas populated by actors inside and outside of the nation state. These norm-making processes are complex in the sense that the identification of

---

95 See G. Hadfield, 'The Public and the Private in the Provision of Law for Global Services' in Gessner, op. cit., n. 11, pp. 239–56.

either coordinative (facilitating) or regulatory (redistributing) functions can no longer occur on the basis of distinguishing between the public or private nature of the actors involved.[96] Instead, the norm-making processes have to be seen as *law generating* when and where we are willing to recognize the inseparability of the coordinative/regulatory dimension from the authority/ affectedness dimension of these processes. This connection distances the RCRC process from a new institutional economic assessment of formal/ informal rule creation and ties it into a comprehensive and interdisciplinary investigation into the foundations and processes of global law making as currently pursued by sociologists, political scientists, and philosophers as well as legal pluralist scholars.

Against this background, what can be learned from this example for other contemporary forms of law making? Recognizing a growing interest among legal scholars in the origins and prospects of what is conventionally referred to as a 'privatization of law',[97] it is necessary to emphasize that the *regulatory* function of the Code does not follow from the state's enactment of a statutory disclosure obligation, as was repeatedly argued by those identifying the Code as a public regulatory instrument. What constitutes an unsatisfactory answer to the question whether or not the Code is law resulted from the recognition that, in fact, not only the underlying drafting process but also the envisioned enforcement mechanism are intriguingly complex and arguably open-ended for a reason. The government did not make the Code directly or indirectly enforceable when it enacted the disclosure requirement, as it did not itself enact an ultimately effective sanctioning mechanism in the case of non-disclosure or deficient disclosure. Instead, the government's action in this regard illustrates a particular set of features that characterize law making in the area of corporate governance and many other regulatory areas today. The Code can only fulfil its function of influencing corporate behaviour and, as such, rendering German corporations more competitive, if a sufficient number of market participants endorse the Code's rules to make them matter. In that sense, a *rough consensus* regarding the Code's normative obligations must exist for it to have any influence on the corporate landscape. This rough consensus must not encompass each and every of the Code's recommendations or, perhaps even less, its suggestions. Instead, it suffices that there is among market participants a far-reaching agreement – a rough consensus – as to the binding quality of the Code's content. That this is the case has been verified by a number of empirical studies since its publication.[98] Secondly, the particular quality of the Code's

---

96 But see Hadfield, id. and Hadfield and Talley, op. cit., n. 22.
97 J. Köndgen, 'Privatisierung des Rechts. *Private Governance* zwischen Deregulierung und Rekonstitutionalisierung' (2006) 206 *Archiv für die cilivilistische Praxis [AcP]* 477–525; G. Borges, 'Selbstregulierung im Gesellschaftsrecht – zur Bindung an Corporate Governance-Kodices' (2003) 32 *ZGR* 508–40.
98 Van Kann and Eigler, op. cit., n. 78.

three-pronged regulatory nature of information (restatements), recommendations, and suggestions in connection with the statutory disclosure
requirements for recommendations leads to a complex constellation of the
Code's regulatory impact. Where a rough consensus is being attained, it
might set into motion the generation and crystallization of a *customary law*
of corporate governance norms, namely, with the passage of time and an
increasing acceptance of the Code among market participants. With the
crystallization of certain corporate governance rules, parts of the law of
corporate governance can develop into a regime which can further develop
and solidify in the future. In light of such an incremental growth of norms
through piloting (drafting a code), implementing (publishing it), and
enforcing them (through a communication obligation set by the state on
the one hand, and a market shaming process on the other), the Code can
contribute to the growth of a corporate governance regime, which can
become ever more comprehensive, while at the same time being more
flexible, open, and adaptive to changes than a statutory provision would be.

Seen in this light, the Code is illustrative of how recommendations can be
made to enter a regulatory realm which is occupied by both public and
private norm-entrepreneurs, including the state that is pursuing corporate law
reform, and private actors such as banks, investments funds, and expert
groups calling for new rules to govern corporate conduct but also other
stakeholders such as unions and business ethics propagators. From this
perspective, the Code denotes how recommendations can increasingly be
recognized as 'rules to be followed', long before they may grow into widely
accepted norms of 'good governance'. That the latter is not oriented towards
a reductionist concept of market efficiency is maintained by connecting the
coordinative/regulatory dimension with that of authority/affectedness. It is
against this background, then, that we need not only to return to the original
question of whether the Code is law, but also dare to inquire whether we
have been asking the right question.

As suggested, the perspective taken vis-à-vis reform issues related to
corporate governance has been informed by both a public-private, official-
non-official distinction between law and non-law, on the one hand, and a
deeply felt scepticism about the chances for the law reform of historically
grown, path-dependent norms and institutions, not only in 'Germany
Incorporated',[99] on the other. And, indeed, the legacies with which we have
been struggling, are weighty. In contrast to the institutional and methodological side of norm setting and law making in the context of increasingly
'privatized' law-making forms, most contemporary commentators of
corporate law reform have not yet begun to embrace such a perspective. As
it stands, law reform continues to be conceptualized largely with regard to a

---

99 P.A. Hall and D. Soskice, 'An Introduction to Varieties of Capitalism' in Hall and
Soskice, op. cit., n. 54, pp. 1–68.

dualistic perception of state regulation and 'intervention' on the one hand and market order and self-regulation on the other. Traditionally, the German choice was thus: 'To regulate or not to regulate'. And, the traditional answer was, indeed, to regulate.[100] The realm of options for the protection of shareholders' interests have thus been perceived to range from coercive, binding law ('vested rights') to an approach of entrusting this protection to the capital market.

But it is against this background that – on both sides of the Atlantic, and beyond – the search for 'good governance' in company law will continue. It will do so by involving the wide range of public, private, and hybrid law-making forms to which we have increasingly grown accustomed. For this, valuable lessons can be drawn from earlier examples of commercial self-regulation (for example, standard contracts), as well as from other, contemporary developments in other fields (environmental law, commercial arbitration[101]). The rich spectrum of experiences on the national, European, and international level is reflective of an on-going search for ways to adequately mobilize societal knowledge while being aware and conscious of divergent national trajectories of socio-legal and economic development. The enactment of the Corporate Governance Code and the installation and, indeed, highly effective continuation of a 'standing commission' to review its acceptance and the need of amendments are both illustrations of a change in approaching law reform in a politically highly contested area. At the same time, the development of codes, in Germany as in many other countries, by private and public actors, both domestically and transnationally, suggests the emergence of legal regimes that can no longer adequately be explained with reference to the 'state' or the 'market'. Instead, the emergence of a transnational law of corporate governance is characterized by an intricate combination of public and private agency, but also of a variety of regulatory, evolving instruments.

As corporate governance scholars continue to sharpen their analytical lenses for the study of formal/informal norm creation and the particular socio-economic cultures[102] in which different hybrid regulatory approaches

---

100 See the brillant account by G. Spindler, 'Deregulierung des Aktienrechts?' (1998) 43 *Die Aktiengesellschaft (AG)* 53–74, 53 ff., 57, stressing the different approach taken by American corporate law, which – for the most part – is state law, which is, in turn, 'enabling' law, giving firms great discretion in designing their governing law. 'Corporate law' as such, then, serves for one as a framework providing default rules, while, on federal level, it contains a considerable number of binding rules to safeguard investors' interest and trust in the capital market.

101 See, for example, F. De Ly, 'Lex Mercatoria (New Law Merchant): Globalisation and International Self-Regulation' in *Rules and Networks. The Legal Culture of Global Business Transactions*, eds. V. Gessner, R.P. Appelbaum, and W.F. Felstiner (2001) 159–88.

102 See A.N. Licht, 'The Mother of all Path-Dependencies: Towards a Cross-Cultural Theory of Corporate Governance Systems' (2001) 26 *Delaware J. of Corporate Law* 147–205.

emerge, it becomes evident to which degree 'comparative corporate govern-ance'[103] is being transformed into an inter-disciplinary regulatory analysis. Our focus on the way in which corporate governance principles are migrating between different national political economies, on the one hand, and newly forming regulatory spaces,[104] on the other, informs and accentuates our perceptions not only for the existing *differences* in national corporate laws, but more importantly for the fact that conventionally viewed 'national corporate governance systems' have long become transnationally constituted spaces of institutional and normative interaction and contesta-tion. They are, thus, anything but peaceful, embedded legal orders. Instead, they are marked by a fundamental regulatory transformation in which social norms and 'soft law' become intertwined, changed, adapted, and interwoven within a regulatory environment of 'hard' law which itself is no longer stable.

The case of corporate governance reform, which I have highlighted in this paper, illustrates the degree to which the contested issues and the successively made proposals that grew out of a far-reaching and open-eyed gathering of information and evidence by national and supranational policy makers, expert committees, and scholars were of a veritable *transnational* nature, emerging from parallel reform efforts in other countries, among private and non-state actors around the world. In that sense, domestic company law reform must be seen as part of an emerging transnational legal pluralism. Its defining feature is the fundamental contestation of the very distinction that legal pluralism has always struggled with: that between law and non-law.

CONCLUSION

Corporate governance norms provide a telling example of the transformation of traditional state-originating, official norm setting in favour of increasingly decentralized, multi-level processes of norm production. At the same time, not only are norms produced on more levels: the nature of these norms themselves changes dramatically. This constellation, however, suggests nothing less than a fundamental contestation and erosion of boundaries between state and non-state actors, between official and unofficial law, between public and private ordering, and it is here where we see a recurrence but also a reformulation of Polanyi's astute observations as to the pressures

---

103 M.J. Roe, 'Comparative corporate governance' in *The New Palgrave Dictionary of Economics and the Law*, ed. P. Newman (1998) 339–46.

104 M. Amstutz, 'In-Between Worlds: Marleasing and the Emergence of Interlegality in Legal Reasoning' (2005) 11 *European Law J.* 766–84; see, also, M. Amstutz and V. Karavas, 'Rechtsmutation: Zu Genese und Evolution des Rechts im transnationalen Raum' (2006) *Rechtshistorisches J.* 14–32.

73

on market regulation to answer to the dynamics of what he called the danger of disembedding the market from society and of the 'double movement' of both emancipatory and containing liberalization.[105] The novelty of this blurring of boundaries between traditional norm creating and executing spheres appears as a direct result of a specific historical experience of a particular framework of socio-economic, political-legal regulation that characterized the twentieth-century rise of the social and welfare state.[106] This experience was aptly identified and premeditated by turn-of-the-century sociologists and lawyers, and powerfully captured by Max Weber's sobering assessment of the disenchantment of modernity.[107] Irredeemably thrown into the iron cage of modern rationalization,[108] contemporary hopes are pinned – if at all – on a transformative realization of emerging self-regulatory potentials. Current attempts to rethink legal regulation as 'regulatory governance', 'regulatory capitalism', or 'rough consensus and running code' should be seen in this light.

The framework of transnational corporate governance regulation can only be understood against the background of, and in light of, the complex, intertwined nature of corporate governance regulation as it unfolds in a context marked by tensions between national and, for example, European aspirations for market competitiveness, market and polity integration dynamics, and the increasingly transnational nature of firms' operations and regulations. A viable theory of transnational law making must seek to acknowledge these contextual tensions and draw on the various learning experiences with regard to market regulation in order to integrate them productively into an enriched concept of regulatory governance. Such a theory might then be able to capture the particular dynamics of transnational corporate governance regulation through its structuring capacities for distinguishing between the substantive and procedural dimensions of con-temporary norm creation. The particular promise of a theory such as RCRC here lies in its capacity to draw conceptual lines between the experi-

---

105 Polanyi, op. cit., n. 33.
106 N. Luhmann, *Political Theory in the Welfare State,* tr. by J. Bednarz Jr. (1990); M. Stolleis, 'Die Entstehung des Interventionsstaates und das öffentliche Recht' (1989) 11 *ZNR* 129–47.
107 M. Weber, *The Protestant Ethic and the Spirit of Capitalism,* tr. by T. Parsons (1930); M. Weber, *On Law in Economy and Society,* tr. by E. Shils and M. Rheinstein (1967); D. Trubek, 'Max Weber on Law and the Rise of Capitalism' (1972) *Wisconsin Law Rev.* 720–53; R. Wiethölter, 'Proceduralization of the Category of Law' in *Critical Legal Thought: An American-German Debate,* eds. C. Joerges and D. Trubek (1985) 501–10; G. Teubner, 'Substantive and Reflexive Elements in Modern Law' (1983) 17 *Law & Society Rev.* 239–85; G.-P. Calliess, *Prozedurales Recht* (1999); P. Zumbansen, *Ordnungsmuster im modernen Wohlfahrtsstaat. Lernerfahrungen zwischen Staat, Gesellschaft und Vertrag* (2000).
108 R. Sennett, *The Culture of the New Capitalism* (2006); T. Judt, *Ill Fares the Land* (2010).

mentation with norm-creating processes, which are understood as contextualized learning processes ('rough consensus'), on the one hand, and the assessment of emerging normative bodies on the other ('running code'). The promise of RCRC lies in its sensitivity with regard to knowledge emanating from concrete regulatory contexts that are recognized as norm proposals. Within the process of disseminating such norm proposals, they are gradually evolving into programmes of regulation. Emerging into a still-evolving running code, such norm programmes remain fully assessable from any factual or normative standpoint, while not sacrificing their ongoing regulatory function. As such, this model strives – not unlike competing governance concepts – for coherence, applicability and, ultimately, legitimacy.

JOURNAL OF LAW AND SOCIETY
VOLUME 38, NUMBER 1, MARCH 2011
ISSN: 0263-323X, pp. 76–95

The Crystallization of Regulatory Norms

Donal Casey* and Colin Scott*

This article investigates the processes through which regulatory norms generally, and in the context of transnational private regulation (TPR) in particular, become effective. We argue that institutionalization – the embedding of norms within some wider structures which impact upon their distribution, enforcement, and mode of transmission – is generally central to the processes through which regulatory norms are crystallized. We note that, within processes of crystallization of TPR norms, the potential for managing legitimacy has been exploited through the institutionalization of policies, structures, and processes which are responsive to the beliefs, expectations or interests of the relevant legitimacy communities. However, we suggest that the focus of such legitimating strategies on the making of rules and standards exposes weaknesses and limits to the potential of such legitimation attaching to actions which implement such norms through monitoring and enforcement, particularly where such processes are embedded within supply-chain contracts.

INTRODUCTION

A central problem of regulatory governance is seeking to understand the conditions under which regulatory rules are followed. Within regulatory research, this is often expressed in terms of the problem of compliance. Furthermore, there has been growing interest in the role played by a wide variety of norms in steering regulatory regimes. Whilst these issues are of importance for regulatory regimes generally, they take on particular

* UCD School of Law, University College Dublin, Belfield, Dublin 4, Ireland
donal.casey@ucdconnect.ie   colin.scott@ucd.ie

Earlier versions of this paper were presented at the ECPR Joint Sessions, Lisbon, 2009 and at the first annual conference of the Hiil-funded project on Transnational Private Regulatory Regimes. We thank the following for comments on earlier drafts: Joel Anderson, Daniel Friedrich, Robert Goodin, Tony Prosser, Linda Senden, Nicholas Southwood, Kai Spiekermann, and Andrew Woods.

76

significance in regimes which are one step removed from national legislative systems, as with those which are substantially supranational or substantially non-state or private in origins. Regimes which combine both these elements, being both transnational and non-governmental, are the core set of transnational private regulatory (TPR) regimes. TPR regimes, accordingly, present a particularly acute challenge.[1] A central problem of such regimes is to understand the conditions under which the variety of norms secure conformity, and to distinguish these circumstances from those where, although a variety of governing norms are available, none consistently steer behaviour.

We argue in this paper that a central aspect of regulatory compliance is the institutionalization and embedding of norms within some wider set of structures. Classically the crystallization of norms occurs within the processes for legislating or rule making, such that the regulatory rules are recognized as valid legal rules requiring obedience to them. The challenge to state sovereignty associated with increasing emphasis on supranational and non-state governance of economic and social life requires a degree of rethinking of how norms become effective. A wide array of rules within TPR regimes do not have an authoritative legal source and are crystallized within other institutional structures, such as those of social groups or markets. From this starting point, the focus of this paper is on setting out the variety of norms which shape behaviour within regulatory regimes generally, and TPR regimes in particular, and seeking some understanding of the conditions under which norms 'crystallize', to take on de jure or de facto binding properties.

Crystallization is the process through which fluids are solidified, starting from a nucleus and then growing in a fashion which assumes a regular pattern in a very marked contrast to the boundaries of the fluid from which it emerged. A process of crystallization thus gives shape to what was previously shapeless, defining and giving significance to elements of the structure. Drawing on this process, our particular understanding of the crystallization of norms suggests a process by which norms take on regulative effects.

Whilst the article contributes to the widespread challenge to the centrality of official or formal law in contemporary regulatory governance, it suggests that there is significance in the institutionalization of rule-making processes external to the state, long held to be a central property of official law.[2] We argue that institutionalization, by which we mean the embedding of norms within some wider structures which impact upon their distribution, enforcement, and mode of transmission generally is central to the effects of regulatory norms (that is, norms which have been set with the intention of

---

1 J. Black, 'Constructing and Contesting Legitimacy and Accountability in Polycentric Regulatory Regimes' (2008) 2 *Regulation and Governance* 137–64, at 144.

2 B. Tamanaha, 'Law and Society', St. John's Legal Studies Research Paper no. 09-0167 (2009).

producing particular effects) and that this is of equal importance to the crystallization of other kinds of norms than law. This paper starts with the case for a broad analysis of norms within regulatory settings and the assortment of mechanisms through which such norms are promulgated. We follow this with a discussion of the problem of crystallization of norms – what are the processes through which norms are linked to the modification of an actor's behaviour? From this analysis we examine the issues of legitimacy and legitimation in the context of the crystallization of norms in TPR regimes. Here, we address how we conceptualize legitimacy and the role legitimacy plays in the processes of crystallization.

A SPAGHETTI BOWL OF NORMS

We are concerned in this article substantially with norms which have regulatory intentions or effects on social and economic behaviour. Thus, we are not concerned with norms governing such matters as identity, values or common sense in themselves. The norms which steer behaviour take a variety of forms and originate from a multitude of sources. Such norms have been subject to numerous taxonomies and analytical schema. Regulatory norms comprise prescriptions of behaviour, to which sanctions of one kind or another are attached for breach.[3] In the paper, 'A Typology of Norms', Morris establishes a classification which attends to the 'salience of norms' rather than 'content criteria'.[4] Morris's typology, we argue, is fundamentally concerned with regulatory norms and is suggestive of a series of continua which address the *distribution* of a norm (extent of knowledge, acceptance, and application), its *enforcement* (rewards and punishments, enforcing agency, extent of enforcement, source of authority, degree of internaliza- tion), mode of *transmission* (socialization process and degree of reinforce- ment by subjects), and *conformity* to the norm (amount of conformity and deviance by objects and kind of deviance).[5]

Morris's typology is valuable in explicating the parameters of norms with regulatory intentions or effects. However, it says little about the context in which norms are likely to be: more or less widely known; more or less widely accepted; more or less conformed to, and so on. These are key issues at the heart of the problem of crystallization. Within this spaghetti bowl, the norms which govern a particular social actor's conduct will depend upon a number of relational factors. A social actor's participation within a specific jurisdiction, agreement, community, and/or market setting will dictate which norms may be applicable to their conduct. Following a well-established

---

3 R.T. Morris, 'A Typology of Norms' (1956) 21 *Am. Sociological Rev.* 610–13, at 610.
4 id., p. 612.
5 id.

three-way analysis of social ordering generally – hierarchy, market, and social ordering – we can think of three main categories of norms, namely, legal, social, and market.[6]

Legal norms in regulatory governance settings classically originate from the decisions of legislatures (or ministries and agencies under delegated legislative powers) to prescribe or prohibit certain conduct, to attach sanctions for breach and, sometimes, to establish machinery for detecting deviations from the norm which has been set (for example, an agency with duties to monitor behaviour and powers to investigate, delegation to a non-state body such as a professional organization, and sometimes incentives to,[7] or requirements on third parties to enforce).[8] It is clearly a prerequisite to the operation of such regimes that there is a commitment amongst the targeted community to the law-making process. The absence of such commitment is a key factor in explaining the limited reach of law in international regimes.[9] The limits of public international law are demonstrated by long-standing frustrations over the effects and effectiveness of norms on human rights which have the status of public international law but which are routinely breached by many, if not all, signatory states.[10]

TPR regimes have emerged which are also underpinned by law. However, these regulatory regimes' reliance on law tends to derive from the contractual relationships between the actors involved rather than from public law instruments. Such regulatory regimes include those based on individuated contractual relations (as when standards are included in supply-chain contracts which also outline modes of monitoring, such as third-party certification,[11] and mechanisms for dealing with non-compliance) and on associational contractual relations (as when members of an association agree to be bound by the association's code).[12]

In many situations legal rules are not the predominant steering mechanisms which guide a social actor's behaviour. Rather, social norms which emanate from communities govern much human behaviour. Regimes based on social norms emerge in the community at large and, in particular,

6 R.E. Goodin, 'Democratic Accountability: The Distinctiveness of the Third Sector' (2003) 44 *European Archives of Sociology* 359.

7 J. Braithwaite, *Regulatory Capitalism: How it Works, Ideas for Making it Work Better* (2008) ch. 3.

8 J.A. Gilboy, 'Compelled Third-Party Participation in the Regulatory Process: Legal Duties, Culture, and Non-Compliance' 20 *Law and Policy* 135–55.

9 K.W. Abbott and D. Snidal, 'Hard and Soft Law in International Governance' (2000) 54 *International Organization* 421–56, at 422.

10 G. Teeple, 'Honoured in the Breach: Human Rights as Principles of a Past Age' (2007) 1 *Studies in Social Justice* 136–45.

11 M. Blair, C.A. Williams, and L.W. Lin, 'The New Role for Assured Services in Global Commerce' (2007) 33 *J. of Corporate Law* 325–60.

12 C. Scott, 'Private Regulation of the Public Sector: A Neglected Facet of Contemporary Governance' (2002) 29 *J. of Law and Society* 56–76.

communities such as those based around professions. A core feature of social norms is their *normativity*. By this, we mean that social norms are prescriptions or proscriptions embedded in a society or community of what *ought* to be done (or not done).[13] Despite this, what *ought* to be done is not necessarily what is *actually* done. As such, the existence of a social norm, in and of itself, does not say anything about the regulatory effects of such norms. While there may be a social norm in many societies which may take the form of 'you ought not to litter' or 'in restaurants, you ought not to talk on your mobile phone', we still see litter on the streets and people talking on their phones in restaurants. However, failure to follow social norms can elicit responses that may involve signs of disapproval, ostracization, and other measures. Breaches of social norms may be characterized as anti-social (as opposed to illegal) behaviour.

The effectiveness of social norms is a central theme of Lisa Bernstein's study of the evolution and application of non-legal norms in the New York diamond trade.[14] The system of regulation which she describes originated within a relatively homogeneous group of diamond traders capable of enforcing their own social norms. Enforcement depended both on agreements by dealers on joining the club to submit all disputes to the club's arbitration process, and the reputational effects associated with conduct breaching the norms. Thus, there was a strongly institutionalized system for enforcement of norms in a very tight-knit, though gradually fragmenting group of traders. Whilst Bernstein claims that the bonds of this community are one of the central characteristics underlying its effectiveness, institutionalization of social norms may occur in more fragmented settings. Indeed, Bernstein highlights how technology has been used to bolster the effectiveness of the social norms upon the industry in the face of the global fragmentation.[15] In the context of TPR regimes more generally, a highly diffused picture of regulatory capacity has emerged with non-governmental organizations (NGOs), businesses, and associations of businesses having varying degrees of involvement in hundreds and perhaps thousands of different regimes, some exhibiting a degree of overlap and even competition for adherents. Other things being equal, those regimes which exhibit a degree of tightness in their social organization (for example, because they are oriented around a particular profession or specialized market) are likely have greater capacity for implementing social norms distinct from the legal obligations of participants.

13 J. Woodward, 'Why Do People Cooperate as Much as They Do' in *Philosophy of the Social Sciences: Philosophical Theory and Scientific Practice*, ed. C. Mantzavinos (2009).
14 L. Bernstein, 'Opting Out of the Legal System: Extralegal Contractual Relations in the Diamond Industry' (1992) 21 *J. of Legal Studies* 115–57.
15 id.

Norms which emerge from within markets are classically set through the interaction of many buyers and sellers, and most centrally relate to the price/quality ratio of goods and services. Other matters too may be the subject of market norms, such as dispute resolution procedures. In some instances, what we might think of as pure market processes for establishing and enforcing norms proves inadequate. For the millions of people who buy and sell regularly on eBay, there are risks involved which relate to non-delivery, poor quality, non-payment, and so on. eBay has developed clear norms and a mechanism under which buyers rate sellers. This information underpins an enforcement mechanism where sellers with few or poor ratings may need to sell at a lower price (if they can sell at all) than would be the case if they had better ratings.[16] This simple enforcement mechanism incentivizes compliance and permits sellers who build up strong ratings to sell successfully.

Processes of technical standardization have emerged also as mechanisms for addressing weaknesses in the coordinating capacity of markets, and as alternative mechanism for setting norms for market actors, with the standard-setting process involving key industry actors, through decisions on adoption or not of norms which occur in market settings.[17] In the case of technical standardization, the process for the making of norms is more of a social than a market process, involving deliberation by groups of key industry actors. Nevertheless, the success or failure of a technical standard is largely determined by its take-up within a particular market through, for instance, its adoption both in production processes and in the specification within supply contracts. In addition to technical standards, other kinds of norms are also incorporated within contracts. Such norms include those that require suppliers to comply with ethical rules governing employment of workers.[18]

It is clear that the range of norms which are *available* to govern an actor's conduct does not automatically answer the question of which norms *actually* govern that actor's behaviour. Whilst a wide variety of norms may exist within fluid governance settings, only a proportion may crystallize into a system in which expectations are set by the norms. Indeed, empirical research has shown that, in particular contexts, both contractual and regulatory, while legal rules may be applicable to a specific action of a certain social actor or actors, for instance, through contractual agreement or legislation, these legal rules are not relied upon to steer their conduct.[19]

---

16 D. Lucking-Reiley, D. Bryan, N. Prasad, and D. Reevers, 'Pennies from eBay: The Determinants of Price in Online Auctions' (2007) 55 *J. of Industrial Economics* 223–33.
17 K.T. Hallström, *Organizing International Standardization: ISO and IASC in Quest of Authority* (2004).
18 C. McCrudden, 'Using Public Procurement to Achieve Social Outcomes' (2004) 28 *Natural Resources Forum* 257–67.
19 P. Grabosky and J. Braithwaite, *Of Manners Gentle: Enforcement Strategies of Australian Business Regulatory Agencies* (1986); S. Macaulay, 'Non-Contractual Relations in Business: A Preliminary Study' (1963) 28 *Am. Sociological Rev.* 55–67.

Furthermore, although a legal rule may have been promulgated by a legislator, it may not have crystallized to guide social actors' behaviour. In such cases, social norms may guide the specific conduct of the actor. The implication of this observation is that the mere categorization of norms according to their source is not sufficient to identify their actual effects. We argue that what is important when evaluating norms is not their source. Rather, the crux lies in whether such norms have crystallized so as to govern behaviour. In other words, whether what ought to be done, is in fact done.

THE DYNAMICS OF CRYSTALLIZATION

A wide variety of norms are available for the governance of social and economic behaviour in national and transnational settings. We suggest that the processes of crystallization are central to shaping the effects of norms on behaviour. The central problem associated with crystallization is to understand the factors which result in conformity, more or less, with a norm. There is no single answer to the question of how various norms crystallize and produce binding effects upon those actors to whom they are addressed. Rather, norms may crystallize through a variety of mechanisms. Some clues are to be found in analyses which set down parameters relating to both the nature and extent of institutionalization of regulatory norms. These parameters are indicative not of a sharp distinction between norms which are crystallized and those which are not. Rather, they highlight a number of continua within which any particular norm may be located. These factors can be broadly understood as relating to the extent to which a norm has been distributed, the degree of enforcement of the norm, and its mode of transmission. From such a perspective, conformity is the dependent variable which may be explained by reference to distribution, enforcement and/or mode of transmission.

Analysis of the distribution of a norm relates to the extent to which it is known, accepted, and applied. Knowledge of a norm is frequently not only a product of its promulgation. Training and education for those involved in applying the norm and sometimes information campaigns and notices may also play a key role in building such knowledge. By contrast, it may be argued that social norms by their very nature imply that what ought to be done is known by the community in which norms operate. Acceptance of a norm may involve consideration of both the process through which it emerges, its content, and its likely effects. Crystallization of norms is therefore heavily reliant upon the instruments which can transmit information that educates actors about not only the substantive content of rules, but also the objectives which underlie norms and methods by which norms can be complied with. In respect of application, the classical conception of law was that of universal applicability. A widespread observation associated with the emergence of both welfare and regulatory states

82

has been the application of more materialized or highly specified rules to sub-sections of society.[20]

Analysis of the enforcement of a norm is concerned with the rewards and punishment associated with following the norm, the mechanisms and extent of enforcement, the source of authority, and the degree of internalization. A classical regulatory regime involves the oversight of compliance with regulatory rules by a unit within a ministry or a specialized agency, with powers to gather information and to apply sanctions. A considerable volume of empirical evidence in the United States, the United Kingdom, and Australia suggests that enforcement processes frequently do not involve the stringent application of regulatory rules.[21] Instead, a wide range of approaches, often involving education and advice to those found in breach, are utilized ahead of more stringent actions – warnings, civil or criminal penalties, and license revocations. In their classic model of responsive regulation Ayres and Braithwaite array these potential responses in an enforcement pyramid, combining the empirical evidence of the practice of escalating sanctions with the game-theory arguments as to how and when such escalation should occur.[22] The application of the enforcement pyramid is intended to ensure that regulatees who are fundamentally oriented towards legal compliance receive appropriate advice to enable them to meet this objective. On the other hand, the credible threat of escalation encourages the 'amoral calculators' (who only comply when this is consistent with financial incentives) to comply at the lowest level of the pyramid, because non-compliance would be more costly. Thus, even within classical regulatory regimes, rewards and punishment may occur within the framework of the legislative regime, but not be determined by it. Thus, crystallization does not occur at the legislative moment, but rather in the practices of the overseeing agency and its relations with those whom it oversees.

Within TPR regimes operated under individuated or collective contracts, the authority for oversight and enforcement derives not from legislation but from contract and is frequently linked to market incentives for compliance (or not). Such regimes often involve the crystallization of social norms within particular professional or commercial groupings (as with many professional and standards bodies, or in the case of the New York diamond industry, discussed above). In such regimes, the norms are thus reflected in contractual arrangements and reinforced through participation in markets.

Social norms may be crystallized to the extent that they trump legal norms. An intriguing example is presented by Robert Ellickson's famous study of neighbour disputes in Shasta County. Ellickson was interested in

20 G. Teubner, 'Juridification: Concepts, Aspects, Limits, Solutions' in *A Reader on Regulation*, eds. R. Baldwin, C. Scott, and C. Hood (1998).
21 Grabosky and Braithwaite, op. cit., n. 19; R. Cranston, *Regulating Business: Law and Consumer Agencies* (1979).
22 I. Ayres and J. Braithwaite, *Responsive Regulation: Transcending the Deregulation Debate* (1992).

testing the Coase theorem, which was based around an example of neighbour disputes, and observed the norms surrounding the consequences when cattle broke out of their ranches causing damage to the land of other farmers. Within Shasta county, two different legal regimes were operating – one of strict liability caused by stray cattle and the other denying liability. Even those ranchers aware of this distinction were found to operate their practices and dispute resolution on the basis that it is wrong to let cattle stray.[23] Within this meta-norm exist subsidiary social norms requiring notification to ranchers when their cattle stray and a quick response and apology from the offending cattle-owner. Minor harm is lumped rather than pursued and stray cattle are boarded without charge, often for many weeks, until a convenient time for their return is agreed.[24] Where the social norms are persistently breached there is the potential for an escalating set of sanctions against the deviant, starting with social sanctions (such as negative gossip) and which may eventually reach a formal legal claim.[25] Within TPR regimes, similarly, it is likely that social norms frequently underpin the reasonable operation of a regime by the parties with a degree of reinforcement through market sanctions and/or the possibility of resort to legal sanctions for significant or harmful deviation from such norms.

Whilst the institutionalization associated with legal, social, and market norms are quite varied when considering the distribution and enforcement of norms, it may be quite similar when considering modes of transmission. Socialization is the process through which we learn about norms which apply to our conduct. Flowing from this, reinforcement may be conceived of as the process by which others enhance the impact of such socialization processes. Socialization affects how we act, not only in respect of social norms, but also legal and market norms. Such processes involve those with whom we are in direct contact – in family, education and peer-group settings. In addition, a central role in this process may also be played by the mass media. Governments are particularly cognisant of this dimension of making norms effective. For example, substantial criminal penalties for driving with blood-alcohol above minimum levels are backed up with advertising campaigns that go beyond informing drivers of the penalties and seek to affect both socialization processes and the reinforcement of messages surrounding the social unacceptability of drink-driving. The introduction of a levy on plastic bags supplied in retail premises in Ireland created a modest financial incentive to reuse plastic bags rather than dispose of them after a single use.[26] The effects of this widely accepted levy have, arguably, been magnified by the

23 R.C. Ellickson, 'Of Coase and Cattle: Dispute Resolution Amongst Neighbours in Shasta County' (1986) 38 *Stanford Law Rev.* 623–87, at 673.
24 id., p. 674.
25 id., p. 677.
26 F. Convery, S. McDonnell, and S. Ferreira, 'The Most Popular Tax in Europe? Lessons from the Irish Plastic Bag Levy' (2007) 38 *Environmental and Resource Economics* 1–11.

84

emergence of social norms which reject the taking of plastic bags, even where the taker complies with the requirement to pay a levy.

To take a further example, a central mechanism of contemporary regulatory governance is supply-chain contracts which specify standards or norms with which the contractor must comply. Such contracts are frequently used to import norms developed in other contexts which are less than fully institutionalized. Whilst supply-chain contracts are one individuated mechanism for institutionalizing standards, an alternative and more general mechanism is the specification of compliance with technical standards in legislative instruments making particular standards mandatory as a condition of market participation or, alternatively, incentivizing take-up of such standards by providing that compliance with a technical standard will be deemed to comply with some broader legal principles, such as product safety

The take-up of standards in supply-chain contracts is not restricted to technical standards, as traditionally conceived, and extends also to broader non-state governance regimes, such as those applying to issues of environmental protection and fair trade. In the case of the standards set by the Forest Stewardship Council, these were adopted by major retailers in their supply-chain contracts because of market pressures to show strong environmental performance – a process described as Non-State Market-Driven Governance.[27] The incorporation of standards into supply-chain contracts is transparent to the parties and has been subject to well developed mechanisms of monitoring and enforcement (for example, through third-party certification).[28] Accordingly, there is frequently a high degree of institutionalization.

Knowledge and acceptance of a norm is part of the process of entering into a contract. While entering into a contract (and indeed the terms) are classically treated as voluntary matters by the parties, the voluntary character has long been questioned.[29] It is possible to imagine circumstances where a contractor enters into the contract without being fully accepting of the detailed terms. Furthermore, the authority for enforcing supply-chain contracts is the contract itself, which will frequently provide terms relating to monitoring and sanctions for breach, and additionally create the potential for not renewing a contract where compliance has not been satisfactory. Empirical research in the United States and the United Kingdom automotive industries has found that contracting parties frequently do not rely on the law

---

27 B. Cashore, 'Legitimacy and the Privatization of Environmental Governance: How Non-State Market-Driven (NSMD) Governance Systems Gain Rule-Making Authority' (2002) 15 *Governance: An International J. of Policy, Administration and Institutions* 503–29.
28 Blair et al., op. cit., n. 11.
29 A. Stinchcombe, 'Contracts as Hierarchical Documents' in *Organizational Theory and Project Management,* eds. A. Stinchcombe and C. Heimer (1985); R.L. Hale, 'Coercion and Distribution in a Supposedly Non-Coercive State' (1923) 38 *Pol. Sci. Q.* 470–8.

or lawyers in resolving disputes over breaches – widely understood as the product of their relationship being institutionalized socially and economically, as much as legally.[30] So, within such contractual settings, we should not assume that the contract is the instrument of institutionalization which it appears to be.

With supply-chain processes the dimension of socialization and reinforcement occurs largely through market processes – the acceptable modes of negotiating and treating contractual obligations (whether they are treated in formal or informal terms). Just as the Shasta County ranchers largely resolve cattle trespass disputes informally, so with business-people operating in this manner, there is frequently the potential to pursue formal sanctions, held in reserve, for anti-social actors who do not follow the applicable social norms in their relationships. Pressures to ensure strict compliance may be external. For example specification of ethical norms relating to fair trade or labour rights within supply-chain contracts may form part of the expectations of consumers associated with products.[31] More generally, Gunningham et al. have extended the idea of companies being governed by an implicit 'social licence to operate' as underpinning the legitimate operation of companies, beyond the extractive industries from which the idea emerged.[32]

THE LEGITIMATION OF NORMS

In this section we argue that processes of legitimation are fundamental to the crystallization of regulatory norms. A number of questions assist in illuminating the significance of legitimacy and the legitimation of regulatory norms in the context of crystallization. First, what do we mean when we assert that a regulatory norm is legitimate? Secondly, what is the importance of legitimacy and what role does legitimacy play in the crystallization of regulatory norms? Thirdly, what are the possible reasons which underlie the legitimacy of regulatory norms and regulatory regimes? Finally, how can regulatory regimes seek to achieve the legitimation of the norms which they produce? This section will address each of these questions.

---

30 Macaulay, op. cit., n. 19; H. Beale and T. Dugdale, 'Contracts Between Businessmen' (1974) 2 *Brit. J. of Law and Society* 45–60. Macaulay's empirical research highlighted that contract law is often times ignored in favour of non-legal norms in business transaction, By contrast, Beale and Dugdale buttressed this observation by identifying that, in many cases, businessmen expressly agreed upon primary obligations only, while issues related to the business relationship were left to be regulated by tacit non-legal norms.
31 D.A. Kysar, 'Preferences for Processes' (2004) 118 *Harvard Law Rev.* 526–642.
32 N. Gunningham, R. Kagan, and D. Thornton, 'Social License and Environmental Protection: Why Businesses Go Beyond Compliance' (2004) 29 *Law and Social Inquiry* 307–41.

86

The legitimacy of regulatory norms may be addressed from a normative and a sociological perspective. In normative terms, legitimacy speaks of the acceptability of regulatory norms, and whether or not such norms can be justified by reference to certain predetermined 'standards and criteria of legitimacy'.[33] One can identify four broad criteria which are frequently prescribed to evaluate the legitimacy of regulatory norms and regimes: constitutional; democratic; functional and performance-based; and values- and objectives-based.[34] Constitutional evaluations of regulatory norms and regimes emphasize issues such as fair procedures, due process, consistency, coherence, proportionality, and the existence of 'oversight from constitutionally established bodies such as national courts, legislatures or executives or international organisations'.[35] Where such norms and regimes are assessed by reference to democratic standards, the extent and effectiveness of participation, transparency, accountability, and deliberation in the norm-formation process are given prominence.[36] Normative evaluations, which stress the values and objectives of regulatory norms, focus on the underlying ends which the norms and the regulatory regime seek to achieve, for example, fair trade, good agricultural practices, market efficiencies, and sustainable development.[37] Finally, functional and performance-based appraisals point to issues such as the degree of expert involvement in the production of regulatory norms, and the effectiveness and efficiency of such norms in achieving the objectives which they pursue.[38]

By contrast to these normative and essentially prescriptive approaches to legitimacy, the sociological perspective embraces the view that '[l]egitimacy is a quality that society ascribes to an actor's identity, interests, or practices, or to an institution's norms, rules or principles'.[39] Hence, legitimacy is conceived of as an objective constituent that may or may not be present in a particular regulatory norm or regime. In line with our thinking in relation to the crystallization of regulatory norms, we conceptualize legitimacy as an empirical phenomenon rather than a normative abstraction. Drawing on

33 J. Steffek, 'The Legitimation of International Governance: A Discourse Approach' (2003) 9 European J. of International Relations 249–75, at 253.
34 J. Black and D. Rouch, 'The Development of the Global Markets as Rule Makers: Engagement and Legitimacy' (2008) 2 Law and Financial Markets Rev. 218–33.
35 id., p. 225.
36 M. Zürn, 'Democratic Governance Beyond the Nation State: The EU and Other International Institutions' (2006) 6 European J. of International Relations 183–221; T. Risse, 'Transnational Governance and Legitimacy', and K.D. Wolf, 'Private Actors and the Legitimacy of Governance Beyond the State', both in Governance and Democracy: Comparing National, European and International Experiences, eds. A. Benz and Y. Papadopoulos (2006) 179–99, 200–27; F.W. Scharpf, Interdependence and Democratic Legitimation (1998).
37 Black and Rouch, op. cit., n. 34.
38 N. Brunnson and B. Jacobsson, A World of Standards (2000).
39 C. Reus-Smith, 'International Crises of Legitimacy' (2007) 44 International Politics 157–74, at 159.

Suchman's schema, we argue that a regulatory norm is legitimate where there is a 'generalised perception or assumption' that the norm is 'desirable, proper, or appropriate within some socially constructed system of norms, values, beliefs, and definitions'.[40] Thus, for a regulatory norm to be legitimate, it must be accepted by those to whom it is addressed. The underlying rationales for acceptance and, therefore, the legitimation of a regulatory norm lie in the existence of congruence between the norm and actors' 'beliefs or expectations or ... interests'.[41] To some extent socially accepted norms overlap with social norms. Nevertheless, it is perfectly possible for norms generated other than through social processes to be accepted too, and it is the variety of mechanisms through which acceptance of norms generally occurs which are of interest here.

What is the importance of legitimacy and what role does legitimacy play in the crystallization of regulatory norms? The answers to these questions lie in the way in which actors react to regulatory norms which they perceive as legitimate. Here, 'the central empirical premise of legitimacy is well supported – legitimacy is an effective influence strategy'.[42] This empirical premise rests on a number of observations which are fundamentally important to the crystallization of regulatory norms. First, legitimacy creates a sense of obligation, upon those that confer a regulatory norm with legitimacy, to act in accordance with the particular norm. While a sense of obligation does not necessarily lead to compliance, it does increase the likelihood that a regulatory norm will be obeyed. As such, the legitimation of a regulatory norm may obviate the need for extensive and inefficient monitoring and enforcement mechanisms within a regulatory regime. Secondly, a regulatory regime which has been legitimated will be able not just to foster passive support for its norms but will also be able to garner active support from those actors which it seeks to steer through its norms.[43] This is of particular importance in relation to regulatory norms which seek to steer behaviour as active support is a 'critical element in motivating behavioural responses'.[44] While individuals may agree to be bound by a contract, it does not necessarily follow that their actions will change in line with contractual obligations. Where active support is granted to the regulatory norms contained within contracts, however, active compliance with contractual obligations in the absence of coercion can be enhanced.

---

40 M. Suchman, 'Managing Legitimacy: Strategic and Institutional Approaches' (1995) 20 *Academy of Management Rev.* 571–610, at 574.

41 Black, op. cit., n. 1, p. 144.

42 T.R. Tyler, 'Psychological Perspectives on Legitimacy and Legitimation' (2006) 57 *Annual Rev. of Psychology* 375–400, at 392.

43 Reus-Smith, op. cit., n. 39, p. 163; Suchman, op. cit., n. 40, p. 575; R. Hülsse, 'Even Clubs Can't do without Legitimacy: Why the Anti-Money Laundering Blacklist was Suspended' (2008) 2 *Regulation and Governance* 459–79.

44 Black, op. cit., n. 1, p. 148.

Thirdly, by providing a 'reservoir of support',[45] legitimacy can lead to the stability and persistence of regulatory norms even when they attempt to shape behaviour in ways which are immediately undesirable.[46] This aspect of legitimacy, therefore, enhances the persistence of regulatory norms in situations where they no longer serve the immediate interests of their intended audience. Tyler concludes that legitimacy is central to:

> whether or not authorities in organised groups are effective in shaping the voluntary behaviour of group members. Such voluntary behaviour is, in turn, central to the effectiveness of authorities because, although authorities typically have some ability to reward rule following and punish rule breaking, leadership based on reward, coercion, or both is difficult and often ineffective.[47]

As such, legitimacy is of crucial important to the processes of the crystallization as it can create a sense of obligation and bolsters active support for regulatory norms while aiding the persistence and stability of such norms.

As noted above, legitimacy as we conceive it refers to a quality which is attributed to a regulatory norm or regime where there is congruence between the norms or regime and actors' 'beliefs or expectations or ... interests'.[48] This conjunction may exist at a normative, pragmatic and/or cognitive level.[49] Legitimacy may be provided because aspects of the regulatory norm relating to how it was created, and/or its substantive content, are aligned with the particular normative evaluative criteria of those actors to whom the norm are addressed. Therefore, our conceptualization of legitimacy is not insulated from normative concerns such as those rooted in constitutional, democratic, performance- or value-based evaluative criteria. Nevertheless, such evaluations are empirically grounded in the specific normative concerns of the actors whose behaviour the regulatory norm seeks to shape. A 2007 survey carried out by ISEAL, an alliance of social and environmental TPRs, spotlighted the important role which such normative evaluations play in the legitimation of standard-setting organizations, including TPRs.[50] The survey results showed that inclusiveness, participation, fair representation, and independence of auditing all played a crucial role in the assessment of the credibility of standards which, in turn, feeds into the legitimacy of TPRs. Indeed, the Marine Stewardship Council, established by the World Wildlife Fund and Unilever in 1996, was initially criticized due to perceived industry

---

45 M. Weatherford, 'Measuring Political Legitimacy' (1992) 86 *Am. Pol. Sci. Rev.* 149–66.

46 Suchman, op. cit., n. 40, pp. 574–5; Tyler, op. cit., n. 42, p. 381.

47 T. Tyler, 'The Psychology of Legitimacy: A Relational Perspective on Voluntary Deference to Authorities' (1997) 1 *Personality and Social Psychology Rev.* 323–45, at 335.

48 Black, op. cit., n. 1, p. 144.

49 Suchman, op. cit., n. 40.

50 S. Bernstein, 'Legitimacy in Intergovernmental and Non-State Global Governance' (2011) 18 *Rev. of International Political Economy* (forthcoming).

capture and lack of transparency and participation in its standard-setting procedures. In light of these criticisms, the MSC became a fully independent non-profit organization in 1998, and undertook a comprehensive governance reform to enhance participation, representation, and transparency.[51]

One of the most striking examples of TPR over the past two decades has been the emergence of TPR in the policy area of forestry. Within this policy area, the Forest Stewardship Council (FSC), on which the MSC is based, has been the most active of the TPRs in the institutionalization of processes which attempt to increase its legitimacy, and in turn, crystallize the norms relating to responsible forest management. The FSC was created in 1993 by a number of environmental NGOs, some members of the timber industry, and the World Wildlife Fund (WWF), and was formally recognized as a non-profit organization in 1995.[52] In order to address the normative concerns of many of its stakeholders, the FSC has institutionalized an elaborate governance structures which is based upon 'participation', 'democracy', and 'equality'.[53] The FSC has established a tripartite governance structure composed of social, environmental, and economic chambers which have equal voting rights. Within each chamber, there are both north and south sub-chambers with equal voting rights attached to each section irrespective of the number of members. In order for any decision to be made, there is a requirement that two-thirds vote, which necessitates agreement not only between social, environmental, and economic interests, but also between north and south interests. This situation can be contrasted with that of GLOBALGAP, a TPR in the sphere of food safety and quality. While GLOBALGAP has initiated processes to enhance participation in its standard setting, such as notice-and-comment procedures, the Board of GLOBALGAP is still composed of retailer and producer representatives. While GLOBALGAP recognized the need to open up its standard-setting procedure, these actors felt that ultimate control of the organization should remain in the hands of the retailers and producers.[54] Similar arrangements can also be found in industry-led forest certification schemes.[55]

51 L.H. Gulbrandsen, *Transnational Environmental Governane: The Emergenence and Effects of the Certification of Forests and Fisheries* (2010).
52 L.H. Gulbrandsen, 'Organizing Accountability in Transnational Standards Organizations: The Forest Stewardship Council as a Good Governance Model' in *Organizing Transnational Accountability: Mobilization, Tools, Challenges,* eds. M. Boström and C. Garsten (2008).
53 E. Meidinger, 'The Administrative Law of Global Private-Public Regulation: The Case of Forestry' (2006) 17 *European J. of International Law* 47–87; E. Meidinger, 'Competitive Supragovernmental Regulation: How Could it be Democratic' (2008) 8 *Chicago J. of International Law* 513–34.
54 Interview with GLOBALGAP representative (26 March 2010).
55 B. Cashore, G. Auld, and D. Newsom, *Governing Through Markets: Forest Certification and the Emergence of Non-State Authority* (2004); L.H. Gulbrandsen, 'Accountability Arrangements in Non-State Standards Organizations: Instrumental Design and Imitation' (2008) 15 *Organization* 563–83.

In her study of the international standardization organization, the ISO, Tamm Hallström suggests that traditionally, given the industry focus of the ISO, and its core business of setting technical standards, its legitimacy was generally assessed along two lines.[56] First, legitimacy was assessed by the extent to which there was expertise in the standard-setting process, a normatively based evaluation. Secondly, however, the legitimacy of ISO standards were assessed by the degree to which the ISO standards allowed for the rationalization of standards in a particular area, and the associated benefits which flow from such a rationalization. Legitimacy evaluations based upon the ability of TPRs such as ISO to rationalize existing standards highlight the fact that pragmatic or instrumental evaluations may also play an important role in the legitimation of regulatory norms.[57] Pragmatic or instrumental evaluations rest upon whether or not a regulatory norm serves, or is perceived to be a response to, the needs and interests of its intended audience. Cashore, Auld, and Newsom suggested that the key factors which led businesses to support the FSC were based on pragmatic evaluations related to the possibility of either increased market access or the protection of market share, and not through normative evaluations relating to participation, transparency, and so on.[58] In order to manage such evaluations, it has engaged in campaigns which seek to damage the brands of those which do not support the FSC. Pragmatic legitimacy is, in many respects, similar to Scharpf's output dimension of his theory of democracy and legitimate democratic rule.[59] The substantive output aspect of the concept requires authority to be effective in solving the audiences' problems and meeting their needs. Finally, the legitimacy attributed to a regulatory norm may be cognitively based. Cognitive legitimacy may be granted, for example, where a regulatory norm pursues an objective which is socially understood and taken for granted as desirable, proper or appropriate.

Stemming from this discussion is the observation that the legitimation of a regulatory norm may be rooted in one rationale or a number of different ones which may be normatively, pragmatically, and/or cognitively based. In order for legitimacy to be granted to regulatory norms, those regulatory regimes which produce norms must be cognisant of and, responsive to the legitimacy demands of those actors whose behaviour their norms seek to shape. Indeed, regulatory regimes must 'focus on those being led' and '[w]idespread legitimacy will exist only when the perspectives of everyday members are enshrined in institutions and in the actions of authorities'.[60] The extent to

---

56 K. Tamm Hallström, 'ISO Expands its Business into Social Responsibility' in *Organizing Transnational Accountability: Mobilization, Tools, Challenges,* eds. M. Boström and C. Garsten (2008).
57 Black, op. cit., n. 1; Cashore, op. cit., n. 27; Tyler, op. cit., n. 42; Cashore et al., op. cit., n. 55.
58 Cashore et al., id.
59 Scharpf, op. cit., n. 36; Bernstein, op. cit., n. 50.
60 Tyler, op. cit., n. 42, p. 392.

which the multitude of normative evaluations and the degree to which instrumental or cognitive rationales underlie the granting of legitimacy will depend not only on the particular regulatory regime in question, but also may vary between the different actors which are subject to the regulatory norms. For example, effective participation in the standard-setting process and the ability of a technical standard to facilitate market access may be crucial to whether or not suppliers grant legitimacy to the technical standard institutionalized within a supply-chain contract. Nevertheless, in order for purchasers to grant such a standard of legitimacy and to incorporate such a standard within their supply-chain contracts, they may need to be convinced that the standard not only enhances efficiency, but also achieves the objective it pursues, such as the guarantee of product safety. Consequently, a number of different legitimacy demands may be made by those actors to whom regulatory norms are addressed.

As noted above, traditionally the legitimacy of ISO standards was assessed by reference to the degree of expertise and the extent to which ISO standards rationalized technical standards. However, Tamm Hallström offers an example which highlights how a TPR can find itself in a legitimacy dilemma.[61] As the ISO expanded its scope from technical standards and began to develop a social responsibility standard, ISO 26000, expertise and rationalization were insufficient in and of themselves to legitimate the new standard. The ISO recognized that, given the potential users of such a standard, it had to adapt its standard-setting procedure to open it up to wider stakeholders such as NGOs and consumer groups. In order to do this, the ISO set up six specific stakeholder categories and created new procedural rules so that all stakeholder views were represented. By doing so, however, it was faced with new types of stakeholders who had different legitimacy demands from those previously dealt with. In particular, a legitimacy dilemma was created when the NGO and consumer stakeholder groups demanded that the standard-setting process be more transparent and opened to the media. However, the demand for increased transparency was successfully contested by the industry stakeholder groups. The significant point is that legitimacy demands are not homogenous. While there may be congruence, and indeed a certain degree of compatibility between legitimacy demands, it is equally likely these demands will lead to contestation. Such an environment may lead to a 'legitimacy dilemma' for a regulatory regime:

> [W]hat they need to do to be accepted by one part of their environment is contrary to how they need to respond to another ... It is simply not possible to have complete legitimacy from all aspects of its environment.[62]

61 Tamm Hallström, op. cit., n. 56.
62 J. Black, 'Contesting Accountability and Legitimacy in Non-State Regulatory Regimes', Basel Institute of Governance Conference Paper (2007) 7, 8, at: <http://www.baselgovernance.org/fileadmin/docs/pdfs/Nonstate/Paper-Black.pdf>.

Here, regulatory regimes such as standards-setting organizations must make an active choice as to what legitimacy demands they respond to positively, for instance, by introducing greater participation and transparency in the standard-setting process, and which legitimacy demands they choose to dismiss.

The tensions which may emerge in active strategies to manage legitimacy in a transnational private regulatory regime are highlighted by the dependence on others for implementation which characterizes many regimes where the 'peak organization' within the regime is concerned chiefly with the setting of standards. It is not untypical in such regimes that responsibility for monitoring and enforcement is either explicitly or implicitly passed on to others. In some instances, there are private or self-regulatory organizations which may actively manage their legitimacy, but which may also be subject to a degree of steering by the peak organization. A good example of this phenomenon is presented by the variety of self-regulatory organizations for advertising in Europe which have tended to align themselves with the International Chamber of Commerce norms on advertising self-regulation in respect of substantive principles, and with Best Practice Recommendations in respect of regulatory procedures promulgated by the European Advertising Standards Alliance.[63]

Just as common are the regimes where implementation of TPR norms is achieved through their incorporation into supply-chain contracts where a purchaser requires adoption of the applicable standards and engages in monitoring and enforcement either directly or through contracting third-party assurance organizations.[64] Third-party organizations may bring in the norms of their profession, for example, where accounting firms provide assurance services. However, it is clear that bilateral contractual relations within supply-chain contracts present significant problems for the management of legitimacy in terms both of substantive norms and processes, and identifying the level at which such issues are managed.

A documented example of the use of inter-firm contracting to legitimate the governance of a project is presented by the case of the construction of Terminal 5 of Heathrow Airport. Deakin and Koukiadaki have described how the client, airport owner BAA plc, put in place a sophisticated framework for contracting which contained substantive innovations, such as risk pooling between sub-contractors and client, performance monitoring, and also learning mechanisms which provided for 'effective diffusion of information, the use of frameworks, benchmarks and measurement and the operation of integrated teams working'.[65] This contract-based mechanism of

---

63 European Advertising Standards Alliance (EASA), *Blue Book 6: Advertising Self-Regulation in Europe and Beyond* (2010).

64 Blair et al., op. cit., n. 11, pp. 325–60.

65 S. Deakin and A. Koukiadaki, 'Reflexive Approaches to Corporate Governance: The Case of Heathrow Terminal 5' in *Reflexive Governance: Redefining the Public Interest in a Pluralistic World*, eds. O.D. Schutter and J. Lenoble (2010) 108.

governance is said to have allowed the parties to develop a mutual framework of understanding and for adjustment of strategies to address shortcomings. In other words, the construction contracts were transformed, to some extent, from an instrument of hierarchy to an instrument of mutual learning.[66]

The centrality of supply-chain contracts to TPR regimes present significant challenges for legitimating strategies. On a worst-case scenario, they are likely to be experienced coercively by suppliers, resulting in adverse consequences for commitment to the regime. Regimes involving multiple actors, such as where third-party assurance organizations are brought in, increase complexity but also diffuse the responsibility for legitimation. Indeed, the choice of third parties may be part of a legitimation strategy not only vis-à-vis suppliers, but also in respect of ultimate consumers seeking assurance that products are compliant with codes in the manner claimed. To the extent that issues of consumer confidence are significant, there may be strong incentives to manage legitimacy in such a manner. This is a field for further research within particular TPR regimes.

CONCLUSION

The past two decades have witnessed a proliferation of TPR in many significant policy areas. While it is now clear that TPR abounds in global regulatory space, many of the important dynamics of TPR are yet to be sketched out. In this paper, we have addressed one critical dynamic – the process of crystallization of TPR norms. Broadly speaking, crystallization of TPR norms suggests a process by which these norms take on regulative effects and steer behaviour. Our main argument can be broken down into two related parts. Firstly, we argue that the institutionalization of TPR norms – the embedding of norms within some wider structures which impact upon their distribution, enforcement, and mode of transmission – is important in the process of crystallization. Whilst structures which relate to the distribution, enforcement, and mode of transmission of TPR norms are significant, the second aspect of our argument draws attention the critical role played by the institutionalization of the policies, structures, and processes which seek to enhance the legitimacy of TPRs. Here, we perceive legitimacy as a quality which may be attributed to a norm or regulatory regime where there is a perceived congruence between these aspects of a TPR and actors' 'beliefs or expectations or ... interests'.[67] TPR regimes must both recognize and be responsive the expectations of their legitimacy

---

66 See, also, O. Perez, 'Using Private-Public Linkages to Regulate Environmental Conflicts: The Case of International Construction Contracts' (2002) 29 *J. of Law and Society* 77–110.
67 Black, op. cit., n. 1, p. 144.

communities. The importance of legitimacy from the perspective of the crystallization of TPR norms lies in the observations that, where a TPR is perceived as legitimate, a sense of obligation and active support may naturally flow. The potential for managing the legitimacy of a TPR regime has been exploited by such regimes through the institutionalization of policies, structures, and processes which are responsive to the beliefs, expectations or interests of their legitimacy communities and can augment the structures which address the distribution, enforcement, and mode of transmission of norms in crystallizing TPR norms. However, the dependence of many TPR regimes on supply-chain contracts for monitoring and enforcement creates a further significant challenge, beyond the reasonably well developed arrangements for the setting of standards, which has yet to be fully documented and addressed.

JOURNAL OF LAW AND SOCIETY
VOLUME 38, NUMBER 1, MARCH 2011
ISSN: 0263-323X, pp. 96–118

Privatized Sovereign Performance: Regulating in the 'Gap' between Security and Rights?

Fiona de Londras*

This article explores what I term 'privatized sovereign performance': the 'private' operationalization of functions that are intimately connected with the sovereign identity of the state. It is considered in the context of corporate involvement in extraordinary rendition in order to outline the rights-related difficulties it creates or exacerbates, and explore the ways in which transnational private regulatory mechanisms have a role to play in crafting a rights-based response. It argues that the 'public' is saturated in rights-based regulation which pushes a state that wants to conceal its torturous activity into the 'private'; that the conventional private regulatory mechanism of litigation faces significant obstacles and is ineffective in this circumstance; and that transnational private regulation holds potential to align the structural and legal obstructions to torture between the public and private sphere, thus making the 'escape hatch' from rights seemingly presented by the privatization of sovereign performance more difficult to access.

INTRODUCTION

It is trite to observe that states have long acted upon their privatization impulse to outsource the provision of services previously supplied by the

* School of Law, University College Dublin, Dublin 4, Ireland
fiona.delondras@ucd.ie

Earlier versions of some ideas in this paper were presented at the 2009 SLS Annual Conference (Keele), as a Scrymgeour Lecture at Dundee School of Law (September 2009), at the Third Biennial Conference of the ECPR Standing Group on Regulation and Governance (University College Dublin 2010), and at the University of Tilburg (October 2010). My thanks to the participants at these events for their comments, and particularly to Janet McLean, Stephanie Switzer, Aurélie Gilbert, Colin Scott, Aoife O'Donoghue, Linda Senden, Michelle Farrell, and Gavin Simpson. All errors, of course, remain my own.

state[1] and that this movement has for some time exposed the fault lines of human rights law at domestic level. These domestic patterns have been replicating themselves on the transnational and international plane and, for human rights lawyers, the same fault lines and frustrations of enforceability and accountability have emerged. During the 'War on Terrorism' we have witnessed the emergence of particularly worrying forms of privatization; the *Washington Post* recently revealed that '1,931 private companies work on programs related to counterterrorism, homeland security and intelligence in about 10,000 locations across the United States'.[2] While some of these companies provide relatively banal services (such as catering), others present confounding dilemmas for rights-protection. Among them are private companies involved in 'extraordinary rendition'.[3]

This constitutes an example of privatization being used not to 'plug gaps' in state capacity but, rather, in the attempt to exploit the apparently 'private' sphere in order to engage in unquestionably illegal activity, namely, torture. While public law structures (including human rights law) attempt to bolster the absolute anti-torture norm, the privatization of sovereign performance in the context of extraordinary rendition reveals the capacity for that highly structured public sphere's attempts to be frustrated by transferring functions to a 'private' sphere whose regulatory regime enhances the opportunity for such activity to be concealed. It is in that context that one can begin to see how transnational private regulation may constitute part (although not all) of the solution from a rights-protection perspective. Transnational private regulation holds potential for us to ensure an alignment in structural (and legal) obstructions to torture between the public sphere and the private sphere, closing off (or at least making much more difficult to access) the 'escape hatch' seemingly presented by the privatization of sovereign performance.

In this article I begin with a brief outline of the nature of extraordinary rendition and its legal implications. Secondly I trace four parallel developments that, I argue, provide an important context to the analysis of the privatization of sovereign performance that follows. The sum of these two parts is to demonstrate that (a) extraordinary rendition is unquestionably unlawful, and (b) the public sphere, including human rights law, has developed structures in order to support that unlawfulness by placing clear

---

1 See, for example, D. Parker, *Official History of Privatisation: Volume One* (2009); D. Parker and D. Saal (eds.), *International Handbook of Privatization* (2003); M.R. Troillot, 'The Anthropology of the State in the Age of Globalization' (2001) 42 *Current Anthropology* 125–38.

2 'Top Secret America: A Washington Post Investigation' *Washington Post*, 19 July 2010. See <http://projects.washingtonpost.com/top-secret-america/articles/a-hidden-world-growing-beyond-control/>.

3 This is in addition to the long-standing practice of creating 'CIA front companies', which is also thought to take place in the context of extraordinary rendition.

97

rights-based obligations on states, even in times of emergency. A highly developed public sphere from a rights-protection perspective requires states interested in breaching human rights norms to think about how – or, conceptually, *where* – the desired activities can be engaged in with minimal risk to the state. It is in that context that the 'private' sphere can become attractive to a state. This is particularly so if that private sphere is imagined as one that is relatively unregulated from a human rights perspective and sufficiently opaque to significantly increase the chances of concealing unlawful activity. A consideration of some of these 'assumed assumptions' about the imagined transnational private space forms the next part of the article. These two features of the privatization of sovereign performance – transfer and obscurement – are fundamental to understanding both *why* a state might engage in such privatization and *how* we might tackle the vulnerabilities that such privatization highlights in human rights protection.

In outlining the nature of the transnational private space in this context, the article shows that the aviation industry's transnational private regulatory regime is relatively well developed. Less well developed, however, is a rights-based conception of regulation within that regime itself; rather, in this context regulation appears to be particularly efficiency-focused with little factoring in of rights-related concerns. Thus, in some ways, the imagined transnational private space within which corporations can engage in extra-ordinary rendition activities on behalf of states appears to align relatively well with the reality of that transnational private regulatory regime. Reinforced by this, I proceed to suggest some regulatory mechanisms by which that regime might be recalibrated to include a rights-based perspective on its activity. While contracts that effectively facilitate torture are not permitted, the nature of the current private transnational regulatory regime as it applies to aviation and as it is treated by international human rights law fails to construct effective impediments to such arrangements. The concern of this article is with conceiving private regulatory mechanisms that can be used to disincentivize such behaviour.

EXTRAORDINARY RENDITION

Although the term 'rendition' was previously used to describe extradition-type processes, it is now used exclusively in relation to trans-jurisdictional transfers that do not offer the normal processes of challenge, due process, and so on to the transferred individual. In the context of the 'War on Terrorism' it describes the non-judicial transfer of an individual across borders for the purposes of interrogation, almost always while being held incommunicado, and through the use of unlawfully coercive means including torture. It is, therefore, a euphemism for illegal transfer to torture. In international human rights law, the transfer of an individual to another state where there is a real risk that they will be subjected to torture itself

98

constitutes a breach of the anti-torture norm. This principle – known as the principle of *non-refoulement* – occupies a position of absoluteness within the jurisprudence of the European Court of Human Rights[4] and of near-absoluteness in international human rights law.[5] Thus, even if a state does not *directly* torture the individual, the act of transferring an individual to torture is itself a breach of international law and the involvement of other entities, including corporate entities, abets such unlawful behaviour.

Although there is some indication that extraordinary renditions had been carried out prior to the 'War on Terrorism', the rate of rendition appears to have greatly escalated in recent years. While the secrecy that surrounds the practice of extraordinary rendition makes it very difficult to 'count' cases, there are reports of something along the lines of 117 cases of extraordinary rendition since September 2001 with some 53 of those cases concerning the transfer of individuals to a country or base not under the control of the United States.[6] In addition, there is now a significant amount of evidence indicating that corporate entities (including aviation companies and logistics companies) are used by the United States in the performance of extraordinary rendition.[7] This is aptly summarized by Giovani Fava:

> Within the context of the 'extraordinary renditions', the CIA has often used private companies and charter services for aircraft rentals. Through civil flights it is possible to reach places where military aircraft would be considered suspicious … Most of these companies are the so-called 'shell companies': they only exist on paper (post office boxes, for instance) or they have a sole employee (normally a lawyer). These shell companies appear as the owners of aircraft which are systematically the subject of *buy-and-sell* operations. After each transaction, aircraft are re-registered in order to lose their tracks.[8]

4 *Soering* v. *United Kingdom* (1989) 11 EHRR 439; *Chahal* v. *United Kingdom* (1997) 23 EHRR 413; *Saadi* v. *Italy,* App. No. 37201/06, Judgment of the Grand Chamber, European Court of Human Rights, 28 February 2008.

5 In the context of refugee law, *non-refoulement* appears now to have achieved the status of *jus cogens*, although there is less agreement around whether it has a *jus cogens* status in international law generally. On *non-refoulement* and refugee law see, for example, J. Allain, 'The *Jus Cogens* Nature of *Non-Refoulement*' (2001) 13 *International J. of Refugee Law* 533–58; UNHCR, *Advisory Opinion on the Extra-Territorial Application of Non-Refoulement Obligations under the 1951 Convention relating to the Status of Refugees and its Protocol*, 26 January 2007.

6 P. Bergman and K. Tiedemann, 'Extraordinary Rendition by the Numbers', New America Foundation (2008), see <http://www.newamerica.net/blog/files/New%20America%20Foundation%20Extraordinary%20Rendition%20A%20Look%20at%20the%20Data.pdf>.

7 See, for example, S. Grey, *Ghost Plane: The True Story of the CIA Rendition and Torture Programme* (2006); T. Paglen, *Torture Taxi: On the Trail of the CIA's Rendition Flights* (2006); S. Grey, 'The Agonizing Truth About CIA Renditions' *Salon*, 5 November 2007, see <http://www.salon.com/news/opinion/feature/2007/11/05/rendition/>.

8 G. Fava, *Working Document No. 8 on the Companies linked to the CIA, aircraft used by the CIA, and the European counties in which CIA aircraft have made stopovers*, European Parliament, DT\641333EN.doc (2006) 2.

There are three main ways in which private actors are involved in extra-ordinary rendition: the provision of logistics including aircraft and flight planning,[9] the contracting of pilots and other essential professionals for the operation of flights,[10] and the provision of security to state agents on rendition flights.[11] While I do not mean to suggest that private corporations engaged in torture directly, their involvement was fundamental to the state's goal of subjecting individuals to torture in the course of the 'War on Terrorism'.

THE BROADER CONTEXT: FOUR PARALLEL DEVELOPMENTS

In order to understand more fully the use of corporate entities within extra-ordinary rendition there are, I think, four parallel developments with which we ought to concern ourselves: (i) international securitization in the age of human rights; (ii) the destatification of sovereign performance; (iii) the corporatization of sovereign performance; and (iv) the disembodiment of rights. The implication of these four developments, when seen in parallel, seems to invite the privatization by states of the sovereign performance of illegal transnational activity, such as extraordinary rendition, in the attempt to evade discovery and accountability. Thus, these developments provide an important context in which to think about ways in which private transnational regulation might contribute to efforts focused on *effective* rights protection.

1. *International securitization in the age of human rights*

It is broadly accepted that the development of a sophisticated machinery of international human rights law is one of the most significant legal developments of the twentieth century. This has resulted in a plethora of general and specific international covenants dealing with human rights,[12] the

---

9 J. Mayer, 'Outsourcing: The CIA's Travel Agent' *New Yorker*, 30 October 2006.
10 id.
11 M. Arar, 'The Horrors of Rendition: A First Hand Account' *Counterpunch*, 27–29 October 2006, at: <http://www.counterpunch.org/arar10272006.html>. Anecdotal reports suggest, however, that private security personnel did find themselves sometimes having to engage in the control of the rendee.
12 For example, International Covenant on Civil and Political Rights (ICCPR); International Covenant on Economic, Social and Cultural Rights (ICESCR); UN Convention on the Elimination of all form of Discrimination against Women (CEDAW); UN Convention on the Elimination of All Forms of Racial Discrimination (CERD); UN Convention against Torture, and Other Cruel, Inhuman or Degrading Treatment or Punishment (UNCAT); UN Convention on the Rights of the Child (CRC); International Convention on the Protection of the Rights of All Migrant Workers and Members of their Families; UN Convention on the Rights of Persons with Disabilities; European Convention on Human Rights and Fundamental Freedoms (ECHR); African Charter on Human and Peoples' Rights; American Convention on Human Rights; Arab Charter on Human Rights.

concurrent development and increasing effectiveness of various international adjudicatory bodies,[13] and a developing synergy between international and domestic constitutional human rights protections in at least some jurisdictions.[14] Although there can be no suggestion that the development of international human rights law has been an unmitigated success, it has succeeded in inserting rights as a necessary consideration – even if only at a rhetorical level – in states' domestic and international activities.

While the attacks of 11 September 2001 had been preceded by decades of terroristic violence in other jurisdictions, the reaction to those attacks ushered in a period of securitization (at international, regional, and domestic levels) that has become a defining paradigm of the early twenty-first century. At the international level we saw the development of numerous allegedly security-oriented measures such as asset-freezing that rubbed up sharply against human rights protections.[15] Similarly, regional organizations began to concern themselves with the creation and implementation of repressive counter-terrorist systems.[16] In domestic jurisdictions existing counter-terrorism law was developed beyond its previous reincarnations either through a complete reorientation of the counter-terrorist model (such as in the United States)[17] or through the expansion of pre-existing regimes (as in the United Kingdom).[18]

These two developments are in obvious tension with one another. Most counter-terrorism laws and practices demand at least some level of human rights 'sacrifice' and, as the securitization impulse became enflamed, arguments for the 'sacrifice' of more and more rights (including, in some cases, the right to be free from torture) were increasingly made.

13 For an overview of enforcement bodies, including bodies designed to enforce regional human rights standards and critical appraisals of these enforcement systems, see P. Alston and J. Crawford (eds.), *The Future of UN Human Rights Treaty Monitoring* (2000).
14 See, for example, F. de Londras, 'Dualism, Domestic Courts and the Rule of International Law' in *Ius Gentium: The Rule of Law in Comparative Perspective*, eds. M. Sellers and T. Tomaszewski (2010); F. de Londras, 'International Human Rights Law and Constitutional Rights: In Favour of Synergy' (2009) 9 *International Rev. of Constitutionalism* 307–28.
15 See, for example, J. Gurulé, *Unfunding Terror: The Legal Response to the Financing of Global Terrorism* (2009).
16 See, for example, M. den Boer, C. Hillebrand, and A. Nolke, 'Legitimacy under Pressure: The European Web of Counter-Terrorism Networks' (2008) 46 *J. of Common Market Studies* 101–24.
17 R. Chesney and J. Goldsmith, 'Terrorism and the Convergence of Criminal and Military Detention Models' (2008) 60 *Stanford Law Rev.* 1079–134.
18 C. Walker, *The Anti-Terrorism Legislation* (2009).

101

2. The destatification of sovereign performance

The second development with which I am concerned is the steady movement of sovereign performance from the state to other entities. By this I mean not only privatization – which of course is not a new phenomenon – but the decision, in effect, to delegate the performance of deeply sovereign functions to non-state actors. The idea of sovereign performance here requires some elaboration. Although the term 'sovereignty' is of course contested and, perhaps, in some ways outmoded, I employ it in an attempt to transcend the construction of public and private which (as further considered below) is both problematic from a rights-protection perspective and out of step with our modern understanding of the nature of state action. By privatized sovereign performance I mean the 'private' operationalization of functions that are intimately connected with the sovereign identity of the state such as security and entry to or exit from the territory of the state. There is no necessary connection between the sovereign nature of an act and its legality; torture, for example, is a deeply 'sovereign' act as it (re)asserts state authority and power, notwithstanding its absolute illegality.

Destatification of sovereign performance takes place through numerous different mechanisms, not all of which are necessarily of equal concern from the perspective of human rights protection as (depending on its nature) the delegee of sovereign performance might itself have internal and external accountability and legitimacy machinery. Increasing regionalization through formalized institutions and organizations is one example of the destatification of sovereign performance, but this can also occur by means of a transfer of functions or authority from the state to corporate entities.

3. The corporatization of sovereign performance

Corporatization of sovereign performance is the transfer of at least some implementation mechanisms to corporate entities.[19] This has long taken place in the context of prison provision and governance, immigration control, and so on.[20] The degree of the privatization of sovereign performance will differ from case to case. In the context of privatized prisons, for example, states rarely allow the corporate entity to determine *who* is to be incarcerated and over whom this destatified sovereignty is to be performed; rather, those decisions are retained by the state, normally through its criminal justice process. Thus, while liberty is restricted on the authority of the state

---

19 It may also involve changing state providers to profit-making corporate-type entities, but that is not under consideration here.

20 See, for example, J. Gilboy, 'Implications of "Third Party" Involvement in Enforcement: The INS, Illegal Travellers, and International Airlines' (1997) 31 *Law and Society Rev.* 505–30; R. Harding, 'Private Prisons' in *Crime and Justice: A Review of Research, Vol. 38*, eds. M. Tonry and N. Morris (2001).

102

(the assertion of sovereign authority), the operationalization of such restriction is done by a non-state actor (the performance of sovereignty). The destatification and corporatization of sovereign performance is evident in the context of extraordinary rendition.[21] In this context, the decision as to who is to be subjected to extraordinary rendition is not destatified; that decision continues to be made by the state, usually through its security and intelligence services. Unlike in the context of incarceration, however, the normal constitutionalized infrastructure of the state – such as the judiciary – is not available to the individual. Thus there are limited safeguards for individual rights and those who are 'rendered' are effectively incapable of challenging their subjection to such sovereign performance.

Destatification and corporatization (that is, privatization) in the context of extraordinary rendition presents a number of issues and concerns analogous to those apparent in the privatization of prisons or proxy immigration control by airlines. Unlike those situations, however, privatization in this context is determinedly purposive: it is directed at the facilitation, concealment, and execution of absolutely prohibited activity, namely, torture. While corporations neither identify the rendees, nor directly torture detainees, their insertion in the process between the point of identification and the point of torture is distinctly related to the latter.

4. The disembodiment of 'human' rights[22]

Fourthly, the concept of human rights is being progressively disembodied with entities like corporations being recognized as having 'human' rights, in spite of their lack of humanity.[23] This process of disembodiment has serious implications for the language and structure of human rights itself (by facilitating what has been called a 'corporate colonisation'[24] that severely distorts the dignitary paradigm of human rights law[25]), for political processes (by empowering corporate entities to play increasingly influential roles in elections, for example[26]), and for corporations whose reservoir of rights now expands from corporate rights as traditionally understood to 'corporate rights + human rights'.

---

21 See text accompanying nn. 8–11 above.
22 This phrase is based on A. Grear, 'Challenging Corporate "Humanity": Legal Disembodiment, Embodiment and Human Rights' (2007) 7 *Human Rights Law Rev.* 511–43.
23 M. Emberland, *The Human Rights of Companies: Exploring the Structure of ECHR Protection* (2006); *Citizens United* v. *Federal Election Commission* 558 U.S. 50 (2010); T.R. Piety. 'Citizens United and the Threat to the Regulatory State' in *University of Michigan First Impressions* (2010), at <http://works.bepress.com/tamara_piety/8>; J. Barkan, 'Liberal Government and the Corporate Person' (2010) 3 *J. of Cultural Economy* 53–68.
24 Grear, op. cit., n. 22, p. 513.
25 See U. Baxi, *The Future of Human Rights* (2006, 2nd edn.).
26 *Citizens United*, op. cit., n. 23.

103

The combination of these four parallel developments results in a situation where states have heavy rights-protecting burdens in their performance of sovereignty but are enabled to 'off-load' at least some of those burdens by means of privatization to corporations that are imbued with both human and corporate rights but perform sovereignty without being limited by the kinds of rights-protection burdens that inhibit state action. While international human rights law requires states to introduce regulation where services and functions are privatized,[27] that requirement is of little utility where such privatization is undertaken with the purpose of evading human rights obligations.

THE QUESTION OF DIFFERENCE

It might be said that the privatization of sovereign performance presents a challenge to human rights protection in every situation, and that in this sense there is nothing 'different' about extraordinary rendition. In my view, privatizing sovereign performance in this context not only presents a challenge that is located at the most grave point of the continuum that the parallel developments outlined above present, but also illustrates the pur-posiveness of such privatization. This makes the involvement of corporate entities in extraordinary rendition an important and worthwhile locus for study and distinguishes it from, for example, prison privatization. A state does not privatize a prison for the purposes of torturing prisoners; in contrast, it transfers sovereign performance to corporations in extraordinary rendition precisely *in order to* exert sovereignty through torture, either itself or by a proxy. The state is concerned with concealing this activity because being seen to violate the anti-torture norm carries substantial risks for a state's position within the international community. This relates to both the nature of the international prohibition on torture as a human rights norm *and* torture's role within the so-called 'civilizing' narrative of international law.

The prohibition on torture is included in every major human rights docu-ment[28] as well as specific conventions on torture at both the international[29] and regional levels.[30] At all of these levels, the right to be free from torture is

---

27 See, for example, C. Donnelly, 'Positive Obligations and Privatisation' (2010) 61 *N. Ire. Legal Q.* 209.

28 Art. 5, UDHR; Art. 7, ICCPR; Art. 3, ECHR; Art. 5, African Charter on Human and Peoples' Rights; Art. 13, Arab Charter on Peoples' Rights; Art. 5, American Convention on Human Rights; Art. 3, Convention on Human Rights and Fundamental Freedoms of the Commonwealth of Independent States.

29 UNCAT.

30 European Convention for the Prevention of Torture and Inhuman or Degrading Treatment or Punishment (1987); Inter-American Convention to Prevent and Punish Torture (1985).

104

absolute and non-derogable.[31] In addition, the anti-torture norm enjoys *jus cogens* status.[32] As noted above, the prohibition on torture includes a prohibition on *refoulement*, or the transfer or return of an individual to a territory or state where there is a real risk of that individual being subjected to prohibited torturous treatment.

The absoluteness of the anti-torture norm in international law reflects its role as an organizing principle of the international community. The development of international law occurred within a clear (and imperialistic) 'civilization' narrative. Orthodox perspectives see the modern world as starting with a society of states originally confined to European members, and argue that the global political and legal society resulted from the expansion of that society by inclusion of non-European states upon recognition of their sovereignty.[33] Although this orthodox narrative runs the risk of obscuring the older roots of the civilizing narrative of international law's development as well as the internal European civilizing narrative,[34] it nevertheless suffices for the purposes of this article for it shows the centrality of this narrative to the project of constructing an international community. The identification of peremptory norms such as the prohibition on torture marks them as foundational organizing principles of that civilizing narrative. The implication, therefore, is that engaging in such behaviour constitutes counter-civilization. This plays an important role in understanding why a state – such as the United States – might be interested in (at least trying to) conceal its engagement in torture. Even when enterprising human rights activists and, subsequently, Dick Marty of the Council of Europe had gathered sufficient evidence to show that planes chartered and used by the CIA were regularly flying between and to locations where torture was a frequent occurrence,[35] the United States insisted repeatedly and in the strongest possible terms that it did not condone, encourage, engage in, or commission torture. Throughout the 'War on Terrorism' the United States has engaged with the UN Committee on Torture and reiterated the absolute prohibition on torture. Although it may have been attempting to narrow our understandings of what constitutes torture through this involvement, the important point for my purposes is that it did not simply decide to act in a typically hegemonic manner by turning away from

---

31 Art. 2, UNCAT; Art. 3 Common to the Geneva Conventions; Art. 15(2), ECHR; Art. 4(2), ICCPR; Art. 4, Arab Charter on Peoples' Rights; Art. 27, American Convention on Human Rights; and Art. 35(2), Convention on Human Rights and Fundamental Freedoms of the Commonwealth of Independent States.

32 On this see, for example, A. Orakhelashvili, *Peremptory Norms in International Law* (2006) 54–7.

33 See, for example, G. Gong, *The Standard of Civilisation in International Society* (1984).

34 For a far richer narrative, see E. Keene, *Beyond the Anarchical Society: Grotius, Colonialism and Order in International Politics* (2002).

35 D. Marty, *Alleged Secret Detentions and Unlawful Inter-State Transfers Involving Council of Europe Member States* (2006).

international law and rejecting its human rights principles and machinery.[36] The United States, in other words, did not walk away from international law's absolute prohibition on torture: it may have intentionally breached it but its behaviour nevertheless displayed a base-level normative acceptance of its validity and importance as a source of law and of obligations,[37] reflecting its core position within the international community. This goes some way to explaining the concealment rationale for the privatization of sovereign performance in the context of extraordinary rendition.

Privatizing the sovereign performance of extraordinary rendition is, however, complicated by an understanding of the inherently sovereign and demonstrative nature of torture as a state practice. Paul Kahn has recently written that torture was historically a deeply demonstrative act, one through which an endangered and vulnerable state could show to all those who threatened it that it was and remained powerful.[38] Kahn does not claim that there has been any change in the function of state torture. The function of torture is as much, if not more, that of showmanship and demonstration as it is of intelligence gathering; it is a type of state-like strutting and swagger that shows a defiance against those who would try to undermine the state's existence or threaten its sovereignty.[39] The difficulty, of course, for the modern state is that its strut and swagger by means of torture places it in the position of pariah. It can not be revealed, or at least not fully admitted, to the world at large. By claiming documented cases of torture to be the work of 'bad apples' and publicly expressing abhorrence for torture, while simultaneously operating a web of torture flights that it tried to conceal by the use of private entities, the United States could attempt at once to present a normatively sound anti-torture face to the world at large while demonstrating its power and ruthless sovereignty to those it believed to be Al Qaeda and its associates. It did not succeed in concealing its torture-related activities, but what matters from a normative perspective is that it tried to do so by means of privatizing its sovereign performance.

While the nature of the prohibition on torture (including *non-refoulement*) and its role within the international community's exercise of

---

36 N. Krisch, 'International Law in Times of Hegemony: Unequal Power and the Shaping of the International Legal Order' (2005) 16 *European J. of International Law* 369–408.

37 In this respect I now recant somewhat from my more pessimistic view as expressed in F. de Londras, 'The Religiosity of *Jus Cogens*: A Moral Case for Compliance?' in *Religion, Human Rights and International Law*, eds. J. Rehman and S. Breau (2007).

38 P. Kahn, *Sacred Violence: Torture, Terror and Sovereignty* (2008).

39 There is also a significant body of literature arguing that the function of torture is ultimately to reduce the victim to a state of passivity. See, for example, M. Nowak, 'What Practices Constitute Torture?: US and UN Standards' (2006) 28 *Human Rights Q.* 809–41, at 833, and D. Sussman, 'Defining Torture' (2006) 37 *Case Western Reserve J. of International Law* 225–30, at 227.

106

drawing lines identifying which states are 'in' and which are 'out' (so-called 'rogue states') goes some way towards explaining the American decision – paradoxical, at first blush – to privatize the performance of this most sovereign of behaviours, it is not sufficient on its own. It certainly helps, together with the growth of human rights norms, to explain the significant obstacles that existed to open engagement in torture, but something more is needed to understand fully the decision to privatize and – building on that – to conceive of ways that transnational private regulation may become part of the solution to such privatization. The United States must, it seems to me, not only have recognized the importance of appearing not to torture in the international community but also to have assumed that the private transnational space was one in which such performance could take place without detection. We can, from this, infer that the United States made at least some assumptions about the nature of the private transnational space within which aviation companies engaged in extraordinary rendition could operate. This reiterates the point made in the introduction that disparities between regulatory structures in the public and private spheres can create opportunities for what a state may see as 'advantageous' privatization of sovereign performance, in spite of the instinctively paradoxical nature of bringing additional actors 'into' the process of engaging in unlawful activity such as torture.

'ASSUMED ASSUMPTIONS' ABOUT THE PRIVATE
TRANSNATIONAL SPACE

In order for the privatization of such sovereign performance to present itself as a sensible option for a state (that is, an option that facilitates torture and maximizes the potential for concealment), it appears that one must make at least a few assumptions about the nature of the private transnational space. First comes an assumption that the transnational space is deeply committed to a public/private construction in which corporations reside in the 'private' space (where they are relatively unregulated from a rights-based perspective) and states reside in the 'public' space (where they bear relatively heavy rights-based obligations). The second assumption is that within the private transnational space there is a level of opacity that permits of the concealment of this kind of activity. Both of these assumptions require some further elaboration.

1. *International human rights law's public/private construction*

In both domestic and international law, the protection of individual rights has largely been designed and implemented within a state/individual structure, where human rights are primarily conceived of as claims of the individual as against the state. International human rights law does not generally have the

107

capacity to govern the actions of private actors directly[40] because, as part of general public international law, its constituents are primarily states.[41] Although international human rights law has attempted to ensure that states are required to put in place structures, standards, and laws that would – to the extent considered possible – protect individuals from rights violations by non-public actors, those measures are generally focused on responsibilizing the state for private action and not on also responsibilizing (and thereby removing incentives for) rights-endangering 'private' actors.[42] Even in domestic human rights law, the concepts of public act and actor have tended to become conflated in a manner that excuses seemingly private actors (even if carrying out public functions) from rights-based obligations (although there is some variation between jurisdictions[43]).

Within this construction, the state essentially bears all rights-related responsibility and the corporation – itself now bearing some rights – has few if any obligations. This must, of course, be attached with a caveat recognizing the continuing development of soft-law standards relating to corporate social responsibility and the business and human rights movement, and attempts to develop commitment to the Draft United Nations Code of Conduct on Transnational Corporations[44] (which contemplated the introduction of mandatory requirements), although this Code appears to have been replaced with the Norms on the Responsibilities of Transnational Corporations and Other Business Enterprises with Regard to Human Rights[45] (which provide soft-law norms, albeit with an apparent view to formalizing a treaty in the future). Furthermore, the business and human rights movement continues its effort to develop the 'protect, respect and remedy' approach to corporate protection of human rights.[46] This construction of a state/private model

---

40 See, for example, R. Higgins, *Problems and Process: International Law and How We Use It* (1994) 153.

41 This is not to deny the continuing evolution of international law and the role of non-state actors in it, on which see T. Broude and Y. Shany (eds.), *The Shifting Allocation of Authority in International Law: Considering Sovereignty, Supremacy and Subsidiarity* (2008); A. Boyle and C. Chinkin, *The Making of International Law* (2006).

42 See, for example, *A v. United Kingdom* (1998) 27 EHRR 611; *Opuz v. Turkey* (2009) ECHR 33401/22 (9 June 2009); Art. 2, CEDAW; Art. 4(1), UN Convention on the Rights of Persons with Disabilities.

43 Contrast the position under the ECHR Act 2003 in Ireland (F. de Londras and C. Kelly, *The European Convention on Human Rights Act: Operation, Impact and Analysis* (2010) paras. 5.11–5.20), under the Human Rights Act 1998 in the United Kingdom (H. Fenwick, *Civil Liberties and Human Rights*, (2007, 4th edn.) 215–56), and under the state action doctrine in the United States (D. Barak-Erez, 'A State Action Doctrine for an Age of Privatization' (1994) 45 *Syracuse Law Rev.* 1169–92).

44 *U.N. Code of Conduct on Transnational Corporations*, 23 I.L.M. 626 (1984).

45 E/CN.4/Sub.2/2003/12/Rev.2 (26 August 2003).

46 J. Ruggie, *Protect, Respect and Remedy: A Framework for Business and Human Rights* (2008) UN Doc. A/HRC/8/5.

immediately presents the 'private' as a potential 'escape hatch' for states seeking to be released from their rights-related responsibilities. Whether the private sphere really is such an escape hatch in any given situation will depend to a large extent on the regulatory context of that space.

2. *The relative opacity of the transnational private sphere*

The second assumption about the transnational private sphere within which aviation companies operate that would appear to underpin the decision of the United States to involve them in extraordinary rendition is that this sphere is relatively opaque, or at least sufficiently so to allow for state activity to be concealed through the use of civilian aircraft. The Convention on International Civil Aviation 1944 (the Chicago Convention) provides that civilian aircraft are obliged to comply with a number of requirements such as the pre-reporting of flight plans and adherence to consistent identificatory call signs and numbers. In addition, there is no prohibition on the random searching of civilian aircraft by the relevant law enforcement agencies such as the police, customs officials, immigration officials, and so on. Civilian aircraft, therefore, are subject to both reporting regimes and the potential for search that would not seem at first blush to be compatible with a programme of extraordinary rendition. That said, however, one must bear in mind that chartered or rented civilian airlines can carry out activities on behalf of the state that are not immediately obvious as they do not conspicuously present as being involved in security activity. Military aircraft, in contrast, are not susceptible to search. Nor is there any requirement that their flight plans be submitted in advance to air traffic controllers, although special permissions for overflight and some information as to mission must be provided. Thus, military aircraft arguably have a number of advantages over civilian aircraft in an 'extraordinary rendition' programme. Their main *dis*advantage, for the sending state, is the easy identification of military aircraft by standard markings. However, if a state engaging in extraordinary rendition is concerned with concealment of their activities then the use of private airplanes is in fact a more sensible option.[47]

The concealment motivation is relevant here to identifying the paradoxes inherent in the United States' extraordinary rendition programme. The determination to maintain an air of secrecy around extraordinary rendition does not appear to be motivated by a security need. Even if some arguments can be made that the specific types of interrogation methods used ought not to be publically disclosed as such information may enable prospective detainees to 'prepare to resist' such techniques, the same could not be said in

---

47 G. Fava, *Report on the Alleged Use of European Countries by the CIA in the transportation and illegal detention of prisoners*, European Parliament, RR\382246EN.doc (2007).

relation to the general information confirming that the United States engaged in extraordinary rendition.

THE TRANSNATIONAL PRIVATE REGULATORY REGIME OF THE CIVIL AVIATION INDUSTRY

If, as outlined above, public international law does not currently seem to be capable of providing sufficient disincentives to states privatizing the sovereign performance of torture and may, in fact, be an incentive for such behaviour, it behoves us to look at the regulatory regime of the civil aviation industry as it stands, relating to rights-based concerns. As a transnational regulatory regime, it is multi-level and multi-stakeholder, ranging from a specialized agency of the United Nations (the International Civil Aviation Organization (ICAO)), to European regional organizations and industry bodies (both general and relating to specific elements of the aviation industry). Given the nature of aviation as an almost-entirely transnational activity there has, since 1944 (the founding of the ICAO) been some element of transnational regulation, but primarily its focus has been (and continues to be) on organizing and regulating the logistical elements of the industry.

Industry organizations[48] tend to concentrate on ensuring that regulation as it exists in the public sphere does not overly impinge upon competitiveness and profitability within the industry and on harmonizing regulatory requirements. These industry organizations' regulatory activities can be divided into six general areas: safety, security, the environment, finance and operations, sundry standards, and staff. In addition to internal industry regulation in these areas, they tend to identify themselves as having a strong focus on lobbying and representing industry concerns within more formally 'public'

---

48 International Air Transportation Association (established 1945, succeeding International Air Traffic Association, 230 members, including 126 countries. Outside of states, membership comprises airlines, airports, travel agencies, other travel and tour operators and intermediaries, freight forwarders and industry suppliers); International Business Aviation Council (established 1981, 15 members, all business organizations (national and regional)); International Society of Air Safety Investigators (established 1964, mixed membership of individuals/organizations operating in air safety inspection); International Air Carrier Association (established 1971, 33 members, all airlines); International Air Cargo Association (established 1960 as Society of Automotive Engineers, 1990 as International Air Cargo Forum Association, and 1994 as International Air Cargo Association, 218 members listed (see <www.tiaco.org>) ranging from airports, to companies, to universities as educational affiliates); Civil Air Navigation Services Organisation (established 1996, 104 members consisting of air navigation services providers (ANSPs) and associate members, who provide goods and services to ANSPs); the Airport Association of CIS Civil Aviation (established 1990, 258 members, provides services dealing with analysis, assimilation, and introduction of national and world experience into the activity of airport complexes and their infrastructures on the territory of CIS states); the Association of European Airlines (established 2002 as airline lobbying organization, 35 members, all European airlines).

110

transnational organizations such as the ICAO and on education, both within and outside the industry. Common to all of these trade or industry organizations, however, is a distinct lack of focus on traditional rule of law concerns, including on the rights of those who may be affected by industry operations outside of tangential concern therewith through environmental regulation.

In general terms, these organizations deal with individuals as consumers of their products and services rather than as subjects thereof (as is generally the case in extraordinary rendition where the individuals who are 'rendered' are not the clients/consumers of the company involved; rather, the 'rendering state' is). In contrast, the ICAO does list 'rule of law' as one of its strategic objectives, but its own organizational description thereof reads: 'Strengthen law governing international civil aviation'.[49] This is a clearly ambiguous statement and, while it does not necessarily include or omit human rights considerations on its own terms, it does little to suggest that human rights protection or the rights-based governance of state-agency contracts is a primary concern of the organization. However, given its nature as a specialized organ of the UN, the work of the ICAO must be seen in the context of the broader concerns and capacities of the United Nations, including its rights-related competencies and work. The European Union has a number of regional and associated organizations that have some regulatory capacity in the aviation context.[50] As above, none of these organizations have a specific human-rights related orientation of the type we are concerned with in this case study, however, once more, those that are clearly tethered to the European Union must be seen within the context of the EU's broader work and rule of law concerns, including fundamental rights protection under EU law and – from accession to the ECHR – Council of Europe law.

If one of the assumptions incentivizing the privatization of sovereign performance in the context of extraordinary rendition was that the transnational private sphere was relatively opaque and existed within the 'private' sphere as conceptualized within the public/private construction of human rights law, then the transnational private regulatory regime of the aviation industry does little to offer any disincentive or to balance out the rights-related deficiencies identified above. This suggests that public regulatory responses are unlikely to be sufficient on their own; rather, for those concerned with effective rights enforcement and the quarantining of extraordinary rendition to the specific circumstances of the 'War on Terrorism', it mandates at least some private regulatory responses.[51]

---

49 'Strategic Objectives of ICAO for 2005–2010', at <http://www.icao.int/icao/en/strategic_objectives_2005_2010_en.pdf>.
50 European Civil Aviation Conference; European Aviation Safety Agency; EUROCONTROL.
51 Public regulation also plays an important, although unanticipated, role here. Data collected through the regular filing of flight plans is helpful in tracing the 'spider web' of rendition flights in Europe. See D. Marty, *Alleged Secret Detentions and Unlawful Inter-State Transfers Involving Council of Europe Member States* (2006).

One might suggest that litigation is the 'obvious' regulatory response to the aviation industry's involvement in extraordinary rendition; after all, litigation and liability are often described as the type of language that companies understand. There are avenues through which individuals who have been rendered and subsequently released – or, indeed, their families – can attempt to make companies civilly liable for their involvement in rendition. In the United States, the Alien Tort Statute[52] is perhaps the best example of such a litigative tool (although its future potential has recently been called into question[53]). The difficulty, however, with attempting to make such companies liable in this way is that, because the alleged activities and contracts are identified as being within the realm of 'national security', the state is inclined to intervene and use particularly strong public defences to obstruct discovery and frustrate litigation. Thus, even if a court were willing to accept that contracts for transportation services within extraordinary rendition ought not to stand because they endanger the anti-torture norm, this willingness might be frustrated by the simple incapacity to acquire full details of the nature of the contractual relationship and activities in question. The case of *Mohammed et al.* v. *Jeppensen Dataplan Inc* offers an illustrative example of such obstruction.

Jeppesen Dataplan (also known as Jeppesen International Trip Planning) is a wholly owned subsidiary of Boeing whose involvement in the CIA's extraordinary rendition programme, and the knowledge thereof on the part of senior management, was exposed in a *New Yorker* article published in 2006.[54] Following on from these revelations, the American Civil Liberties Union initiated litigation on behalf of five individuals who it was claimed had been subjected to extraordinary rendition and torture. They argued that Jeppesen knew or ought to have known that the services they provided to the CIA would result in the torture of the applicants and, as a result, that Jeppesen was liable in damages under the Alien Tort Statute.[55] The United States government applied for the status of intervener and claimed that the Court ought to dismiss the petition on the basis of the state secrets privilege relating to the nature and extent of the alleged activities, which it invoked on behalf of both itself *and* Jeppesen.

The Court originally acceded to the government's application[56] although,

---

52 28 U.S.C. 1350 (providing 'The district courts shall have original jurisdiction of any civil action by an alien for a tort only, committed in violation of the law of nations or a treaty of the US').

53 *Kiobel* v. *Royal Dutch Petroleum* 2010 U.S. App. LEXIS 19382 (17 September 2010).

54 Mayer, op. cit., n. 9.

55 *Mohamend et al.* v. *Jeppesen Dataplan*, First (Amended) Complaint, Civil Action No. 5:07-cv-02798, 8 January 2007.

56 *Mohammed et al.* v. *Jeppesen Dataplan Inc*, App. C07-02798 JW, US District Court for the Northern District of California.

on appeal, this was reversed with the Appeal Court applying a narrow understanding of the privilege.[57] Following that decision, the government submitted a petition for the rehearing of the application by the full Court, once more arguing that, should the case proceed, information essential to the maintenance of national security would be liable to be exposed thereby jeopardizing national security generally.[58] Jeppesen itself also submitted a petition for rehearing by the full Court, claiming that discovery in the case is impossible as a result of the government's assertion of the state secrets privilege and, secondly, that Jeppesen would be unable to properly and effectively challenge the plaintiffs' assertions as all information on the basis of which they might so challenge them would be information that the government would claim subject to state secrets privilege.[59] In response, the plaintiffs argued that if the government succeeded in its action that would effectively prevent *anyone* from taking an action for damages in respect of torture or inhuman or degrading treatment arising from being subjected to extraordinary rendition and, potentially, even more broadly than that.[60]

On 8 September 2010 the Court of Appeals for the Ninth Circuit released its closely divided (6 to 5) judgment in the case.[61] Upholding the government's invocation of the state secrets doctrine in this case, the Court reiterated long-standing Supreme Court precedent characterizing accession to a state secrets claim as 'exceptional'[62] and as including cases where discovery requirements might result in the exposure of evidence 'revealing military [or state] secrets'.[63] Taking the limits of the privilege into account, the Court concluded that compelling disclosure of evidence about the existence and scope of an extraordinary rendition programme, the role that Jeppesen Dataplan and/or other governments might play in that programme, or any element of the CIA's counter-terrorist activities would result in the revelation of state secrets that it is bound to protect. The effect of that, in this case, was that the entire action was to be struck out and could not proceed.

Although the Court in *Jeppesen* appeared to express regret about the bind that it found itself in, recognized the existence of the extraordinary rendition programme, and noted that a number of non-judicial pathways remain open to the plaintiffs (and, indeed, the government[64]), it nevertheless found itself incapable of allowing the proceedings to progress. The *Jeppesen* litigation

---

57 *Mohammed et al.* v. *Jeppesen Dataplan Inc*, App. No. 08-15693, US Court of Appeals for the Ninth Circuit.
58 Government's petition for a rehearing *en banc*, 12 June 2009.
59 Jeppesen Dataplan's petition for a rehearing *en banc*, 12 June 2009.
60 Plaintiffs' response to petition for a rehearing *en banc*, 6 July 2009.
61 *Mohamed et al.* v. *Jeppesen Dataplan* (8 September 2010), 2010 U.S. App. LEXIS 18746.
62 *Totten* v. *US*, 92 U.S. 105 (1876).
63 *US* v. *Reynolds*, 345 U.S. 1, 6–7 (1953).
64 *Mohamed*, op. cit, n. 61, p. 59.

thus illustrates the capacity of a state that has privatized sovereign performance in this way to use extremely strong public law defences in order to
frustrate transparency, accountability and, ultimately, regulation through
litigation. This forces us then to turn elsewhere for some succour if we are
concerned with the effective protection of individual rights: transnational
private regulation offers significant potential in this respect.

POSSIBLE TRANSNATIONAL PRIVATE REGULATORY SOLUTIONS

It seems to me that there are at least some private transnational regulatory
responses that might be useful for those of us who are interested in the
effective protection of human rights, notwithstanding the practice of
privatizing sovereign performance. Although these should not be seen as
stand-alone proposals that would be sufficient in themselves, if one of the
factors that makes privatization of this kind of sovereign performance
attractive to states is, as I argued above, the perceived opacity and lack of
rights-related responsibility within the 'private' transnational space (even
where the actions complained of are clearly and unquestionably in breach of
international law), it is imperative that we consider means by which that
space can itself be reformed. Thus, rather than suggest that private transnational regulation is the whole answer, I offer these suggestions as part of
an overall answer which goes beyond, but cannot ignore, the transnational
private space.

As illustrated above, there is a pre-existing transnational private
regulatory regime that involves itself to at least some extent in standard
setting. Within this regime there is the potential for the elaboration of rights-
related standards that would be usefully attached to corporations' contracts
with states. These standards ought, at the least, to include an obligation to
engage in a 'rights audit' of prospective contracts and a commitment not to
engage in contracts that implicate the corporation in serious human rights
violations. The UN's Norms on the Responsibilities of Transnational
Corporations and Other Business Enterprises with Regard to Human Rights
offer guidance in this respect.[65] In spite of the existence of such provisions,
however, one of the obstacles to effectively applying rights-based norms to
civil aviation companies' involvement in extraordinary rendition is that the
industry itself may not recognize this as a 'real' problem. This is so, not
because of the nature of the activity but, rather, because many of the involved
entities are what we might call 'rogue companies', established on a very
temporary basis, for the purposes of engaging in a specific one-off contract,
without a large staff and sometimes without premises. They are, in essence,
'front companies' with which the industry may not feel itself concerned or

---

65 See, especially, Norm no. 3.

with which it may not feel an affinity. However, standard setting can fulfil a legitimization function whereby the companies that generate, sign up to, and fulfil the standards can use them as a means of distinguishing themselves from those companies that do not, with those other companies being seen as illegitimate pariah entities. Dealing with those non-compliant or uncertified companies then casts immediate doubt upon a contracting party and, indeed, upon the activities being contracted to. Thus, rights-based standard setting may have some impact on both the pariah entities *and* on situations where a legitimized company might be considering establishing such a company for the purposes of engaging in these kinds of contracts.

A second area for consideration is that of professional standards, particularly applying to lawyers who would be engaged in drawing up the contracts in question. Lawyers, of course, are subject to national professional standards including ethical codes. In the United States, each state Bar has its own ethics rules and codes of conduct. In addition, the American Bar Association in 1983 adopted *Model Rules of Professional Conduct* to provide a model framework for such state-level codes of conduct.[66] There are also some examples of transnational codes of conduct for the legal profession. By means of example, the Council of Bars and Law Societies of Europe has adopted a Charter of Core Principles of the European Legal Profession and Code of Conduct for European Lawyers (2008),[67] which have been adopted at various levels within the European states' own domestic professional associations.[68] The development and enforcement of rights-aware codes of conduct and ethics requirements against lawyers who are not only involved in the creation of these contracts but also, as the extract from the Fava Report considered above shows, sometimes constitute the sole employees of involved 'rogue' companies has significant potential in this context. It is, of course, contingent upon its enforcement and, to date, the indications are that lawyers involved in the 'War on Terrorism' (or at least those employed by the state) may not be subjected to ethics investigations.[69]

Thirdly, we might in this context embrace the growing recognition that fully appreciating the relationships between regulation and human rights

---

66 The *Model Code of Professional Conduct* includes, at rule 1.2(d) that:
> A lawyer shall not counsel a client to engage, or assist a client, in conduct that the lawyer knows is criminal or fraudulent, but a lawyer may discuss the legal consequences of any proposed course of conduct with a client and may counsel or assist a client to make a good faith effort to determine the validity, scope, meaning or application of the law.

67 This Charter names 'respect for the rule of law and the fair administration of justice' as one of the core principles of the European legal profession (p. 4).

68 The CBLSE has itself documented the status of the Charter in the different member states. See <http://www.ccbe.eu/fileadmin/user_upload/NTCdocument/Status_of_the_CCBE_C1_1251875770.pdf>.

69 OPR, *Investigation into the Office of Legal Counsel's Memoranda Concerning Issues Relating to the Central Intelligence Agency's Use of 'Enhanced Interrogation Techniques' on Suspected Terrorists*, 29 June 2009.

may require a reorientation, to at least some extent, of regulatory theory's traditional conceptualization of '"better regulation" [as being] almost invariably conceived in terms of efficiency – seeking the most impact for the least imposition of regulatory burden'.[70] Instead, as Prosser has argued, we should design regulatory approaches in a manner that reflects the fact that protection of human rights is an important regulatory objective.[71] This would dovetail well with a growing recognition of corporate social responsibility and companies' obligations beyond the economic in order to usher in rights-related regulation. The current process of re-regulating private industry (especially, but not exclusively, the financial industry) offers an opportunity to human rights scholars and activists to embed human rights as an important value within private transnational regulatory regimes. It is important to remember that such principles were at one time embedded within the market: after the Second World War there was an emergence not only of a body of human rights law but also of a globalized market, which was based, to some extent at least, on the principle that 'markets that societies do not recognize as legitimate cannot last'.[72] According to Abdelal and Ruggie, who advocate a return to embedded liberalism within the re-regulated global marketplace, '[t]he core principle of embedded liberalism is the need to legitimize international markets by reconciling them to social values and shared institutional practices'.[73] If one of our contemporary 'social values' and 'shared institutional practices' is, as is surely the case, the protection and promotion of human rights and prevention of activity such as torture, then recognizing the capacity of private entities to endanger those rights and placing rights-based regulatory obligations upon them must form a part of the re-regulation process.[74]

Embedding liberalism within the market has the potential to capture the growing movement towards ethical and political consumerism, which has itself been well documented[75] and is being increasingly recognized as a regulatory tool.[76] It is now accepted that consumers have the capacity to

---

70 E. Darian-Smith and C. Scott, 'Regulation and Human Rights in Socio-Legal Scholarship' (2009) 31 *Law and Policy* 271–81, at 272.

71 T. Prosser, *The Regulatory Enterprise: Government, Regulation and Legitimacy* (2010).

72 R. Abdelal and J. Ruggie, 'The Principles of Embedded Liberalism: Social Legitimacy and Global Capitalism' in *New Perspectives on Regulation*, eds. D. Moss and J. Cisternino (2009) 152.

73 id., p. 153.

74 This has clear resonance with the fundamental-rights based limitations in the EU's Inter-Institutional Agreement on Better Law-Making , Official Journal C 321, 31/12/2003 P. 0001–0005 (2003).

75 See, for example, S. Wheeler, 'Political Consumption: Possibilities and Challenges' in *Law in Pursuit of Development: Principles into Practice?*, ed. A. Perry-Kessaris (2010).

76 See, for example, D. Kysar, 'Preferences for Processes: The Process/Product Distinction and the Regulation of Consumer Choice' (2005) 118 *Harvard Law Rev.* 526–642.

shape the market and market behaviour in a manner analogous to how voters can shape politics and political behaviour.[77] Leaving to one side, for a moment, the obvious inequalities in market power between those with resources and those without, this basic conception of market power and ethical or political consumption potentially offers human rights advocates a technique for challenging corporate involvement in extraordinary rendition in a manner analogous to that adopted with some significant success by those involved in the Fair Trade movement. Although the aviation industry does not offer the same range of choice as Fair Trade products such as coffee, this apparent lack of choice does not equate to a lack of consumer power. Consumers can make decisions as to where to invest their funds, if they are private investors, or attempt to put pressure on their fund managers (such as pension funds) to ensure that investments are not made in companies that are implicated in such activities. When ethical consumerism has a 'bottom line' impact, it is likely also to have a behavioural impact. Ethical consumerism in this context should embrace the growing interest in socially responsible investment.[78] A corporation's involvement in state contracts, or the involvement therein of their subsidiaries, ought to become one of the questions to which prospective investors demand answers or, indeed, one of the types of information that must be disclosed to prospective investors. This kind of market-based transparency has enormous potential and, indeed, has been embraced in other contexts such as investment by national pension management funds in munitions companies.[79]

Finally in this relation, there is an appreciable potential for civil society to play an interesting and effective regulatory role in at least attempting to break down the opacity that seems to be allowed by the Chicago Convention considered above and to engage in what we might term 'name-and-shame' initiatives. This can include – as it already has – campaigns of photographing and cataloguing suspect aircraft including attempting to trace the ways in which aircrafts' identificatory call numbers have been changed from one flight to another. In many instances, identifying a particular case in relation to which a substantial amount of information has been gathered, and focusing the campaign on that case can be a particularly effective approach and can lead to the involvement of NGOs and academic centres, which might then help with the preparation of litigation and *amicus curiae* briefs. Even if, as was the case in the *Jeppesen* case, the litigation might not result in the payment of damages or a finding of liability it can attract attention to a company's alleged involvement in extraordinary rendition that may impact on the corporate entity involved. It can also lead to increased public aware-

---

77 F. Fetter, *The Principles of Economics* (1911) 394.
78 See, generally, B. Richardson, *Socially Responsible Investment Law* (2010).
79 See, for example, Part 4 of the Irish Cluster Munitions and Anti-Personnel Mines Act 2008, imposing a duty on investors of public funds to avoid their direct or indirect investment in munitions companies.

117

ness of the kinds of activities being engaged in by corporations and has the potential to develop moral capital – that might well translate itself into consumer pressure – for these corporations to rethink their involvement in such activities. These movements' regulatory potential is only enhanced by the successful ushering of the power of Web 2.0 and citizen journalism through easily established websites, blogs, Facebook campaign pages, Twitter accounts, and Wikipedia pages.[80]

CONCLUSION

While I find it unquestionable that the development of rights-based transnational private regulatory regimes is an indispensable element of responding to the corporatization of sovereign performance, it seems equally certain that such developments would be insufficient on their own, not least because of states' tendencies to undermine accountability endeavours such as litigation. I do not, therefore, contend that developing a rights-based perspective within the aviation industry's transnational private regulatory regime (or, in other circumstances, the transnational private regulatory regime of another industry) would be sufficient on its own. As noted above, it ought to be accompanied by efforts to address the deficiencies within public international law that are likely to also be contributory factors. So too can hybrid responses – such as the development of international standards relating to state contracts to which both states and corporations are party (analogous, perhaps, in its scope to the UN Convention on the Sale of Goods) – play an important role. However, to ignore the potential of transnational private regulation in this context is to deny the human rights scholar and practitioner an important part of the rights-protection toolkit. It is also to ignore the impulses of states to seek out escape hatches from the public law limits by which they are constrained. The decision to privatize sovereign performance in the context of extraordinary rendition may, paradoxically, be a sign of the success of international human rights law at the normative level. A failure to tackle the rights-related vulnerabilities presented by the phenomenon will leave that normative success to stand alone, however, without the effectiveness it needs to be of real and substantive value to how states behave and how individuals enjoy the liberty promised to us all by the 'age of human rights'.

---

80 But compare M. Gladwell, 'Small Change: Why The Revolution Will Not be Tweeted' *New Yorker*, 4 October 2010. For an example of the embrace of online media in order to focus attention on human rights abuses, see the International State Crime Initiative, at <http://www.statecrime.org/> (November 2010) and discussion of its role by the director, Penny Green, interviewed by Human Rights in Ireland: C. Murphy, 'States, Criminality and Civil Society' (14 June 2010), at <http://www.humanrights.ie/index.php/2010/06/14/states-criminality-and-civil-society/>.

JOURNAL OF LAW AND SOCIETY
VOLUME 38, NUMBER 1, MARCH 2011
ISSN: 0263-323X, pp. 119–37

Competition Law and Transnational Private Regulatory Regimes: Marking the Cartel Boundary

Imelda Maher*

Cartels today are prohibited under competition regimes around the world, although seen historically (in Europe at least) as a public good to be tolerated or even encouraged by governments. Despite the prohibition, illegal cartels are still prevalent, and there are circumstances where cartel-like conduct is allowed under competition rules. This article explores the extent to which such conduct can be both subject to one regulatory regime (competition law) while also carrying out regulatory functions, and hence can be construed as transnational private regulatory regimes (TPRERs). There are three categories of cartel-like arrangements: private contractual arrangements that fall outside the realm of competition law; self-regulatory arrangements designed to exclusively advance the interests of regulatees; and hybrid regimes where private arrangements have been co-opted as a form of regulation which operate in the shadow of competition law and are often seen as advancing competition objectives.

Cartels are an indispensable and integral part of economic coordination.[1]

Cartels are cancers on the open market economy.[2]

* UCD School of Law, University College Dublin, Belfield, Dublin 4, Ireland
imelda.maher@ucd.ie

Thanks to participants at the ECPR Regulatory Conference Standing Group Third Biannual Conference who attended and commented on my presentation of an earlier version of this paper there. Special thanks to the editors and Tony Prosser for their comments. The usual disclaimer applies.

1 F.E. Koch, 'Cartels as Instruments of International Economic Organization. Public and Private Legal Aspects of International Cartels' (1945) 8 *Modern Law Rev.* 130, at 137.
2 M. Monti, speech to the Third Nordic Competition Policy Conference, Stockholm, 11 September 2000.

119

© 2011 The Author. Journal of Law and Society © 2011 Cardiff University Law School. Published by Blackwell Publishing Ltd, 9600 Garsington Road, Oxford OX4 2DQ, UK and 350 Main Street, Malden, MA 02148, USA

The OECD in its most recent report on cartel enforcement reiterated the conclusion from its second report that cartels are unambiguously bad, causing harm amounting to several billion dollars every year, affecting developed and developing economies – and especially the latter who lack the resources to tackle them effectively.[3] Cartels are a risk in many sectors, for example, where there are few market players and/or where raw materials are being provided.[4] In some sectors, cartels may be pervasive. For example, the Dutch competition authority in 2005 decided to target cartels in the construction industry and more than 500 companies came forward looking for immunity for notifying the authority about cartel activity under its leniency programme.[5] This indicated that the industry was heavily cartelized. In July 2010 the European Commission imposed fines in excess of €175 million on animal feed phosphate producers for operating a cartel which dated back to 1969. The producers, over a 35-year period, met regularly to allocate market shares and customers, set sales quotas, and coordinate prices and sales conditions where they deemed it necessary.[6] The cartel only came to the attention of the Commission when one of the participants acted as a whistleblower and received full immunity from its fines. One of the largest cartels ever detected was the vitamins cartel where vitamin manufacturers had colluded on market shares and price.[7] First recounts that there were quarterly meetings and an annual meeting of senior executives where prices and budgets for the year were agreed. Efforts were made to disguise the cartel which involved companies in Japan, the EU, Switzerland, and the United States. Very large fines were imposed and senior executives from several of the participating firms were given prison sentences in the United States, where private enforcement actions were also brought. The EU, Australian, and Canadian competition authorities also investigated the cartel.[8] Perhaps the most famous cartel was the lysine and citric acid cartel which was the subject of a Hollywood film in 2009,[9] with one company being investigated for its participation in that cartel while still a member of the vitamins cartel,[10] showing the extent to which cartelization was seen as an attractive business practice for the firm.

These few examples show the extent to which cartels can arise in inter-

3 OECD, 'Hard Core Cartels – Implementation of the 1998 OECD Recommendation' (2006) 8 *OECD J. of Competition Law and Policy* 7–54.
4 See discussion of risk of cartels for the chemical industry in F. Distefano, 'Cartel Risks in the Chemicals Sector – Lessons to Draw from Recent Cases and Areas to Watch' (2011) *European Antitrust Rev.* s. 3.
5 OECD, op. cit., n. 3, p. 16.
6 European Commission, IP/10/985, 23 July 2010.
7 H. First, 'The Vitamins Case: Cartel Prosecutions and the Coming of International Competition Law' (2001) 68 *Antitrust Law J.* 711–29.
8 id., p. 717.
9 *The Informant!* (2009), directed by S. Soderbergh, based on K. Eichenwald, *The Informant* (2000). Both media provide a detailed account of how a major international cartel can work.
10 First, op. cit., n. 7, p. 719.

national business. Illegal cartels are by nature secret. This makes it difficult to calculate the exact costs to the economy. The European Commission suggests that excessive pricing by cartels amounts to 20–25 per cent of a non-cartel price.[11] Specific examples show the level of mark-up. For example, a cartel for replica football shirts in the United Kingdom was shown to have led to a 30 per cent increase in prices. In Korea, a cement cartel was calculated to have raised prices overall by about US$380 million.[12] The very large fines imposed on cartels also are indicative of the extent to which firms have benefited.[13] Thus, despite the modern prevalence of a prohibition on cartels in competition-law regimes, they remain a feature of business practice.

There are other forms of cooperation between firms that do not concern price fixing or market sharing and hence do not constitute hard-core cartel activity. It is less clear whether these forms of cooperation are anti-competitive in themselves and hence they do not necessarily fall within the prohibition or their overall benefits outweigh their competitive disadvantages so they are exempt from or fall outside the prohibition. For example, standard-setting regimes, research and development and innovation agreements, specialization agreements all constitute horizontal agreements. It is in relation to these agreements that we see the interplay of public regulation of cooperative agreements between competitors that constitute transnational private regulatory regimes (TPRERs) and may or may not fall foul of the prohibition on cartels in competition law.

This article argues that despite the ban on cartels being a key feature of competition laws around the world,[14] cooperative agreements between firms

11 European Commission, *Annual Report on Competition Policy*, 23.7.2009 COM(2009) 374 final (2008).
12 OECD, op. cit., n. 3, p. 21.
13 The European Commission imposed fines of €15,937,738,092 (as of 9 November 2010) in 1990–2010. See EC, *Cartel Statistics*, at <http://ec.europa.eu/competition/cartels/statistics/statistics.pdf>.
14 For example, the UNCTAD model competition law suggests a provision along the following lines:
    I. *Prohibition of the following agreements between rival or potentially rival firms, regardless of whether such agreements are written or oral, formal or informal:*
    (a) Agreements fixing prices or other terms of sale, including international trade;
    (b) Collusive tendering;
    (c) Market or customer allocation;
    (d) Restraints on production or sale, including by quota;
    (e) Concerted refusals to purchase;
    (f) Concerted refusal to supply;
    (g) Concerted denial of access to an arrangement, or association, which is crucial to competition.
    II. *Authorization or exemption*
    Practices falling within paragraph I, when properly notified in advance, and when engaged in by firms subject to effective competition, may be authorized or exempted when competition officials conclude that the agreement as a whole will produce net public benefit.

– cartels – can be viewed as transnational private regulatory regimes and that it is not contradictory to treat cartels as both potentially vulnerable to one form of regulation (competition law) while also performing important regulatory functions themselves. Even where cartels are banned, there are still circumstances where cartel-like conduct is allowed. Thus this article, looking at the EU,[15] argues that by prohibiting cartels the EU ensures that it decides to what extent and in what circumstances and under what conditions such potentially powerful transnational private regulatory regimes should be permitted to operate. Such agreements have posed particular regulatory challenges for governments leading to different regulatory responses over time. In the last hundred years, European governments have moved from a position of encouraging cartel activity, to registering cartels, to now seeing them as a major threat to competition. Thus, while at first glance the prohibition of cartels can be seen as a counter-factual to the general trend in favour of private regulatory regimes, in fact the prohibition simply requires any regulatory functions carried out by cartels to operate within the context of a far-reaching prohibition.

The article first examines the nature of cartels and how approaches to cartels have changed – from business activity to be encouraged, to tolerated activity, to illegal and even criminal activity. It then examines the circumstances in which they are legally permitted within the EU before addressing the question of when cartels can constitute TPRERs, looking in particular at the public interest. The article then concludes that horizontal agreements are subject to the constraint of competition law. Within that constraint, they may either be construed as contractual arrangements, self-regulatory (and probably illegal) or co-regulatory with horizontal agreements either not anti-competitive or exempt as their benefit to the public interest outweighs any risk to competition or private gain. Hence, cartels, broadly defined, may still be construed as forms of transnational private regulation.

CARTELS AND THE PUBLIC INTEREST

A public good is something that cannot be excluded and is non-rivalrous in character. It can be norm related (for example, good governance) or physical (clean air).[16] A competition regime can be seen as a public good, that is, a set of norms that facilitates the operation of competitive markets which, as a result of improving consumer welfare, increase general welfare. A com-

---

15 The article looks only at the operation of Article 101, see n. 35 below. It does not address questions of collective dominance by a group of firms under Article 102. On collective dominance, see G. Monti, 'The Scope of Collective Dominance under Article 82 EC' (2001) 38 *Common Market Law Rev.* 131–57.

16 P. Drahos, 'The Regulation of Public Goods' (2004) 7 *J. of International Economic Law* 321–39.

petitive market can be the means through which other goods are delivered, for example, innovation and technology. These are not treated as public goods but instead are left to the market which makes them excludable. Drahos explains that such excludability is justified as necessary to ensure the goods are developed. The characterization of competitive markets as public goods as well as markets being the means through which other goods are delivered highlights the complex interplay between prohibiting anti-competitive conduct and permitting arrangements between competitors that ultimately increase consumer welfare and/or meet other needs such as codifying standards across the EU, thereby integrating the market (seen as a public good under the EU treaties), and improving production and, for example, consumer safety.

The term 'cartel' is usually reserved for illegal cooperation between firms, usually at the same level of the market, for purposes that have unacceptable anti-competitive effects such as removing price competition or creating barriers to entry. Harding and Joshua describe a cartel as:

> an organization of independent enterprises from the same or similar area[s] of economic activity, formed for the purpose of promoting common economic interests by controlling competition between themselves.[17]

This definition is broad and goes much further than hard-core cartels, that is, a group of two or more independent sellers who agree to fix or control prices or output to a given market.[18] While most cartels that come into the public domain and fall foul of competition prohibitions are price-fixing cartels,[19] information sharing may also fall foul of the competition rules.[20] For example, in the 1990s the European Commission found that there was an information-sharing cartel between tractor producers – such agreements having the effect of reducing competition by increasing transparency in the market.[21]

---

17 C. Harding and J. Joshua, *Regulating Cartels in Europe: A Study of Legal Control of Corporate Delinquency* (2003) 12.

18 J.M. Connor, 'Global Antitrust Prosecutions of Modern International Cartels' (2004) 4 *J. of Industry, Competition and Trade* 239–67, at 240, citing A.R. Dick, 'When are Cartels Stable Contracts?' (1996) 39 *J. of Law and Economics* 241–83.

19 Price fixing is problematic under the competition rules even if instituted by government. See the current debate about alcohol pricing in the United Kingdom, at <http://www.alcoholpolicy.net/alocholpricing/> and <http://www.hm-treasury.gov.uk/alcohol_taxation.htm>: efforts to set minimum prices are hampered by the ban on price fixing in the competition laws.

20 See T. Björkroth, 'Exchange of Information and Collusion – do Consumer Switching Costs Matter?' (2010) 6 *European Competition J.* 179–96.

21 *UK Agricultural Tractor Registration Exchange* [1992] OJ L 68/19; [1993] 4 CMLR 358. Confirmed by the General Court and the Court of Justice, see case T-35/92, *J. Deere* v. *Commission* [1994] ECR II-957; case T-34/92, *Fiatagri and New Holland Ford* v. *Commission* [1994] ECR II-905. And for the Court of Justice judgment, see case C-7/95, *J. Deere* v. *Commission* [1998] ECR I-3111; case C-8/95, *New Holland Ford* v. *Commission* [1998] ECR I-3175.

The motivation for hard-core cartelization is that higher prices can be secured where the firms cooperate with consumers (producers further down the supply chain as well as end-users) paying higher prices. These arrangements can be enduring, as the animal feed phosphate producers' cartel shows. This is despite the fact that illegal cartels, in particular, are inherently unstable because firms can agree to hold prices but then undercut their competitors who cannot invoke the legal system to challenge the conduct.

Cartels were in fact viewed as benign for much of the twentieth century in Europe. Koch suggests that while cartels need to be managed in order to ensure that the public – and not exclusively the private – interest is served, nonetheless, they were essential for international trade.[22] In Europe there was a strong ambivalence towards cartels – Harding and Joshua refer to the culture of toleration.[23] At the end of the nineteenth century and right up to the Second World War, cartels were common, especially in continental Europe, with German cartels particularly to the fore. At the end of the nineteenth century they were the preferred means of industrial ordering. Freedom of contract meant firms should be able to cooperate, and, in any event, such cooperation ensured a stable development of the market in an efficient way that, on balance, was benign in relation to the public interest.[24] It was really only after the war, and the realization of the extent to which cartels had been connected to the Nazi regime, that there was a new debate about cartels and their role. Even then, they were not rejected out of hand but instead, a more regulatory approach was adopted with registration schemes becoming widespread. For example, in the United Kingdom, under the old Restrictive Trade Practices Acts, agreements could be registered provided they met certain criteria (called gateways).[25] The degree of public scrutiny was reflected in the European Coal and Steel Community (1952) which gave the High Authority – the precursors of the European Commission – the power to set quotas and maximum and minimum prices which, Harding and Joshua suggest, was in effect a kind of public cartel.[26] Koch, writing in the immediate aftermath of the war, suggested a model for international cartel regulation where cartels would be regulated by an international cartel body.[27]

While cartels are generally prohibited now throughout Europe and are increasingly vigorously pursued by the European Commission, they were a key feature of the business landscape until the recent past. The familiarity of

---

22 Koch, op. cit., n. 1.
23 Harding and Joshua, op. cit., n. 17, p. 52 and, more generally, chs. III–V. See, also, D.J. Gerber, *Law and Competition in Twentieth Century Europe: Protecting Prometheus* (1998).
24 Harding and Joshua, id., pp. 70–1.
25 See, for example, R. Whish, *Competition Law* (1985).
26 Harding and Joshua, op. cit., n. 17, p. 94.
27 Koch, op. cit., n. 1.

cartels is such that there remains ambivalence about them among key actors. The executives involved may suffer no adverse consequence even where firms are subject to fines.[28] Harding and Joshua suggest there is a fundamental difference in attitude – both in popular perception and among state actors – to cartels in the EU and the United States. In the United States, cartel activity such as price fixing is treated in itself as breaching antitrust rules and can attract criminal sanctions and imprisonment. The antitrust regime is concerned with the regulation of delinquency so the focus is on conduct with moral censure as an undertone.[29]

In the EU, the emphasis is on the regulation of undesirable harm – the focus is therefore on outcome rather than conduct. The emphasis, historically at least, has been more on the structure of the market. There are two evidentiary dimensions: economics – concerned with market structure – and material facts (for example, evidence of cartel meetings). Both are necessary in the European Court in order to prove not just the existence of the cartel but the responsibility of individual members.[30] With the reform of competition enforcement in 2003,[31] the Commission has turned its focus onto cartels so that EU law is setting the trend in Europe as one of strong condemnation of cartels, with detection supported by a leniency (whistleblower) programme and very large fines being imposed. Nonetheless, evidence of the operation of cartels over the last 100 years is that they seem to be largely constant.[32]

This brief historical overview suggests that the European approach to cartels has changed. For much of the twentieth century cartels flourished, with a positive attitude only modified after the Second World War to one of greater scrutiny – formally if not substantively – through registration in order to ensure the public interest was protected. That ambivalence has now been largely swept away, especially following the 2003 reform of EU competition law where a more economics-based approach was embraced by the Commission.[33]

---

28 A British Airways executive was given share bonuses the day before he went on trial for price fixing as part of a cartel. See A. Brownsell, 'British Airways Attacked for Executive Share Option Award' *Marketing Magazine*, 6 April 2010. British Airways had previously been fined £121.5 million by the Office of Fair Trading, see its press release, 'British Airways to Pay Record £121.5 million Penalty in Price-Fixing Investigation' 1 August 2007. The criminal trial collapsed: see M. Peel and J. Croft, 'British Airways Price-Fixing Trial Collapses' *Financial Times* 10 May 2010, at <http://www.ft.com/cms/s/0/ee55f16a-5c22-11df-95f9-00144feab49a.html>.

29 Harding and Joshua, op. cit., n. 17, pp. 47, 56–7.

30 id., pp. 56–7, 144–6, 160 and following.

31 Council Regulation 1/2003 of 16 December 2002 on the Implementation of the Rules on Competition laid down in Arts. 81 and 82 of the Treaty [2003] OJ L1/1.

32 Harding and Joshua, op. cit., n. 17, p. 272. These sorts of statements have to be treated with caution, however, given the extreme difficulty of assessing cartels in view of their opaque and private nature.

33 For example, EC Commission, *Guidelines on Article 81(3) of the Treaty* [2004] OJ C101/97, para. 13.

Nonetheless, from a historical perspective, the capacity of cartels to be seen as acting in the public interest, with oversight and even encouragement from government, suggests that whether they can constitute TPRER and not purely sites of self-regulation depends in part on the scope of competition law and the extent to which the self-interest of firms is equated with the public interest in how markets operate.

WHEN ARE CARTELS NOT ILLEGAL NOW?

Even today there are circumstances where cartels are legal. For example, in the United States, which prohibits cartels and frequently imprisons executives of firms that have breached the prohibition, export cartels are expressly allowed, provided they are registered.[34] In the EU, provided the export cartel does not affect inter-state trade (the jurisdictional trigger for the competition rules), it will also fall outside the scope of the EU prohibition.[35] An inter-

---

34 US Pomerene Act 1918 supplemented by the Export-Trading Act 1982 and Foreign Trade Improvements Act 1982. The OECD glossary of statistical terms defines an export cartel as 'an agreement or arrangement between firms to charge a specific export price and/or to divide export markets' (drawn from R.S. Khemani and D.M. Shapiro, *Glossary of Industrial Organisation Economics and Competition Law* (1993)). For a discussion of export cartels, see F. Becker, 'The Case of Export Cartel Exemptions: Between Competition and Protectionism' (2007) 3 *J. of Competition Law & Economics* 97–126.

35 The relevant EU provision is Article 101 TFEU, previously Articles 85 and then Article 81 EC. The text has remained the same:

1. The following shall be prohibited as incompatible with the internal market: all agreements between undertakings, decisions by associations of undertakings and concerted practices which may affect trade between Member States and which have as their object or effect the prevention, restriction or distortion of competition within the internal market, and in particular those which:

(a) directly or indirectly fix purchase or selling prices or any other trading conditions;

(b) limit or control production, markets, technical development, or investment;

(c) share markets or sources of supply;

(d) apply dissimilar conditions to equivalent transactions with other trading parties, thereby placing them at a competitive disadvantage;

(e) make the conclusion of contracts subject to acceptance by the other parties of supplementary obligations which, by their nature or according to commercial usage, have no connection with the subject of such contracts.

2. Any agreements or decisions prohibited pursuant to this Article shall be automatically void.

3. The provision of paragraph 1 may, however, be declared inapplicable in the case of:

– any agreement or category of agreements between undertakings,

– any decision or category of decisions by associations of undertakings,

– any concerted practice or category of concerted practices,

which contributes to improving the production or distribution of goods or to

126

national competition regime would address this phenomenon but attempts to include competition on the WTO agenda in Singapore and Doha failed, leaving competition law as a national (or in the case of the EU) supranational phenomenon.[36]

Crisis cartels can also arise where an industry is contracting. Cartels to reduce overproduction where there is low demand may be allowed, provided they are efficient, soften the impact on unemployment, and facilitate the restructuring so as to enhance competitiveness in the sector.[37] Thus, in the early 2000s in Ireland, beef processors agreed that smaller operators would be paid to leave the market by larger processors, given over-capacity in a shrinking market. This arrangement was challenged by the Irish Competition Authority in the courts. The High Court found no breach of the EU prohibition on restrictive agreements (because most Irish beef is exported in part to other EU states, the arrangement necessarily had an effect on inter-state trade triggering the application of the EU rules).[38] On appeal, the Supreme Court referred the issue to the European Court for assistance on the interpretation of the EU prohibition. The European Court found that an agreement of the type in issue would fall within the prohibition – in fact, its object would be to restrict competition.[39] The matter was referred back to the High Court by the Supreme Court where the question of whether or not it falls within the exemption to the prohibition on restrictive agreements is to be answered.[40]

This legal marathon suggests that it is too simple to dismiss cartels as activities that only serve private interests and are illegal. The High Court and Supreme Court were at pains to point out how different the arrangement was from that of one 'hatched in a smoke-filled room', given the parties were aware that there would be competition issues and had openly approached and discussed the agreement with the Authority before it came into effect. The High Court in fact was critical of the Authority for not negotiating with the parties to secure any necessary changes to the scheme to meet its concerns.

---

promoting technical or economic progress, while allowing consumers a fair share of the resulting benefit, and which does not:
   (a) impose on the undertakings concerned restrictions which are not indispensable to the attainment of these objectives;
   (b) afford such undertakings the possibility of eliminating competition in respect of a substantial part of the products in question.

36 A. Bhattacharjea, 'The Case for a Multilateral Agreement on Competition Policy: A Developing Country Perspective' (2006) 9 *J. of International Economic Law* 293–323; D.J. Gerber, *Global Competition: Law, Markets and Globalization* (2010) 101 ff.; I. Maher, 'Competition Law in the International Domain: Networks as a New Form of Governance' (2002) 29 *J. of Law and Society* 111–36.

37 European Commission, *Twelfth Report on Competition Policy* (1982) paras. 38–40; G. Monti, *EC Competition Law* (2007) 95–6.

38 *Competition Authority* v. *Beef Industry Development Society* [2006] IEHC 294.

39 C-209/07, 20 November 2008.

40 [2009] IEHC 72.

This crisis cartel, while entirely private in nature, was the product of a government ministerial task force and other reports, all of which recognized the over-capacity in the sector and the need for change but change that would not require or receive any public funds. Thus, it has a public element in that the government was supportive in principle, if not in the detail. It is perhaps the hybrid nature of the arrangement that makes it more difficult to discuss as an arrangement outside the public interest.[41] Whether or not the arrangement is deemed to be exempt from the prohibition, the complexity of the litigation in itself is a salutary reminder that cartels cannot be dismissed as always exclusively private arrangements that fall outside the law.

Harding and Joshua's definition of cartels is broad in its remit, referring to the parties' economic interests and the control of competition. The Irish Beef case shows how those who share economic interests and seek to control competition may not necessarily fall outside the law. While export and crisis cartels may well involve hard-core price controls that customarily fall outside legitimate business activity, there are other forms of business cooperation which are recognized as being generally pro-competitive. Thus, in the EU, there has been a long-standing recognition of the importance of horizontal cooperation agreements. Such agreements can enhance efficiency, innovation, and the competitiveness of European firms. They allow for the sharing of risk, savings on costs, increased investment, a pooling of know-how, enhanced product quality, and variety and innovation. However, they may also raise competition concerns because they can result in price fixing, the gaining, maintaining or increasing of market power which, in turn, can impact on price, output, innovation, and/or variety or quality of products.[42] The European Commission has regulated these agreements through a combination of hard- and soft-law measures.

Originally, the Commission was the sole body in the EU that could exempt competition agreements with agreements enjoying immunity from the date of notification.[43] The system was unwieldy, with a permanent backlog of notifications.[44] Part of the response to this was that the Commission was given the power to enact block exemption regulations (BERs) that set out the conditions under which certain types of agreements would be

---

41 For a discussion of hybridity in relation to TPRER, see, further, below at p. 156.
42 European Commission, *Draft Guidelines on the Applicability of Article 101 of the Treaty on the Functioning of the EU to Horizontal Co-operation Agreements* (SEC(2010)528/2) paras. 1.1.2–3. These guidelines will replace the existing ones which lapse at the end of 2010, available at [2001] OJ C 3/2.
43 Regulation 17 [1959–62] IJ Spec. Ed. 87, Article 9.
44 36,000 notifications were made within the first year of Regulation 17. The Commission issued ten to twenty decisions a year and received on average 400 notified agreements. See S. Wilks and L. McGowan, 'Competition Policy in the European Union: Creating a Federal Agency?' in *Comparative Competition Policy*, eds. G.B. Doern and S. Wilks (1996) 250; I. Maher, 'Competition Law and Intellectual Property Rights' in *The Evolution of EU Law*, eds. P. Craig and G. de Búrca (1999).

automatically exempt and would not need to be notified.[45] These BERs and their accompanying guidelines survived the 2003 reforms even though the notification system itself did not.[46] There was, however, a major change in approach to them. Under the old regime, the regulations were highly formalistic and very prescriptive. The agreements to which they applied were narrowly defined; a blacklist of unacceptable provisions and a whitelist of acceptable provisions were provided, the combined effect of which was to impose a standard-form contract on those agreements, severely limiting the circumstances under which the BERs could be invoked.[47] After 2003, the BERs are less formalistic, reflecting the more light-touch approach of the Commission overall to competition, with an emphasis now on firms' self-assessment in relation to competition law compliance. No whitelist is now included, giving firms greater flexibility and the blacklist is shorter and more focused. Nonetheless, the fact that the Commission continues to produce BERs reflects how popular they remain among businesses looking for guidance in relation to the scope of the prohibition on anti-competitive agreements and exemptions. What the prohibition with its exemption has created is a regulatory framework within which potentially suspect activity is provided with general guidance, specific blacklisted provisions, and conditions which must be met for the agreements to meet competition concerns. Thus, competition law constrains the exercise of freedom of contract by prohibiting certain conduct and then exempting it.

Horizontal agreements such as research, development, and innovation (RDI) agreements and specialization agreements (production, purchasing, and marketing arrangements) are all regulated through BERs.[48] Such agreements are contractual arrangements which, because of their innovative potential, are pro-competitive either because they fall outside the cartel prohibition entirely or they meet the conditions set down in the BER. The guidelines address a more extensive list of agreements than those covered in the BER. The guidelines are soft-law measures that are not legally binding

45 Council Regulation 19/65 [1965–66] OJ Spec. Ed. 35.
46 Regulation 1/2003 on the Implementation of the Rules on Competition laid down in Article 81 and 82 of the Treaty [2003] OJ L 1/1. The reforms removed the notification system and introduced dual enforcement of the EU rules by national competition agencies as well as the EC. See D.J. Gerber, 'Two Forms of Modernization in European Competition Law' (2008) 31 *Fordham International Law J.* 1235–65; I. Maher, 'Competition Law Modernisation: An Evolutionary Tale?' in *The Evolution of EU Law*, eds. P. Craig and G. de Búrca (2011, 2nd edn.).
47 See J.-E. de Cockborne, 'Franchising and EC Competition Law' in *Franchising and the Law: Theoretical and Comparative Approaches in Europe and the US*, ed. C. Joerges (1991) 287.
48 Block Exemption Regulation for Research and Development Agreements 2659/00 [2000] OJ L 304/Block Exemption Regulation for Specialisation Agreements 2658/00 [2000] OJ L 304/3. Both regulations expire after ten years, which is the norm for this sort of measure, and drafts have been issued for consultation: see <http://ec.europa.eu/competition/consultations/2010_horizontals/index.html>.

but do have practical effects[49] and are a vital guide to Commission thinking in the field, which is important as there is little or no case law on these matters.[50] Their importance is reflected in that fact that when a draft block exemption is published for consultation, the draft guidelines are also issued for comment.

One particular form of agreement which has received further attention in the most recent iteration of the guidelines, currently under revision, is standardization agreements, that is:

> agreements which have as their primary objective the definition of technical or quality requirements with which current or future products, production processes, services or methods may comply.[51]

The draft guidelines specify under what conditions such agreements fall outside the cartel prohibition entirely, namely, if the process for adoption of a standard are transparent and open, the standard is not mandatory for the product/service to appear on the market, and access to the standard (often technical and involving intellectual property rights) is on a FRAND basis.[52] Where actual or potential competitors are excluded, for example, because the way the standards are set do not allow for recognition of equivalent standards, then they may breach Article 101(1).[53] Exemption under Article 101(3) will be possible if the four conditions of efficiency, indispensability, non-elimination of competition, and benefits passed onto consumers are met to an extent that outweighs the anti-competitive effect of the agreement. These competition rules govern standardization agreements, even where there is co-regulation, provided the regulatory framework does not remove all competition from any of the relevant markets.[54] In particular, the European standard-setting bodies are subject to the competition rules to the

---

49 F. Snyder, 'The Effectiveness of European Community Law: Institutions, Processes, Tools and Techniques' in *Implementing EC Law in the United Kingdom: Structures for Indirect Rule*, ed. T. Daintith (1995) 64.
50 On absence of case law, see R. Whish, *Competition Law* (2009, 6th edn.) 573.
51 EC Commission, 'Draft Guidelines on the applicability of Article 101 of the Treaty on the Functioning of the European Union to horizontal co-operation agreements' SEC(2010) 528/2 ('*Guidelines*') para. 252.
52 On a fair, reasonable and non-discriminatory basis. For a discussion on FRAND see, for example, P. Chappatte, 'FRAND Commitments – the Case for Antitrust Intervention' (2009) 5 *European Competition J.* 319–46; D. Geradin and M. Rato, 'FRAND Commitments and EC Competition Law: A Reply to Philippe Chappatte' (2010) 6 *European Competition J.* 129–74; P. Chappatte, 'FRAND Commitments and EC Competition Law: A Rejoinder' (2010) 6 *European Competition J.* 175–8.
53 *Guidelines*, op. cit., n. 51, para. 315.
54 id., para. 21; Case C-198/01 CIF [2003] ECR I-8055 para. 56–8. For a discussion of the application of the competition rules to public or private standardization bodies, see F. Cafaggi, 'Self-Regulation in European Contract Law' (2007) *European J. of Legal Studies* 1–52, at 31.

130

extent that they are undertakings or associations of undertakings.[55] If the standards are produced exclusively as an exercise in public power then competition law does not apply.[56]

The Commission Department of Enterprise is also reviewing standardization of ICT (information and communication technology) at the time of writing. In its White Paper, it sets out the criteria to be met by standardization processes[57] while noting that its discussions are subject to the operation of the competition rules: thus, standardization in general is seen as pro-competitive but must comply with the competition rules.[58] The risk of firms using the standardization process in order to reduce competition and ultimately increase their own profits or to exclude competitors with alternative standards is reduced within this regulatory framework. The criteria set down are designed to ensure that the public interest of competition and standardization outweighs the private interests of the parties.

The particular form of regulation used by the EU ensures (some) control of even pro-competitive agreements by the Commission. The strong prohibition is softened in the treaty itself by an exemption provision. This has then been elaborated on in relation to horizontal cooperation agreements through guidelines (non-binding soft-law instruments) setting out Commission thinking of when such agreements are outside the prohibitions entirely, when within the prohibition but exempt, and when prohibited entirely. These, in turn, are complemented by two specific block exemption regulations. Thus, the question of whether cartels are ever legal can be answered positively, provided we understand cartels in the wider sense provided by Harding and Joshua and not simply as hard-core price-fixing arrangements between parties. This then raises the question to what extent can such horizontal cooperation agreements be seen as TPRER?

<hr />

55 *Guidelines*, id., at para. 253. See Annex I of Directive 94/98EC laying down a procedure for the provision of information in the field of technical standards and regulations, [1998] OJ L 204/37, 21 July 1998, which lists the EU standard-setting bodies: CEN, CENELEC, and ETSI. A list of national bodies is provided in Annex II.

56 *Guidelines*, id., para. 253. The regulation of the liberal professions is also excluded. They have been subject to separate scrutiny by the Commission both through individual decision and through advocacy, with a report published on the liberal professions in 2004: see EC Commission, 'Report on Competition in Professional Services' COM(2004) 83 final, and the follow-up to it, 'Professional Services – Scope for more reform' COM(2005) 405 final. Competition law constrains those professional activities that may have an effect on the market and are not ethical/public law activities.

57 Openness, consensus, balance, and transparency. These norms are the same as those of the WTO: see EC Commission, 'Modernising ICT Standardisation in the EU – The Way Forward', COM(2009) 324 final (2009) s. 2.1.

58 This discussion has focused on Article 101 and anti-competitive agreements. However, where a firm with a dominant position in the market is deemed to have abused it through the standard-setting procedure, then it may be investigated under Article 102TFEU which prohibits such abuse.

As public control of particular market sectors, and especially utilities, has changed, the interplay between competition policy and regulation has become more significant. If regulation is cast (at its widest) as standard setting, monitoring, and enforcement, then competition law can be seen as part of a continuum that has tight, command-and-control regulation at one end and unfettered markets at the other.[59] This is not to say regulation and competition law are the same, but simply that a crude dichotomy may not fully explain the relationship between the two. In fact, cartels are both subject to regulatory control, through the cartel prohibition, and may also perform important regulatory functions such as standardization.

Self-regulatory bodies, whose power is sustained by freedom of contract, tend to represent the interests of their members, and the challenge is to achieve better regulation by relying on those private actors with the relevant expertise and knowledge while constraining them so as to ensure that public-interest objectives are realized.[60] Cafaggi identifies competition law as one of these constraints and there is an extensive body of case law addressing the limits of the discretion of regulatory bodies in relation to competition.[61] Thus, competition law significantly affects decisions about to whom and how private regulatory power should be allocated.[62] This can be seen in the guidelines on standardization agreements discussed above. At the same time, freedom to contract and freedom of association are important tools in private regulation which the state seeks to exploit. If the constraints imposed by competition law are too severe, the regulatory outcome sought will not be achieved. This was the experience under the old EU system of block exemption regulations.

There are also other constraints on private regulation which are important to protect the public interest. Private regulatory regimes need to meet certain rule of law principles such as transparency, consistency, and accountability: the argument is that, as regulatory functions are in essence public in nature, they should be subject to the sorts of constraints imposed on the exercise of public power.[63] From a functional perspective, given they are regulatory in

---

59 H. Collins, *Regulating Contracts* (2002) 58–9 where he rejects the markets/regulation dichotomy. For a more extensive discussion of this, see I. Maher, 'Regulating Competition' in *Regulating Law*, eds. C. Parker, J. Braithwaite, C. Scott, and N. Lacey (2004).

60 F. Cafaggi, 'Rethinking Private Regulation in the European Regulatory Space', EUI Working Paper no. 2006/13 (2006).

61 id., pp. 31, 35. See, for example, T-128/98 *Alpha Flight Services/Aéroports de Paris* [2000] ECR II-3929; case 96/82 etc *IAZ International Belgium Sa* v. *Commission* [1983] ECR 3369.

62 Cafaggi, op. cit., n. 60, p. 35.

63 See C. Scott, F. Cafaggi, and L. Senden in this volume, pp. 1–19, and C. Harlow, 'Global Administrative Law: The Quest for Principles and Values' (2006) 17 *European J. of International Law* 187–214.

nature, they should also be effective: there is no point delegating the exercise of public authority to a private body if it is not effective to do so. Thus, rather than evaluating the desirability of regulation on the basis of whether it is public or private, the test can be one determined by function, where effectiveness and compliance with the rule of law are key considerations. If TPRER can be shown to meet these standards, then their private nature should not really render them unacceptable.

Bartley's working definition of TPRER as systems where coalitions of non-state actors codify, monitor, and in some cases certify firms' compliance with labour, environmental, human rights or others standards of accountability[64] is also used by the editors of this volume. Transnational, I suggest, means either that the actors engaged in the conduct are domiciled in two different states or that the conduct of two actors in one state has an effect outside that state. More fundamentally, the editors remind us that transnational differs from international in that the conduct is not the result of state cooperation reflected in treaties (or MOUs). Thus, public cartels like OPEC are not included within this definition.[65]

Bartley refers to standard setting in several non-market fields such as human rights and environment. Nonetheless, he also refers to a catch-all of 'other standards of accountability'. If the (non-definitive) list he provides is characterized as standards in the public interest, then it can include competition, market integration (a public good in the EU), and public health and safety standards, among others. This suggests that horizontal cooperation between firms within the same sector may or may not constitute TPRER. We can see three broad categories here.

First, those agreements in relation to RDI, for example, that operate to develop new products or improve existing products may be viewed as private contractual arrangements between a small number of firms and other economic actors (including universities)[66] that still operate within the context of the competition rules. Whether these contracts can constitute TPRER will depend on the extent to which they can be seen as setting/codifying/imposing standards, establishing mechanisms for monitoring for compliance, and enforcing such standards. As many RDI agreements are at the experimental phase and very early in any production phase, such fully developed regulatory characteristics are unlikely.

Second, hard-core cartels are a form of self-regulation where activities are

---

64 T. Bartley, 'Institutional Emergence in an Era of Globalization: the Rise of Transnational Private Regulation of Labor and Environmental Conditions' (2007) 113 *Am. J. of Sociology* 297–351, at 298.

65 Scott et al., op. cit., n. 63.

66 The EU prohibition on cartels applies to 'undertakings', a term that is very broadly defined to refer to any economic activity (profit-making is not required), see, generally, O. Odudu, *The Boundaries of EC Competition Law: the Scope of Article 81* (2006) ch. 3.

performed exclusively for the benefit of regulatees.[67] The successful operation of the cartel requires the firms to set standards (or at least prices and
market shares), monitor and enforce compliance through regular reporting
and meetings, with sanctions (such as reduction of market share or refusal to
share price-sensitive information) imposed where there is non-compliance.
Thus, the hard-core cartel requires internal regulatory systems to operate
effectively.[68] Nonetheless, the cartel is exclusively self-regulatory as
membership is limited to those whose interests are advanced by participating
in the cartel or their facilitators, be they trade associations or consultants.[69]
The price-fixing cartel is not perceived today as serving any public interest –
although historically this was not the case (see the discussion above).

Finally, private arrangements have been co-opted to set standards, for
example, in standardization agreements. These hybrid regulatory forms of
co-regulation or delegated self-regulation formalize interaction between the
legislature and private actors in order to maximize industry expertise, reduce
regulatory drag, generate greater ownership of the standards industry, and
hence improve compliance while also protecting the public interest.[70] They
operate in the shadow of competition law and, in the EU, within structures
laid down under the Single Market Programme.[71] On the one hand, these
agreements are generally seen as having positive effects on competition by
opening new markets, lowering costs, and ensuring interoperability and
improving safety, thereby benefiting consumers.[72] On the other, the context
of discussion of standard setting creates opportunities for other more
damaging agreements; the more restrictive the standards, the more likely that
they may dampen innovation and agreed standards and create considerable
barriers to entry for alternative technologies and standards. Thus, standardization agreements are co-regulatory in nature and characterized by four
features: openness (of decision making and membership for all interested

---

67 For a discussion of self-regulation. see Cafaggi, op. cit., n. 60, p. 18 and Cafaggi, op.
cit., n. 54.
68 S.J. Evenett, M.C. Levenstein, and V.Y. Suslow, 'International Cartel Enforcement;
Lessons from the 1990s' in *The World Economy: Global Trade Policy*, eds. P. Lloyd
and C. Milner (2002) 4.
69 For trade associations, see Whish, op. cit., n. 50, pp. 102–4, 545–52. In relation to
other organizations, see T-99/04 *AC-Treuhand AG* v. *Commission* [2008] ECR II-
1501 where the General Court confirmed that a consultancy firm which facilitated the
operation of a cartel infringed Article 81(1). See C. Harding, 'Capturing the cartel's
friends: cartel facilitation and the idea of joint criminal enterprise' (2009) 34
European Law Rev. 298–309.
70 See, for example, the Product Safety Directive, 2001/95/EC [2004] OJ L 151/83, 30
April 2004 Article 4; Cafaggi, op. cit., n. 60. A less hybrid and less harmonized
approach has been adopted in the United States: see C. Koenig, 'Competition Law
Issues of Standard Setting by Officially-Entrusted Versus Private Organisations'
(2010) 31 *European Competition Law Rev.* 449–58.
71 See Cafaggi, id., pp. 31, 35.
72 *Guidelines*, op. cit., n. 51, para. 258.

134

actors), consensus (no particular stakeholder interest favoured), balance (participation is available at any stage in the decision-making process), and transparency.[73] The requirements of transparency and openness[74] also reflect the rule of law requirements that Harlow suggests should apply to private regulators carrying out what is in effect a public function.[75]

Cafaggi sees self-regulation as a form of private regulation, although he does draw a distinction between that and participatory private regulation – where actors other than regulatees are represented. Bartley, on the other hand, does not see self-regulation as form of private regulation. In his view, self-regulation implies standard setting, monitoring, and enforcement carried out by a group where members share common characteristics, while private regulation includes other stakeholders such as NGOs and consumer groups. This difference in approach is explained by reference to membership, with Bartley seeing exclusive membership as a key determinant of whether or not the arrangement can be seen as private regulation. Cafaggi, on the other hand, argues that it is still possible for other interests to be pursued even in a self-regulatory regime, while accepting that it will mainly reflect the interests of the regulatees.[76] Thus, he places less emphasis on membership and recognizes the possibility of self-regulation being more open than Bartley allows. This wider focus is preferable.

The fact that there are criteria standardization agreements need to meet in order to fall within the constraint of competition law means that the regulatory space created by the agreements is contested. Thus, cooperation cannot be exclusively self-interested and instead reflects what Bartley refers to as agendas and struggles about the distribution of power in society.[77] Institutions are seen as settlements of conflict among actors with different power and competing frames.[78] On this analysis, hard-core cartels evade becoming sites for such political struggles between different actors by remaining secretive and self-regulatory.

One of the features of TPRER that is not addressed by Bartley in his working definition, but is a relevant consideration, is the degree of voluntariness for an arrangement. Scott[79] notes that compliance with standards set by a TPRER may in fact be essential to participate in a market, so even those not privy to an agreement may have to comply with the standards to gain access. If the standard becomes de facto compulsory, this then raises

---

73 See, for example, EC Commission, op. cit., n. 57, s. 2.1, drawing on WTO criteria for standardization agreements.
74 *Guidelines*, op. cit., n. 51, para. 278 ff.
75 Harlow, op. cit., n. 63.
76 Cafaggi, op. cit., n. 60, pp. 13–14.
77 Bartley, op. cit., n. 64, pp. 310, 340.
78 id., p. 309.
79 C. Scott, 'Regulatory Governance and the Challenge of Constitutionalism' in *The Regulatory State: Constitutional Implications*, eds. D. Oliver, T. Prosser, and R. Rawlings (2010) 31.

important questions as to the freedom of contract and market foreclosure, essentially making whoever approves the standard and compliance with it a gatekeeper. Market foreclosure raises questions of anti-competitiveness, with the draft guidelines noting that such foreclosure is fatal to exemption and this is without regard to the prohibition of abuse of market dominance (which such a gatekeeper role may create) under Article 102 EU.

Thus, horizontal agreements range from contracts, to self- (and/or private) regulation to co-regulating TPRER, and from legal to illegal. Legality turns on the extent to which such agreements are deemed to be for the public benefit, with policy having changed over time.

CONCLUSION

Cartels (broadly construed) may be both subject to competition (arguably one form of regulation) while also performing an important regulatory function themselves. In recent years in Europe (and for longer in the United States) the public interest has been defined in such a way that agreements on price fixing, market quotas, market sharing, and production restrictions will almost certainly fall foul of competition law. Where cartels are tolerated, they are usually subject to public regulation. Thus, the prohibition of cartels in the EU is softened by an exemption provision that allows the Commission to set in place regulatory frameworks (a mix of hard and soft law) that set down the criteria under which horizontal cooperation between firms may take place, either outside the competition prohibition or under the exemption, because they are seen to provide important public benefits. Thus, by prohibiting cartels, the EU reserves to itself greater control over the circumstances where such horizontal agreements will be allowed.

We see a historical trajectory that runs counter to that more generally for TPRER which have become more evident and more widely accepted as forms of regulation in recent years. For cartels, tolerance has become much more limited with tighter control reflecting a shift in competition policy away from toleration of cooperative business behaviour to greater prohibition. Nonetheless, there are still forms of horizontal agreements – especially in the field of RDI – that can fall outside the competition prohibition entirely, as they are some distance from the final stages of production. Hardcore cartels can be seen as a form of self-regulation (with some debate in the literature as to whether or not self-regulation can be construed as form of private regulation or not) where membership is closed and members interests are advanced with costs externalized.

Finally, the expertise and knowledge of industry is harnessed by the EU notably in relation to standard setting where a hybrid form of regulation applies with principles established through statute but executed in the private realm. This form of co-regulation seeks to ensure that the largely horizontal agreements involved remain aligned with the public interest, now clearly

136

defined as requiring the advancement of competition. It is in this last category that we see TPRER and cartels coming together, albeit where competition provides a stringent regulatory context and where the public interest requires strict criteria that remove the character of exclusivity, and gatekeeping that defines those cartels that remain beyond the pale for modern competition law.

JOURNAL OF LAW AND SOCIETY
VOLUME 38, NUMBER 1, MARCH 2011
ISSN: 0263-323X, pp. 138–62

The Meta-regulation of Transnational Private Regulation

JACCO BOMHOFF* AND ANNE MEUWESE**

This article starts from the assertion that Transnational Private Regulatory Regimes (TPRERs) construct relationships of recognition with the plurality of public and private normative orders and actors that surround them. We argue that the strategies and norms adopted to manage these relationships are reflexive responses to competing legitimacy demands and to issues of regulatory conflict and that they have a meta-regulatory character. More specifically, we explore two disciplines and professional fields, Better Regulation (BR) and Private International Law (PIL), as direct sources of meta-norms and as more indirect sources of inspiration for meta-regulatory strategies. Building on literature that has cast transnational governance and conflict of laws thinking as abstract repositories of potentially useful meta-regulatory ideas, we explore the actual potential for – and limitations of – the migration of disciplinary practices and perspectives in the context of TPR.

INTRODUCTION

Transnational Private Regulatory Regimes (TPRERs) operate in a heterarchical environment characterized by a plurality of public and private normative orders and actors. Within the relevant literatures on transnational and supranational regulation, we identify two main perspectives for the observation of relationships between TPRERs and this environment. The first is the idea that multiple public and private regulators in the transnational sphere

* Department of Law, London School of Economics, Houghton Street, London WC2A 2AE, England
j.a.bomhoff@lse.ac.uk
** Tilburg Law School, Tilburg University, P.O. Box 90153, 5000 LE, Tilburg, The Netherlands
anne.meuwese@uvt.nl

The authors would like to thank the editors of the special issue, as well as an anonymous referee, Julia Black, Aukje van Hoek, and Peer Zumbansen. The usual disclaimer applies.

will 'compete for business and legitimacy'[1] – in short, for a share of trans-national 'regulatory space'.[2] The second is the suggestion that the plurality of actors, norms, and rationalities in the transnational sphere will lead to the emergence of a new form of 'intersystemic conflicts law', through which different actors and logics will be able to operationalize their 'mutual observation'.[3]

These two projects are intimately related in a number of ways. First, both focus primarily on the *interaction of regimes with their surroundings*, rather than on their internal organization or regulatory activity.[4] Second, they share an understanding that a central dimension of this interaction will concern the question of the *recognition of regimes by their environment*,[5] and an assumption that regimes' quest for recognition will have implications for the way they organize and present themselves. Recognition in this sense, therefore, is a reflexive practice with intertwined extra- and intra-regime dimensions. And third, both projects have a built-in appreciation for the extraordinary *normative and institutional diversity of the environment* these regimes are faced with – composed of constituents, intended regulatees, public bodies, state legal actors, rival and complementary regimes, and so on – and of the fact that the nature of the interaction between the regime and each of these components is likely differ.[6]

The norms and strategies involved in both the extra- and intra-regime dimensions of these relationships of recognition can be captured within the concept of *the meta-regulation of transnational regulation*. This, not just in the literal, reflexive sense that they concern the regulation of regulation, but also in the sense of regulation through *meta-norms* – norms of conflict-management that different actors can 'sign up' to, without betraying loyalty to their own rationalities.[7] Legal academic work on this type of conflict

1 E. Meidinger, 'Competitive Supragovernmental Regulation: How Could It Be Democratic?' (2008) 8 *Chicago J. of International Law* 518.
2 Compare J. Black, 'Legitimacy and the Competition for Regulatory Share', LSE Working Paper 14/2009 (2009). For the concept of 'regulatory space' see C. Scott, 'Analysing Regulatory Space: Fragmented Resources and Institutional Design' (2001) *Public Law* 329. 'Regulatory space' is a metaphor used to express a state of fragmentation of resources, information, and de facto regulatory power among a group of regulatory constituents.
3 A. Fischer-Lescano and G. Teubner, 'Diversity or Cacophony?: New Sources of Norms in International Law' (2004) 25 *Michigan J. of International Law* 999–1046, at 1018.
4 In this respect the perspectives differ from the Global Administrative Law (GAL) movement and global constitutionalism. For a call for greater emphasis on plurality and interaction within GAL, see K. Nicolaïdis and G. Shaffer, 'Transnational Mutual Recognition Regimes: Governance Without Global Government' (2005) 68 *Law & Contemporary Problems* 263–317.
5 Compare Black, op. cit., n. 2, p. 2; C. Joerges, 'Free Trade with Hazardous Products – The Emergence of Transnational Governance with Eroding State Government' (2005) 10 *European Foreign Affairs Rev.* 553.
6 Compare Black, id.; Fischer-Lescano and Teubner, op. cit., n. 3.
7 For example, Joerges, op. cit., n. 5, p. 562.

management has sought inspiration for the nature and functioning of such 'meta-regulation' and 'meta-norms' primarily in the operation of innovative modes of norm generation in supranational and cross-rationality contexts – for example, the by now classic example of comitology within EU governance[8] – and in the venerable techniques of trans-jurisdictional conflict resolution found in the discipline of private international law, or the conflict of laws.[9]

This paper further develops this meta-regulatory approach to the interaction between transnational regulatory regimes and the 'regulatory space' they inhabit. We lay the conceptual groundwork in section I, after which we extend the analysis in two directions. First, our ambition is to supplement accounts of *the generation of meta-regulatory norms and strategies*. In our approach, not only are the relevant modes of regime/environment interaction themselves social processes – with actors selectively responding to competing legitimacy claims, evaluating opportunities for collaboration or competition with rival regimes, and so on – but so are the disciplinary perspectives by which these forms of interaction are framed and evaluated. Our ambition is to take seriously the impact of the 'professional performances' and 'professional vocabulary' that come with different disciplinary and professional lenses through which these interactions are viewed.[10] It may be hypothesized that the impact of differences in disciplinary backgrounds and favoured conceptual analogies will be especially pervasive in this area, given the relative novelty of the TPRER phenomenon. Whereas earlier studies have generally cast transnational governance and conflict of laws thinking as *abstract repositories* of potentially useful meta-regulatory ideas, we are interested in a critical analysis of the *actual* potential for – and limitations of – the migration of disciplinary practices and perspectives. The disciplines selected are 'Better Regulation' (BR), as a prominent contemporary site for the development of practices and ideas on the regulation of regulation, which is discussed in section II and Private International Law (PIL), as the oft-turned to 'queen mother of all transnational legal thought',[11] discussed in section III.

8 C. Joerges, '"Good Governance" through Comitology' in *EU Committees: Social Regulation, Law and Politics*, eds. C. Joerges and E. Vos (1999) 311. Another example is the work Joerges, Dehousse, Sabel, Zeitlin, and others have done on the Open Method of Coordination as a new way of norm generation in the face of inter-jurisdictional conflicts: see, for an overview, C.F. Sabel and J. Zeitlin, 'Learning from Difference: The New Architecture of Experimentalist Governance in the EU' (2008) 14 *European Law J.* 271–327.

9 For a collection encompassing both dimensions, see R. Nickel (ed.), *Conflict of Laws and Laws of Conflict in Europe and Beyond: Patterns of Supranational and Transnational Juridification* (2009).

10 D. Kennedy, 'When Renewal Repeats: Thinking against the Box' (2000) 32 *New York J. of International Law and Politics* 337, at 338. See, also, D. Kennedy, 'New Approaches to Comparative Law: Comparativism and International Governance' (1997) *Utah Law Rev.* 545–638, at 582.

11 C. Joerges, 'Rethinking European Law's Supremacy', EUI Working Papers 2005/12 (2005) 7.

Second, within an approach concerned generally with the interaction between regulatory regimes and their surroundings, we focus specifically on questions raised by the emergence of transnational *private* regulatory regimes. In contrast to the Global Administrative Law (GAL) approach[12] and literature focusing on *transgovernmental* networks,[13] our current focus requires special attention to the particularities of the various modes of interaction of private regimes with other normative orders and actors. Questions we address – in section IV – include the role of norms and strategies of PIL in effectuating a 'touchdown' of transnational private actors and the capacity of BR strategies to channel the legitimacy demands of the diverse constituencies of TPRERs. Viewed from the perspective of meta-regulation and meta-norms – many of which were developed against explicitly public backgrounds – an important question in this area is the extent to which meta-regulatory norms and strategies can be *privatized*, that is, applied within private regimes and to private inter-regime relations.

I. META-REGULATION AND META-NORMS

1. *Defining meta-regulation*

The concept of meta-regulation reflects the idea that it is possible to regulate behaviour without doing so directly. The original meaning given to the term 'meta-regulation' in academic literature was rather specific: steering self-regulatory capacity in society (that is, 'regulating self-regulation').[14] Regulation scholars have pointed out that meta-regulation implies that direct intervention and enforcement are replaced with 'allegedly lighter demands on economic actors to institutionalize processes of self-regulation'.[15] Meta-regulatory strategies in this sense are contingent on the relevant substantive area of regulation; for instance, in the context of the regulation of com-

---

12 B. Kingsbury, N. Krisch, and R.B. Stewart, 'The Emergence of Global Administrative Law' (2005) 68 *Law & Contemporary Problems* 15–61.

13 See, for example, A. Hamann, and H. Ruiz Fabri, 'Transnational Networks and Constitutionalism' (2008) 6 *International J. of Constitutional Law* 481–508; A. von Bogdandy, *The Exercise of Public Authority by International Institutions* (2010). See, for a broader perspective that does include private regulation, for example, C. Joerges, I.-H. Sand, and G. Teubner (eds.), *Transnational Governance and Constitutionalism: International Studies in the Theory of Private Law* (2004); L. Catá Backer, 'From Constitution to Constitutionalism: A Global Framework for Legitimate Public Power Systems' (2009) 113 *Penn State Law Rev.* 671–732, at 694.

14 C. Parker, *The Open Corporation: Effective Self-Regulation and Democracy* (2002).

15 J. Jordana and D. Levi-Faur, *The Politics of Regulation in the Age of Governance* (2004) 6–7.

petition, meta-regulation might mean governmental monitoring of organizations' own competition compliance programmes.[16]

A second meaning the term meta-regulation has been given in the literature is that of an explicit governmental strategy to regain control over the whole regulatory environment by using horizontal tools such as regulatory impact assessment (regulation of regulation).[17] More substantively defined, this is the reflexive systematization of regulatory policy through a 'set of institutions and processes that embeds regulatory review mechanisms into the every-day routines of governmental policy-making'.[18] This definition of meta-regulation was originally closely associated with 'the imposition of the competitive ethos of market dynamics'[19] and how this 'can restrict the exercise of public powers'[20] but – as we will show in section II – more general and proceduralist ideas about 'good regulation' increasingly play an important role.

In both versions, meta-regulation is portrayed as a strategy that regulatory actors themselves 'naturally turn to' given 'the realities of the regulatory state and the regulatory society' they face.[21] We argue in the next sub-section that a fruitful way to study the efforts by TPRERs to structure and legitimize their exercises of authority is to conceptualize them as a 'search for meta-norms'.

2. Locating meta-norms

In the context of the governance of trade conflicts, Joerges has specified the concept of a 'meta-norm' as a norm to which parties can commit without betraying their loyalty to their own legal systems.[22] In the TPR context a similar commitment logic may be at work: many transnational actors too

---

16 For one of the best known outcomes of this research agenda, see J. Braithwaite, 'Meta Regulation for Access to Justice', presentation to General Aspects of Law (GALA) Seminar (2003), available at: <www.law.berkeley.edu/cenpro/kadish/gala03/*Braithwaite*%20Kent.pdf>.

17 C.M. Radaelli, 'Regulating Rule-Making Via Impact Assessment' (2010) 23 *Governance* 89.

18 B. Morgan, *Social Citizenship in the Shadow of Competition: The Bureaucratic Politics of Regulatory Justification* (2003) 55.

19 B. Lange, 'Regulatory Spaces and Interactions: An Introduction' (2003) 12 *Social & Legal Studies* 411–23.

20 id.

21 C. Parker et al. (eds.), *Regulating Law* (2004). For more on the reflexive aspects of meta-regulation see C. Scott, 'Reflexive Governance, Regulation and Meta-Regulation: Control or Learning?' in *Reflexive Governance: Redefining the Public Interest in a Pluralistic World*, eds. O. de Schutter and J. Lenoble (2010).

22 C. Joerges, 'Constitutionalism in Postnational Constellations: Contrasting Social Regulation in the EU and in the WTO' in *Constitutionalism, Multilevel Trade Governance and Social Regulation*, eds. C. Joerges and E.-U. Petersmann (2006) 505.

have a dual allegiance: to their (domestic and/or other) constituencies and to the common policy goal.[23] Any meta-regulatory framework will have to accommodate this duality. As part of this *process of accommodation,* TPRERs – in spite of their autonomy – 'build on the assumption of common reference points', an assumption that has been accurately recognized as 'an operative fiction'.[24] As a next step, each participant in the regime 'can subordinate themselves to a, necessarily abstract, seemingly common philosophical horizon, to which they orient their own rule-making'.[25] This acknowledgement of 'network logic' has implications for the disciplinary rooting of legal research on TPRERs.

So far, many debates on the transnational search for meta-norms have been positioned within the GAL project.[26] An increasingly rich body of literature, GAL can be seen as a 'quest for principles and values',[27] and the project's 'potential for transforming our collective sense of the meaning and normative significance of the new juridical objects by recoding them in old terms'[28] has been widely recognized. However, in response to criticisms that the original project might have unfounded totalizing implications, the GAL literature has become increasingly heterogeneous.[29] We suggest it is time to take this trend one step further and to locate the search for meta-norms outside of administrative law discourse. Notwithstanding the importance of disciplinary framing, no 'master discourse of law' can be imposed. On a practical level, the transplantation of domestic legal or regulatory concepts can certainly be helpful, but there is no reason to take inspiration exclusively from administrative law. An additional reason to broaden the search for meta-norms beyond GAL is the necessity to incorporate network logic, since administrative law traditionally is less than comfortable with horizontal structures. Whereas in typical GAL approaches TPRERs would need to be turned into 'something like' administrative law bodies, the starting point of meta-regulatory approaches is that:

> all social and economic spheres in which governments or others might have an interest in controlling already have within them mechanisms of steering – whether through hierarchy, competition, community, design or some combination thereof.[30]

---

23 See, also, Hamann and Ruiz Fabri, op. cit., n. 13, p. 481.
24 Fischer-Lescano and Teubner, op. cit., n. 3, p. 1033.
25 id.
26 In the typology of 'meta-principles of authority' devised by Neil Walker, GAL is part of the 'legal-field discursive' approach. See N. Walker, 'Beyond boundary disputes and basic grids: Mapping the global disorder of normative orders' (2008) 6 *International J. of Constitutional Law* 376.
27 C. Harlow, 'Global Administrative Law: The Quest for Principles and Values' (2006) 17 *European J. of International Law* 187–214.
28 Walker, op. cit., n. 26, p. 389.
29 Nicolaïdis and Shaffer, op. cit., n. 4, p. 263; N. Krisch, 'The Pluralism of Global Administrative Law' (2006) 17 *European J. of International Law* 247–78.
30 C. Scott, 'Regulating Everything', UCD Geary Institute Discussion Paper (2008).

By making this assumption it becomes possible to monitor 'under the radar' development of meta-norms within TPRER – with consolidation of the norm only taking place when there is an incident or a conflict which makes it necessary to point out to those involved in the regime that their commitment to existing standards in fact implies a commitment to further standards.

II. 'REGULATION STUDIES' AND 'BETTER REGULATION'

1. *Regulation as a discipline*

For all the controversy surrounding the qualification of TPRERs as 'law', the qualification of the phenomenon as 'regulation' is 'straightforward' and not only in an intuitive sense: as this section will argue, the way TPRERs operate is partly framed by the normative expectations and disciplinary preoccupations of regulation studies. This influencing occurs because, alongside the academic discipline, 'regulation' has developed into a policy discourse.[31] As Julia Black has put it, '[t]he "how" of regulation, or more particularly "how to do it better", is a burgeoning policy area and deserves separate consideration in its own right'.[32] The main label for the policy discourse which considers 'regulation in general' as an activity that can be regulated and which promotes a set of explicit policies to that end is 'Better Regulation' (BR).[33] This term originated in the European Commission as a brand name for a strategy to improve EU lawmaking without making any explicit constitutional changes, but became a perceived 'common language' for an eclectic community of states, stakeholders, and observers.[34] As such, it can be seen as a next stage in the European history of governance experiments.[35] We explore the style of meta-regulation that has surfaced in Better Regulation discourses and then return to the disciplinary identity of (Better) Regulation and its role as meta-regulation.

31 See M. Lodge, 'Regulation, the Regulatory State and European Politics' (2008) 31 *West European Politics* 280–301 for a comprehensive literature review. For a reference to 'better regulation doctrine', see Scott, op. cit., n. 21, p. 60.
32 Black, op. cit., n. 2, p. 15.
33 Although the European Commission recently has made an effort to change the label to 'Smart Regulation'; European Commission, *Communication on 'Smart Regulation in the European Union* (COM/2010, 8 October 2010) 543.
34 An example of a forum where the 'Better Regulation community' shapes this common language is the annual International Regulatory Reform Conference, which started out as a private initiative of the Bertelsmann Foundation, and was most recently co-organized by the OECD, 28–29 October 2010 in Paris.
35 See n. 8.

2. Better Regulation as a policy discourse

The growing attention for regulation has resulted in the development of dedicated policies concerned with 'regulation in general' on various governance levels (OECD, European Union, and at national levels). At first – in the early 2000s – it seemed that the BR approach was all about a renewed focus on *output*. Most observers emphasized the importance of efficiency in BR discourse[36] and BR proponents played into the sentiment that the issue of regulating at the transnational level is a technical rather than a political matter.[37] Although the 'deregulatory version' of BR claiming that regulation is over-extensive and can be reduced through the 'lifting of burdens' enjoys enduring popularity, we find an increased emphasis on *input*, in line with the findings in regard to BR's intellectual and institutional predecessors 'comitology' and the OMC.[38]

It is now more and more common among regulators and governments to think more reflexively and strategically about regulation and to design dedicated policies for it. BR is, in essence, a set of ideas about what 'good regulation' means. And as these ideas are being floated across transnational forums, BR – and impact assessment in particular as its most successful 'best practice' – is turning into an accepted 'template' for assessing regulatory solutions. The template includes questions such as 'what problem are we trying to solve?', 'what are our regulatory goals?', 'what is the intervention logic?', 'what regulatory techniques could possibly solve the problems and achieve the objectives?', 'how are we going to measure the success of our policy?', and 'what are the impacts of various policy options?'.[39] BR also involves the promotion of various types of tests for law making: substantive tests for regulation (often but not necessarily of a quantitative nature, for example, cost-benefit analysis or administrative burden targets) and procedural standards (for example, public and open consultation). The result is that 'Better Regulation' has become an umbrella term for a variety of discourses, which – in line with the findings of the broader governance literature – share a set of defining and inter-related characteristics: an emphasis on institutionalization, positioning as an alternative to legal governance, and proceduralization as a conflict management strategy.

36 B. Morgan, 'The Economization of Politics: Meta-Regulation as a Form of Nonjudicial Legality' (2003) 12 *Social & Legal Studies* 489–523; E. Darian-Smith and C. Scott, 'Regulation and Human Rights in Socio-Legal Scholarship' (2009) 31 *Law & Policy* 271–281.

37 S. Picciotto, 'Liberalization and democratization: the forum and the hearth in the era of cosmopolitan post-industrial capitalism' (2000) 63 *Law & Contemporary Problems* 157–78.

38 See n. 8 above.

39 See, for example, European Commission Impact Assessment Guidelines, SEC(2009) 92, 15 January 2009, at: <http://ec.europa.eu/governance/impact/commission_guidelines/docs/iag_2009_en.pdf>, which read as an introductory handbook on regulation.

145

First, we observe efforts towards *institutionalization* in order to 'operationalize' – to use a word from the BR vocabulary – the normative ideas about regulation through programmes, networks, guidelines, impact assessment frameworks, control of regulatory quality by oversight bodies, and peer review processes such as those organized by the OECD. A certain degree of institutionalization is needed in order to provide 'an opportunity structure to handle a whole set of specific instruments, such as co-regulation, self-regulation, market-friendly alternatives to classic command and control regulation, consultation and economic analysis'.[40]

Second, BR strategies are put forward as *an alternative for legal governance*. Better Regulation programmes as they became popular in Europe in the last decade, were inspired by a frustration with the more 'technical-legal' improvement strategies for regulatory quality from the 1990s, or more generally, by a widely felt need to supplement 'legal reason with a more explicitly economic rationality'.[41] For some legal and political actors, the new 'rules for rule making' that were put forward, arose out of the ongoing deadlock in efforts to codify administrative law mechanisms to improve regulatory processes.[42] Also, given the deregulatory roots of the BR movement, there is a distinct 'anti-public law' flavour to the discourse.[43] Apart from the odd reference to a shared 'regulatory philosophy', BR does not assume agreement on a certain vision of legitimacy that comes with a set of legal mechanisms as GAL approaches tend to do.

This brings us to the third and related characteristic: *proceduralization* is used to handle the – implicit or explicit – conflicts about regulatory ends among participants in a regulatory regime.[44] This includes conflicts about whether or not BR strategies as such have a deregulatory purpose. Some proponents take a pragmatic approach ('whatever works') to the 'best norm' whilst others see BR programmes as a chance to put welfare economics into practice. BR promotes the idea that we can identify the 'best norm' in an instrumental sense – thus fully identifing with the 'regulatory perspective on law' – but avoids explicit substantive choices in the identification process. For instance, instead of choosing a particular decision criterion for the BR framework, it is common – and promoted as good practice[45] – to have a list

40 C.M. Radaelli and A.C.M. Meuwese, 'Hard Questions, Hard Solutions: Proceduralisation through Impact Assessment in the EU' (2010) 33 *West European Politics* 136–53.
41 Morgan, op. cit., n. 18, p. 31.
42 A.C.M. Meuwese, Y.E. Schuurmans, and W.J.M. Voermans, 'Towards a European Administrative Procedure Act' (2009) 2 *Rev. of European Administrative Law* 3–35.
43 Although at the most recent International Regulatory Reform Conference held in Paris 28–29 October, the alleged importance of the BR project for upholding the rule of law suddenly appeared in several presentations. See, also, n. 34 above.
44 Radaelli and Meuwese, op. cit., n. 40.
45 See, for instance, the 'Best Practice Library' of the European Commission, at <http://ec.europa.eu/governance/impact/commission_guidelines/best_pract_lib_en.htm>.

of 'possible decision criteria' (efficiency, effectiveness, coherence, fundamental rights protection, and so on) and sophisticated procedures for
communicating how they have been applied (for example, the 'decision
matrix' designed to 'highlight trade-offs' from the European Commission's
IA template).[46]

The following illustration of how regulatory actors resorting to BR
strategies rely on an incremental build-up of structures containing prosaic
norms as a way to get legitimacy off the ground is taken from the European
Union context. The 'high-level' legal-political debate on whether stakeholders in EU regulation should be protected by wider standing rules in front
of the Court or by stronger participation rules has proven difficult to resolve.
In the meantime, BR tendencies have led to the implementation of 'good
practices' relating to reporting on consultation. The reasoning behind the
introduction of such norms is the following: 'nobody wants rent-seeking and
one way to counter it, regardless of the legal system, is enhanced transparency'. Such BR norms are often 'enforced' by further meta-norms, in this
case non-binding 'peer review' of the quality of the IA and consultation
processes.[47] This example illustrates how BR-style meta-regulation can be a
way forward whenever we are unable to agree on administrative law solutions, as will often be the case in transnational constellations. It also suggests
that, even where administrative law is capable of regulating, there may still
be reasons to introduce BR requirements because the latter may provide
more appropriate incentives (for example, if consultation requirements are
supposed to counter rent seeking, peer review may render the responsible
institutional actors more conscious of this aim, compared to the prospect of
judicial review). Finally, we have seen how proceduralization (through
'templates' and new mechanisms for non-judicial review) is an inevitable
path, even for fields such as BR, which started out as being all about better
substantive regulation

3. *Better Regulation as meta-regulation*

In assessing the state of BR as a policy discourse and a discipline we
encounter a paradox: the global pervasiveness of the BR discourse is related
to its aura of 'sound substantive theory on regulation' but, in practice, BR

---

46 See, also, the observation by Haines and Gurney that many 'meta-regulatory
strategies are designed to gloss over regulatory conflict, or to delegate the
responsibility for dealing with conflicting regulatory goals on to regulatees'. F.
Haines and D. Gurney, 'The Shadows of the Law: Contemporary Approaches to
Regulation and the Problem of Regulatory Conflict' (2003) 25 *Law & Policy* 353–80.
47 By the Impact Assessment Board. See, also, J. Wiener and A. Alemanno, 'Comparing regulatory oversight bodies across the Atlantic: The Office of Information
and Regulatory Affairs in the US and the Impact Assessment Board in the EU' in
Comparative Administrative Law, eds. S. Rose-Ackerman and P. Lindseth (2010).

strategies rely heavily on procedural mechanisms. Encouraged and guided by the BR movement, many regulatory actors are now using 'systems of public consultation, decision-making, and reporting which go well beyond those required by law'.[48] Indeed, the movement has done more than translate insights from regulatory studies into legislative guidelines: BR has a meta-regulatory effect by embedding the 'regulatory approach' into the daily routine of policy-makers and, increasingly, legislative draftsmen, parliamentary aides, and lobby groups. Arguably, BR can be credited with having help turn 'regulation' into a profession.

The rise of the 'Better Regulator' as a professional illustrates how BR is a form of meta-regulation in both of the senses introduced in section I. BR strategies borrow heavily from the literature on 'meta-regulation' in the sense of 'regulation of self-regulation': they teach regulatory actors to give regulatees incentives and tools to use their own inherent 'regulatory capacities'. It is also clearly a strategy to 'regulate' regulatory activity across the board by using 'tools', 'templates', and 'procedures'. Used as a lens for the nature and structure of authority of TPRERs, the two senses of meta-regulation even meet: BR-inspired strategies consisting of 'shared templates' (for example, for IA) and 'normative commitments (for example, to consultation procedures) steer the self-regulatory capacities of (private) regulators. Given the important role that self-regulatory organizations also play increasingly in the 'epistemic communities that frame debates of regulatory design',[49] the distinction between the two definitions of 'meta-regulation' is further diluted.

The observations on the meta-regulation of regulation take on a greater salience in the context of TPR. Whereas for public regulation BR provides mere 'added legitimacy', for private regulatory actors, relying on collected insights from 'regulation studies' is 'core business'. As we will assert in section IV, the marketing of BR as a 'shared language' in transnational forums can also play an important role in helping transnational private actors harvest credit from domestic actors for having implemented certain BR-style procedures.[50]

---

48 Black, op. cit., n. 2, p. 16.
49 J. Braithwaite and P. Drahos, *Global Business Regulation* (2000) 481.
50 See, also, the HiiL project case study on accounting standards: A.J. Richardson and B. Eberlein, 'Legitimating Transnational Standard-Setting: The Case of the International Accounting Standards Board' (2010) *J. of Business Ethics* (online pre-print, July 2010, DOI: 10.1007/s10551-010-0543-9).

III. (META-)REGULATION AND THE DISCIPLINE OF PRIVATE INTERNATIONAL LAW

1. *Introduction: PIL and transnational regulation*

The interaction between the discipline of PIL, or the conflict of laws, and the themes of transnational regulation and legitimacy beyond the state is puzzling in at least three dimensions. First, scholars of transnational regulation commonly neglect PIL's contribution to the conditioning of cross-border private regulatory activities – that is, they ignore PIL's role as *mechanism*. Second, mainstream European PIL scholarship is itself deeply ambivalent about any regulatory and meta-regulatory dimensions inherent in PIL theories and doctrines. Third, at the same time, however, in a minority line of scholarship, PIL is drawn upon as a prime source of inspiration for a new 'conflicts law' that is meant to play a key role within post-national pluralist constellations. This section aims to show how ambivalences about PIL's regulatory and meta-regulatory dimensions raise doubts about the viability of this latter project.

2. *PIL as mechanism: 'touchdown' and 're-statement'*

Analysts of transnational (private) regulatory activity have, on the whole, shown surprisingly little interest in the field of PIL. Standard treatments of transnational regulation,[51] or of post-national legal pluralism, rarely devote sustained attention to discussion of PIL matters. This disposition may in part be a reflection of a broader lack of interest in PIL within the regulation literature more broadly.[52] Such neglect notwithstanding, PIL instruments and doctrines play an important background role in conditioning cross-border private regulation. One important mode of TPR, for example, concerns the inclusion of labour or environmental standards in supply contracts between buyers in developed countries and suppliers in developing countries.[53] The effectiveness of such contractual standards is to a large extent dependent on PIL norms (are the parties allowed a free choice of applicable law? What is the applicable law in the absence of choice? What is the influence of mandatory norms of the forum or of the place of performance? To what extent can judgments on contractual performance be enforced in other

---

51 See, for example, R. Wai, 'Transnational Private Law and Private Ordering in a Contested Global Society' (2005) 46 *Harvard International Law J.* 471–88, at 472, giving the example of Braithwaite and Drahos, op. cit., n. 49.

52 To give just one example: the volume *Regulating Law*, by Parker et al., op. cit., n. 21, a collection of examinations of different legal subject fields 'through a regulatory lens', while including what the editors identify as 'the main subject areas' in legal curriculums, omits a discussion of PIL.

53 See, for example, M.P. VandenBergh, 'The New Wal-Mart Effect: The Role of Private Contracting in Global Governance' (2007) 54 *UCLA Law Rev.* 913–70.

jurisdictions?). Regulatory innovations in this area, for example, the creation of exceptions to privity of contract to allow third-party consumer associations standing to enforce these contractual standards, would similarly require detailed attention to PIL rules for their effectuation. More institutionalized forms of transnational private governance, such as the certification scheme operated under the aegis of the Forest Stewardship Council (FSC), also depend on PIL rules. The firms or non-profit associations responsible for standard-setting and accreditation within such schemes need to be incorporated in a particular jurisdiction, which will provide basic rules for their governance structures, reporting requirements, and so on.[54] The certificates given out within these schemes are contractual arrangements which, similarly, will be embedded within an applicable system of (state) law, to be determined by PIL choice of law rules.

The neglect of PIL's role within these various forms of TPR has at least two important implications. First, because PIL is the primary means by which state legal systems effectuate a 'touchdown' (Wai) or a 're-statement' (Michaels) of cross-border private activity, leaving out PIL from discussions of TPR understates the extent to which state law is still relevant for norm creation and enforcement beyond the state.[55] Realizing that TPR is still in many ways connected to state law through PIL 'opens the possibility that the constitutional law of states retains a degree of complementarity to the transnational law of commerce' and of other cross-border private activity, with potentially important ramifications for the legitimacy of TPR.[56] Second, sidelining PIL means ignoring the socio-economic and political implications of the choices behind PIL instruments and doctrines. This increases the risk that, as was the case with domestic private law in the early twentieth century, these choices will be ignored for what they are, and that the rules that embody them will be treated simply as *data*; as neutral 'baselines' that require no justification.[57]

---

54 The FSC regime, for example, relies on, among other entities, a 'civil association' under Mexican law, and a German for-profit company (Accreditation Services International, GmbH) based in Bonn.

55 See, for example, R. Wai, 'Transnational Liftoff and Juridical Touchdown: The Regulatory Function of Private International Law in an Era of Globalization' (2002) 40 *Columbia J. of Transnational Law* 209–74; R. Michaels, 'The Re-Statement of Non-State Law: The State, Choice of Law, and the Challenge from Global Legal Pluralism' (2006) 53 *Wayne Law Rev.* 1209–59.

56 R. Michaels, 'The True Lex Mercatoria: Law Beyond the State' (2007) 14 *Indiana J. of Global Legal Studies* 447–68, at 467.

57 On baselines, see C.R. Sunstein, 'Lochner's Legacy' (1987) 87 *Columbia Law Rev.* 873–919. See, also, H. Collins, 'Regulating Contract Law' in Parker et al., op. cit., n. 21, pp. 13–23 (describing the classic, non-regulatory view of private law as a 'pre-political settlement').

3. A 'regulatory' perspective in PIL?

In parallel with regulation scholars' neglect of PIL, orthodox writing within the European PIL scholarly community has itself shown very little interest in incorporating any 'regulatory perspective'. This section will argue that the disciplinary discourse of PIL outside the United States[58] represents, in its dominant approaches,[59] an almost complete negation of any 'regulatory perspective'.[60]

(a) In contrast to a regulatory perspective 'designed *to emphasize the instrumental quality of legal reasoning*', European PIL is *fiercely autonomous* and *actively anti-instrumental*.[61] Within European PIL, there is a long and distinguished line of contributions emphasizing the autonomous nature of the discipline. PIL, in a famous depiction, is seen as 'mere law' for 'mere jurists'.[62] In common law jurisdictions, the primary manifestations of such assertions of autonomy are those directed against legislative intervention, by domestic statute or by European instruments.[63] More generally, orthodox PIL's aspirations of autonomy and non-instrumentality find their expression in adherence to the ideals of *'substantive neutrality'* (or 'substance neutrality') and 'decisional harmony'.[64] To an important degree, the history of European PIL in the second half of the twentieth century revolves around the position of substantive neutrality as an appropriate ideal for choice of

---

58 See, for example, Joerges, op. cit., n. 22, at p. 503 (conceding that his 'narrative is more American than European').

59 Self-styled critical (minority) approaches, such as those informed by law and economics, for example, are an important exception.

60 This notwithstanding recent suggestions of a transformation of European PIL. On these changes, see, for example, H. Muir Watt, 'The Role of the Conflict of Laws in European Private Law' in *The Cambridge Companion to European Union Private Law*, ed. C. Twigg-Flesner (2010) 44; R. Michaels, 'The New European Choice-of-Law Revolution' (2008) 82 *Tulane Law Rev.* 1607–44.

61 On these contrasting perspectives, see Collins, op. cit., n. 57, pp. 13–23 (emphasizing the 'legal' perspective on private law as playing an 'essentially facilitative' role). On the idea of normative autonomy, see, for example, C. Parker, C. Scott, C. Lacey, and J. Braithwaite, 'Introduction to Regulating Law' in Parker et al., op. cit., n. 21, p. 3.

62 G.C. Cheshire, Preface to *Private International Law* (2008, 14th edn.).

63 For a recent example, see A. Briggs, Preface to *The Conflict of Laws* (2008).

64 See, for example, J. Kropholler, *Internationales Privatrecht* (2006, 6th edn.) 36 (describing '*Entscheidungseinklang*' as the 'formal ideal' of PIL); M. Reimann, *Conflict of Laws in Western Europe* (1995) 110–11. Within the common law world, see, for example, C. Forsyth, 'The Eclipse of Private International Law Principle? The Judicial Process, Interpretation and the Dominance of Legislation in the Modern Era' (2005) *J. of Private International Law* 93–114 ('the quest for uniformity of decision is a fundamental – indeed the central – purpose of [PIL]. This is an orthodox, though not universal, point of view'). To a limited extent, legal certainty goals are being restyled as regulatory objectives: see R. Fentiman, 'Choice of Law in Europe: Uniformity and Integration' (2008) 82 *Tulane Law Rev.* 2021–52.

151

law. This concept is still very much part of European orthodoxy and can be seen at work in the main rules for choice of law in contract and tort in European codifications.[65] Besides this direct presence, its influence can be felt in at least two additional ways. The first is a general reticence to allow substantive policies to intrude upon the choice-of-law analysis. While institutional and economic changes are seen by many as putting a strain on the 'specifically European brand of conflicts thinking ... focused on ... familiar "private law" objectives as ... the question for decisional harmony or the "interests of international trade"',[66] prominent conflicts scholars still habitually deplore the intrusion of instrumentalist reasoning into choice of law. Modifying choice-of-law instruments so that they promote the 'polluter pays' principle in environmental tort cases, for example, is denounced by leading writers on PIL as 'a perversion of choice-of-law reasoning'.[67] Secondly, whenever substantive policies *are* given a place in choice-of-law reasoning, these policies and the rules that give effect to them sit in an uneasy relationship with traditional, substantively neutral, choice-of-law rules. 'Contemporary choice of law', it is thought, has become 'a hybrid; some of its rules are meant to further substantive policies, others are ... indifferent to the end result, and serve no further purpose (apart from harmony)'.[68] While conflicts lawyers are, on the whole, resigned to having 'to learn to live with' this binary nature of PIL,[69] the idea of a field of law that actively aims to compartmentalize its instrumentalist and its 'pre-political' reasoning sits in a complicated relationship with a 'regulatory perspective' on law.

(b) PIL is a self-consciously legal-technical discipline,[70] heavily focused on conventional legal values and specifically legal techniques. Conflict of laws is, in many ways, as might be expected of what is after all a 'law of laws', a true lawyers' law.[71] The discipline revels in its complexity and in the technicality of its tools, and attaches fundamental importance to conventional legal values. PIL, to outsiders, often comes across as 'essentially meaningless – as a morass of highly technical, atheoretical doctrines developed by largely unknown academics in relative isolation from the

---

65 See the multi-lateral choice of law rules for contract (art. 4, Rome I Regulation) and tort (art. 4, Rome II Regulation).
66 Muir Watt, op. cit., n. 60, p. 44.
67 A. Briggs, 'Evidence to UKHL Select Committee hearing on proposed Rome II Regulation', UKHL 2004/66.
68 T. De Boer, 'The Purpose of Uniform Choice of Law Rules' (2009) *Netherlands International Law Rev.* 295–332, at 298.
69 Kropholler, op. cit., n. 64, p. 23 (referring to the '*Zweipoligkeit*' of PIL'). The literature on what is often called '*Methodenpluralismus*' in PIL is vast.
70 A. Riles, 'Taking on the Technicalities: A New Agenda for the Cultural Study of Law' (2005) 53 *Buffalo Law Rev.* 973–1033, at 977.
71 See Kropholler, op. cit., n. 64, pp. 2–3, (arguing that PIL 'moves on a higher level of abstraction than individual material legal orders').

political process'.[72] PIL literature constantly reinforces a self-perception among conflicts scholars of their field as a technical, impenetrable area that is best left to specialists.[73] PIL's attachment to conventional legal values is evident from the centrality of classic jurisprudential debates – on rules versus standards, legal certainty versus flexibility, 'theoretical purity' versus 'practical results' – in PIL discourse.[74] In particular, the certainty versus flexibility dilemma is central in PIL writing and legislative drafting to an extent that is not commonly seen in other areas of law.[75]

(c) PIL embodies an almost exclusively court-centered, state-law oriented perspective. A regulatory perspective on law commonly emphasizes the ways in which law and enforcement through courts coexists and conflicts with other mechanisms of social ordering.[76] Orthodox European PIL, in contrast, is heavily focused on dispute resolution through courts and on the binary allocation of legislative and adjudicatory jurisdiction among state legal orders. PIL, in addition, is generally very uncertain or even defensive about admitting a role for non-state norms, such as those of *lex mercatoria* or of religious legal systems.[77]

4. *PIL as anti- and as meta-regulation*

While the dominant self-perception of the discipline can be characterized as in various ways *anti*-regulation, both this orthodox conception itself and a number of alternative, minority strands contain important elements of a perspective that can be labelled as *meta*-regulatory.

An updated interpretation of the classic Savignian paradigm for choice of law, on the one hand, furnishes ideas on (meta-)regulation through *depoliticization*. In this conception, orthodox European PIL purposefully aims to be 'merely facilitative' and 'non-instrumental' – that is, anti-regulatory – in order to achieve a settlement between legal orders that is actively apolitical. The centrality of debates over legal techniques and legal

---

72 Riles, op. cit., n. 70, p. 978.
73 The classic source of such references is T. Prosser, 'Interstate Publication' (1953) 51 *Michigan Law Rev.* 959–1000, at 971.
74 See, for example, J.W. Singer, 'Real Conflicts' (1989) 69 *Boston University Law Rev.* 1–130.
75 See, for example, S. Symeonides, 'Rome II and Torts Conflicts: A Missed Opportunity' (2008) 56 *Am. J. of Comparative Law* 173–222, at 175; R.J. Weintraub, 'The Choice-of-Law Rules of the European Community Regulation on the Law Applicable to Non-Contractual Obligations: Simple and Predictable, Consequences-Based, or Neither?' (2008) 43 *Texas International Law Rev.* 401–26.
76 See Parker et al., op. cit., n. 21, p. 3 (discussing 'how law ... interacts with other forms of regulation or normative ordering').
77 Under the Rome I Regulation for choice of law in contracts, for example, the parties can only choose a domestic system of contract law. An EC Commission proposal to allow choice for non-state law was rejected during negotiations. See J. Hill and A. Chong, *International Commercial Disputes* (2010) 505.

values, from this perspective, should be seen as a reflection of an – often perhaps only partly conscious – effort to depoliticize through legal technicality and professional discipline.[78] Attempting to be anti-regulation is, then, in this conception, precisely the way orthodox PIL regulates.[79]

A collection of minority approaches, on the other hand, largely abandons the Savignian model, and sees conflict of laws as a storehouse of ideas and practices for the elaboration of 'meta-norms', 'to which parties can commit themselves in search for a solution to their conflict without betraying the loyalty to their own law'.[80] These alternative approaches are generally heavily focused on *proceduralization* and *reflexivity*, framing conflict of laws as a 'law of law-making',[81] in which the recognition of claims to authority depends primarily on their underlying 'norm-generation processes'.[82]

These minority views on the meta-regulatory capacity of PIL have generated considerable interest for their potential to constitute the foundations for a broadly conceived new form of 'conflicts law'. PIL, it is thought, could furnish ideas and practices for the coordination of the interaction between plural legal orders – be they public or private, domestic, supranational or transnational – and their rationalities.[83] We do not deny the potential for such explorations in principle – a very similar, partly PIL-inspired, search for meta-norms is in fact undertaken below, in section IV. We do suggest, however, that this turn to PIL thinking in transnational governance theory should be treated with considerable caution, particularly in the European context. For one thing, these various projects invoke conflicting background substantive meta-principles – ranging from an ideal of '*deference to municipal concerns*', based on the belief that 'effective regulation or democratic control ... [are] best protected through domestic laws and institutions',[84] to a project of '*taming the national state*' by

---

78 Compare S. Picciotto, 'Networks in International Economic Integration: Fragmented States and the Dilemmas of Neo-Liberalism' (1997) 17 *Northwestern J. of International Law and Business* 1014–56, at 1037 (referring to attempts to 'depoliticize issues by developing technical ... or professional techniques', in the context of transnational regulation).

79 In the traditional Savignian conception, private law – and private international law – *were* neutral and apolitical. In this updated version, it is recognized that depoliticization is itself not a neutral project.

80 Joerges, op. cit., n. 22, p. 505.

81 C. Joerges, 'Integration through De-Legalisation?' (2008) *European Law Rev.* 291–312, at 304. See, also, Fischer-Lescano and Teubner, op. cit., n. 3, p. 1016.

82 See, for example, C. Joerges, 'Sozialstaatlichkeit in Europe? A Conflict-of-Laws Approach to the Law of the EU and the Proceduralisation of Constitutionalisation' (2009) 10 *German Law J.* 335–60, at 354.

83 Fischer-Lescano and Teubner, op. cit., n. 3; R. Wai, 'Conflicts and Comity in Transnational Governance: Private International Law as Mechanism and Metaphor for Transnational Social Regulation Through Plural Legal Regimes' in *Constitutionalism, Multilevel Trade Governance and Social Regulation,* eds. C. Joerges and E.-U. Petersmann (2006) 262.

84 Wai, op. cit., n. 55, pp. 244, 239 (emphasis added).

154

ensuring 'that "foreign" identities and their interests are taken into account'.[85] More importantly, however, these alternative visions are fundamentally at odds with the anti-regulatory disciplinary identity of orthodox European PIL. This causes tensions not only in the formulation of these theories themselves[86] but – crucially – also in the potential for their reception. Ultimately, the PIL-inspired 'conflicts law' project to 'strengthen mutual observation between network nodes' in transnational governance, is a social undertaking, dependent for its effectuation on its adoption by regulatory and legal-disciplinary elites. TPR theorizing, it is submitted, will have to come to terms with the fact that a body of law that offers some of the most practically relevant rules for transnational private actors – those structuring their contractual regimes, liability, corporate structure, and so on – *and* that has inspired some of the most sophisticated analyses of post-national heterarchical regulatory ordering, is deeply bound up within a long disciplinary tradition that is diametrically opposed to core elements of a 'regulatory perspective'.

IV. THE SEARCH FOR META-NORMS

1. *Elements of meta-norms*

In this section we discuss the search for 'legitimacy-generating'[87] and 'conflict-resolving'[88] meta-norms as one set of responses to 'the absence of hierarchy' that characterizes TPRERs and their regulatory environment. We distinguish between some general elements of meta-norms, touching also upon the involvement of states in transnational regulation and the idea of 'privatized' meta-norms, encapsulated in the question 'what norms and strategies do TPRERs come up with to structure their interactions with their surroundings and legitimize their regulatory activities?'.

Norms suitable for the heterarchical, normatively diffuse context of transnational regulation may have to be distinctive not only in their substantive content (b), but also in their authoritative base (a) and their mode of operation (c).

(a) The sources of both PIL and BR are uncommonly diffuse and both disciplines are – to some extent – used to working with clusters of norms in

---

85 C. Joerges and J. Neyer, 'From Intergovernmental bargaining to Deliberative Political Processes' (1997) 3 *European Law J.* 273–99, at 293 (emphasis added). Joerges and Wai use very similar PIL analogies: Joerges, op. cit., n. 22, p. 505; R. Wai, 'Private International Law Analogies: A Comment on Christian Joerges' Rethinking European Law's Supremacy', EUI Working Paper 2005/12 (2005).
86 See, for example, Joerges, id., p. 503, fn. 43 on the American background to his conflict-of-laws analogy.
87 Black, op. cit., n. 2.
88 Joerges, op. cit., n. 22, p. 560.

varying constellations. PIL, it is often remarked, is not strictly speaking international law, nor entirely congruent with, or part of, domestic private law.[89] PIL scholars are often uneasy about this duality. 'The considerations going into choice-of-law rules', it has been said, 'are not firmly connected with those of substantive law nor those of international law'.[90] This position is sometimes described as a 'third school' of private international law. As for BR, the meta-framework is not laid down in a 'constitutional text' and does not consist of traditional checks and balances or judicial review but can be found in 'guidelines' and lends legitimacy from transparency requirements and quality control by an independent body. One example of a BR-inspired[91] change in legislative guidelines is a provision in the *Cabinet Directive on Streamlining Regulation*, expressing a preference for using 'non-domestic' regulatory standards, essentially placing a burden of proof on the national regulator if it wants to introduce 'unique-to-Canada' regulation.[92] We discuss this example throughout this section to illustrate various elements of meta-norms at the intersection of BR and PIL. What is striking under the current heading is the unspecified nature of the 'non-domestic' norms that policy makers are encouraged to adopt. Cherry-picking from diffuse sources seems problematic from state oriented hierarchical perspectives. But if, as Fischer-Lescano and Teubner have argued, 'the unity of global law is no longer structure-based',[93] then BR and PIL offer useful experiences on how to work with the reality of overlapping reflexive norm systems. The diffuse nature of authority and of normative sources may in fact be especially well suited to the terrain.

(b) Conflict of laws is in the business of managing conflicts. Conflict-of-laws inspired literature contains numerous examples of scholars turning to PIL for inspiration on how to manage conflicts between different legal

---

89 For an extensive discussion, see A. Mills, *The Confluence of Public and Private International Law* (2009); J. Paul, 'The Isolation of Private International Law' (1988) 7 *Wisconsin International Law J.* 149–78.

90 Michaels, op. cit, n. 60, p. 1615.

91 A PowerPoint presentation promoting this meta-norm received considerable interest at the International Regulatory Reform Conference in Berlin in 2008. The presentation and part of the debate can be viewed at< http://www.youtube.com/watch?v=Um9Mk5rfSa8>.

92 *Cabinet Directive on Streamlining Regulation*, at <http://www.regulation.gc.ca/directive/directive01-eng.asp>:
    Departments and agencies are to take advantage of opportunities for cooperation, either bilaterally or through multilateral fora, by:
    . . .
    ■ limiting the number of specific Canadian regulatory requirements or approaches to instances when they are warranted by specific Canadian circumstances and when they result over time in the greatest overall benefit to Canadians; and
    ■ identifying the rationale for their approach, particularly when specific Canadian requirements are proposed.

93 Fischer-Lescano and Teubner, op. cit., n. 3, p. 1007.

156

orders.[94] Conflict management, in Joerges's view, should be concerned with 'ensuring the co-existence of different constituencies' through a model that replaces hierarchy and uniformity with 'compatibility'.[95] Others entrust 'meta-norms' with enabling 'governance within and between social systems, including through allowing and sometimes facilitating conflict and contestation',[96] or with jurisdictional 'conflict management'.[97] Within PIL, a concept traditionally centrally concerned with conflict management is the idea of 'comity'.[98] Comity has long played a crucial but contested role within PIL, with many PIL scholars uncomfortable with its ambivalent legal status. The example of the Canadian guidelines is arguably an instance of 'regulatory comity' and we observe that any discomfort is quickly overcome when a meta-norm is introduced as part of the BR discourse.

(c) A third commonality between BR and PIL as inspirational fields for meta-norms can be found in the focus on process. PIL-inspired approaches to transnational governance are clearly process-oriented but the tendency towards proceduralization can also be found in the classic PIL paradigm. A recurring research finding on BR strategies is that they become heavily proceduralized over time.[99] As we have seen in section II, BR often combines proceduralization with institutionalization. However, it is the incremental nature of the institutionalization that is characteristic here. For instance, BR is not just about 'consulting' or even about the 'obligation to consult' but about all the expectations that are triggered once a decision-making body has said it will consult. Also, 'consultation' is not just a non-distinct term that can cover a wide range of practices, nor is it a concept defined by administrative law; rather, actors tie it to a transnationally defined 'best practice' consisting of consultation codes, minimum periods, and consultation reporting in impact assessment. To return once more to the Canadian example: the casual bracketing of issues of democracy, competence, and sovereignty is quite stunning. In the BR forum where the meta-norm of 'discouraging domestic norms' was presented, the discussion moved very quickly from the question whether such a norm is a good idea at all to suggestions for a good test for determining whether domestic regulation is

---

94 For example, C. Joerges, 'Challenges of Europeanization in the Realm of Private Law: A Plea for a New Legal Discipline' (2004) *Duke J. of International Law* 149–96, at 183.

95 C. Joerges, 'European Challenges to Private Law: On False Dichotomies, True Conflicts and the Need for a Constitutional Perspective' (1998) *Legal Studies* 146–66, at 160. See, also, at p. 196: 'Europeanization is about social learning through conflict management' designed to 'both accompany and legitimate social change'.

96 Wai, op. cit., n. 51.

97 J. Goldsmith, 'Against Cyberanarchy' (1998) *University of Chicago Law Rev.* 1199–250, at 1205.

98 For a general discussion, see, for example, J. Paul, 'The Transformation of International Comity' (2008) 71 *Law and Contemp Problems* 19–38.

99 Radaelli and Meuwese, op. cit., n. 40.

still acceptable and for a good system to enforce such a norm.[100] None of this is to imply that this sweeping regulatory idea will be implemented any time soon (or at all) in domestic legal orders. But ideas like this do shape a generation of 'regulatory actors' who are being influenced in this way as to what standards should guide lawmaking and who gets to decide this.

2. *Privatizing meta-norms*

Some years ago, Fischer-Lescano and Teubner predicted that the functional fragmentation of global law and the emergence of 'sectoral interpendences' in post-national regulation would lead to the emergence of a 'wholly new form of conflicts law'; a PIL-like, reflexive body of norms and practices aimed at achieving 'a weak normative compatibility of the fragments' and a 'loose coupling of colliding units'.[101] While diversity and conflict among transnational regulatory regimes is both a social reality and a normatively defensible position, we argue in this final sub-section that the extent to which *private regimes* will indeed develop conflict techniques associated with increased 'mutual observation' is an empirical question for which an affirmative answer is by no means clear as of yet. We also suggest that this may be an area in which further empirical research, able to differentiate among various modalities and intensities of interaction and overlap,[102] may yield especially fruitful insights. Following one possible entry point for systematization, we look at the strategies that can be observed vis-à-vis various categories of actors that inhabit the diverse normative and institutional environment TPRERs operate in, of which we highlight two: (a) state legal actors and (b) rival regulatory regimes.

(a) State legal actors

What can be observed most easily are efforts within TPRERs to increase their chances of recognition by *state and international legal systems*. As the example above on the Canadian restriction of 'unique to Canada' regulation shows, states are receptive to rules that TPRERs generate, which also means that the process of recognition is a two-way street. One way for TPRERs to facilitate recognition is 'to demonstrate equivalence (*not sameness*) to accepted procedural norms of standard-setting in domestic constitutional settings'.[103] Also within this first category of state actors as potential

---

100 See n. 91.
101 Fischer-Lescano and Teubner, op. cit., n. 3, pp. 1000–4. Compare, also, Wai, op. cit., n. 83, pp. 261–62. On conflict between 'self-referential systems', see Walker, op. cit., n. 26, p. 382.
102 For one such typology, see Walker, id.
103 Richardson and Eberlein, op. cit., n. 50 (emphasis added). This in addition to attempts by TPRER to increase normative connectivity to state and international law by way of direct substantive reference and incorporation. For example:

constituencies, their normative expectations have a meta-regulatory effect, as the normative judgement whether 'transnational due process' is still enough or should be supplemented by hierarchical controls is made as part of an incremental, social process.[104] Another example of a meta-regulatory norm that TPRERs use to retain or to win recognition from state actors is 'information disclosure', a well-known instrument used for substantive regulatory purposes, but one that can also be applied to the regulatory process itself. A case study on the Equator Principles – a set of transnational private standards for regulating social and environmental risk in project financing – found that, when the principles were updated, a reporting requirement was added and coupled that finding with a call for a further meta-norm of 'consistency of reporting'.[105] Such a meta-norm is inspired by BR thinking along the lines of 'by publishing what we do step by step we give all stakeholders the opportunity to explain why they disagree'. It also cleverly fits in with state actors' instincts to accept private norms as long as some kind of monitoring can be carried out.

(b) Rival regulatory regimes

As the area of forestry certification is marked by the existence of numerous private regulatory initiatives – a result of earlier failed (inter-)governmental efforts – it makes a good case study on the use of meta-regulatory strategies vis-à-vis rival TPRERs, in particular, those that can be captured under a heading of 'mutual observance'. The two main transnational private regimes are the Forest Stewardship Council (FSC) and the Programme for the Endorsement of Forest Certification Schemes (PEFC).[106] In the literature we find that evidence of competition and irritation – the two main modes of mutual observance[107] – among these regimes abounds. PEFC, which consists of a mutual recognition system of voluntary national certification schemes, and other similar systems in North America, were set up 'in direct response

Principle 1 of the FSC principles for sustainable forestry demands conformity with 'applicable national law and international conventions' ('Forest management shall respect all applicable laws of the country in which they occur, and international treaties and agreements to which the country is a signatory . . .'). FSC Principle 3, in addition, refers to the 'legal and customary rights of indigenous peoples').

104 See Richardson and Eberlein, id.: in the case of the IASB there was political pressure (especially post-financial crisis) to complement due process with direct accountability to regulators. Incidentally, it may be that the potential contribution of GAL constructs in transnational private governance can be suitably framed as reflexive attempts by TPRER to increase the potential for their recognition by state legal orders.

105 Principle 10, 'Each EPFI commits to report publicly at least annually about its Equator Principles implementation processes and experience': P. Puri, presentation at HiiL workshop, Dublin, June 2010.

106 Formerly the Pan-European Forest Certification Council (PEFCC).

107 Compare Fischer-Lescano and Teubner, op. cit., n. 3, p. 1018.

159

to the possibility that economic actors or states could lose control over forest governance due to the creation of the FSC'.[108] The emergence of the FSC as a 'default global standard setter'[109] triggered a process of questioning its 'legitimacy, cost-effectiveness, scientific merits, and legality',[110] and the rise of rival regimes which ended up, however, supporting many of the same values and procedural requirements.[111] In turn, it has been noted that the emergence of these alternative regimes prompted the FSC itself to step up its game.[112]

One of the most visible and far-reaching meta-norms governing the 'mutual observance' between TPRERs would be some form of regulatory comity, extending to formalized mutual recognition.[113] PIL-inspired approaches often have high expectations for the development of such norms among regulatory regimes. It seems, however, that as far as private regimes are concerned, comity and mutual recognition are still in their infancy, with their future potential uncertain. It is important to distinguish between two kinds of mutual recognition in the transnational sphere. The first is between private standards developed within national regimes, that is, mutual recognition along territorial lines. There is quite a lot of evidence for this happening. The PEFC regime is a prominent example in the forestry sector,[114] but many other instances of such 'private mutual recognition agreements' exist, for example, between professional bodies.[115] More

108 S. Gueneau, 'Certification as a New Private Global Forest Governance System: The Regulatory Potential of the Forest Stewardship Council' in *Non-State Actors as Standard Setters*, eds. A. Peters, L. Koechlin, T. Förster, and G. Fenner Zinkernagel (2009) 397. See, also, E. Meidinger, C. Elliott, and G. Oesten, *Social and Political Dimensions of Forest Certification* (2003) 17–18.

109 R. Lipschutz, 'Paper or Plastic? The Privatization of Global Forestry Regulation', UC Santa Cruz Working Paper (2005) 21.

110 J. McNichol, 'Transnational NGO certification programs as new regulatory forms: Lessons from the forestry sector' in *Transnational Governance. Institutional Dynamics of Regulation*, eds. M.-L. Djelic and K. Sahlin-Andersson (2006) 362.

111 id., p. 372.

112 id. See, also, T.M. Smith and M. Fischlein, 'Rival Private Governance Networks: Competing to Define the Rules of Sustainability Performance' (2010) 20 *Global Environmental Change* 511–22, at 519 (discussing private regulatory regimes' responsiveness to competition).

113 Compare Walker, op. cit., n. 26, p. 379 (placing 'system recognition' at the 'high connective intimacy' end of his scale of forms of overlap and interaction between legal orders).

114 'PEFC is a global umbrella organisation for the assessment of and mutual recognition of national forest certifiation schemes', PEFC website, cited in Lipschutz, op. cit., n. 109, p. 22.

115 Nikolaïdis and Schaffer have noted that the term 'mutual recognition agreement' (MRA) originally referred to agreements among private bodies and was only later applied to agreements among public authorities. The latter use currently seems prevalent. Nikolaïdis and Schaffer, op. cit., n. 3.

research will be needed to uncover the impact of such agreements, and the conditions for their development and their optimal functioning.

On the other hand, preliminary research suggests that there is little evidence for the emergence of mutual recognition among alternative TPRERs, along sectoral or functional lines. In the case of forestry, there has been sustained interest from the UN Food and Agriculture Organization (FAO)[116] and the World Bank Group to promote comity and mutual recognition among rival certification schemes.[117] Despite these efforts, however, there remains 'a vast gulf' between FSC and PEFC, which is deemed 'likely to prevent formal mutual recognition' between the two certification schemes.[118] The potential for such mutual recognition and other forms of private regulatory comity, too, will require further research, in particular, on the conditions for the emergence of successful comity and recognition strategies, notably with regard to the potential role for *public* authorities in mandating or facilitating – or preventing (see the contribution in this volume by Imelda Maher, pp. 119–37) – cooperation among private standard setters.[119]

116 Seminar on 'Building Confidence among Forest Certification Schemes and their Supporters, Rome, February 2001.
117 C. Fischer, F. Aguilar, P. Jawahar, and R. Sedjo, 'Forest Certification: Toward Common Standards?' Foreign Investment Advisory Service, World Bank Group Discussion Paper 05-10 (2005). See, also, J. Griffiths, 'Proposing an International Mutual Recognition Framework', Report for International Forest Industry Roundtable (2001).
118 Gueneau, op. cit., n. 108, p. 398. Compare E. Meidinger, '"Private" Environmental Regulation, Human Rights, and Community' (2000) 7 *Buffalo Environmental Law J.* 123–238, at 226–7 (discussing possible future for coexistence of rival regimes: 'the programs are ... at odds with each other, and it may be in the interest of at least some of the programs not to have a single system emerge.'). For a recent study of 'competing private governance regimes' in various sectors of environmental standard setting, confirming responsiveness to competition but offering little or no evidence for the emergence of alternative conflicts norms, see Smith and Fischlein, op. cit., n. 112. For anecdotal evidence from the forestry sector, see, also, 'Certification an Urban Myth or a Rural Reality: Street Talk' *Timber & Forestry E-News*, September 2010: 'What promised to be a confrontational debate about forest certification between two global leaders of different schemes failed to materialise ...'.
119 In the United States, for example, the recent American Recovery and Reinvestment Act, which requires federally funded building projects to adhere to 'green building' standards, has permitted certification through the PEFC system alongside the FSC standard, even though the dominant 'green building' standard itself (the LEED system) currently only permits FSC certification. The FSC is said to be 'fighting back to protect its monopoly'. For this debate, and for discussion of the roles of public authorities in engaging with competing private regulatory regimes, see Smith and Fischlein, id., p. 519.

161

CONCLUDING REMARKS

The legitimacy and effectiveness of TPRERs are centrally dependent upon the manifold relationships of recognition that these regimes are able to construct with their surroundings. Much of the character of these relationships can be captured through study of TPRERs reflexive responses to competing legitimacy demands – through techniques ranging from information disclosure to impact assessment – and through the generation of various forms of normative connectivity with coexisting normative orders, ranging from state law to rival private regimes. The strategies and norms governing these intra- and extra-regime processes of recognition are, we have argued, *essentially meta-regulatory*, and are simultaneously more modest, more reflexive, and more pluralist than dominant alternatives.

In this paper, we have explored a conceptual triangle of meta-regulation, Better Regulation (BR), and Private International Law (PIL), using each to illuminate perhaps less easily seen characteristics of the others – and invoking all three to gain new insights on TPRERs and the way they deal with their surroundings. Viewing BR and PIL as meta-regulation brings out the distinct way in which both these fields operate on the basis of a commitment logic that allows for the resolution of rationality- or system-conflicts in conditions of endemic pluralism and heterarchy. Juxtaposing BR and PIL, in turn, has highlighted the connections between the intra- and extra-regime dimensions of the interaction of TPRERs with their environment. As a side benefit, this juxtaposition may in the future bring out a more reflexive side to PIL and, perhaps, a view of BR as a new form of 'conflicts law'.

The principal concern of this paper, however, has been to look at TPRERs from within BR and PIL as disciplines and professional fields. BR and PIL, we have argued, are principal repositories of norms and strategies through which actors inside and outside TPRERs – selectively – frame their relationships of recognition. Both fields, we argue, clearly have much to offer, in terms of experience with working with diffuse normative sources, techniques for the proceduralization of conflict resolution, and in effectuating 'loose couplings' between competing rationalities and normative systems. But there are also grounds for caution, and questions for further study. As an empirical issue, preliminary research suggests that predictions for the emergence of a new form of conflict law may need to be qualified in so far as *private* transnational governance is concerned. This empirical point may have important normative implications. It is simply not clear as of yet how far norms and strategies required for the successful management of relationships of recognition in the private sphere – of the kinds identified within BR and PIL – still depend on the presence of a normative and institutional background of *public* law.

162

JOURNAL OF LAW AND SOCIETY
VOLUME 38, NUMBER 1, MARCH 2011
ISSN: 0263-323X, pp. 163-88

Public Accountability of Transnational Private Regulation: Chimera or Reality?

DEIRDRE CURTIN* AND LINDA SENDEN**

The legitimacy of transnational private regulation is contested where authority is exercised by private actors adopting rules and being involved in processes of implementation and enforcement. We eschew a general discussion of legitimacy in this context in favour of the more manageable sub-component, 'accountability'. Drawing on the work of political scientists, we conceptualize public accountability both as a virtue and as a mechanism and explore its relevance with regard to transnational private regulation as opposed to its normal habitat, public regulation and authority. This article highlights the relevance and potential of accountability from both a democratic and a constitutional perspective to the realm of transnational private regulation.

I. ACCOUNTING FOR TRANSNATIONAL PRIVATE REGULATION

The role of private actors in governance is neither marginal nor restricted to the implementation of private rules and regulations. Private actors increasingly exercise authority by adopting rules (or standards) as well as being involved in wider processes of implementation and enforcement[1] in

---

* Faculty of Law, University of Amsterdam, Oudemanhuispoort 4-6, 1012 CN, Amsterdam, The Netherlands
d.m.curtin@uva.nl
** Department of European and International Public Law, Tilburg Law School, Tilburg University, P.O. Box 90153, 5000 LE, Tilburg, The Netherlands
l.a.j.senden@uvt.nl

We thank Colin Scott, Fabrizio Cafaggi, Hans Lindahl, Lokke Moerel, Martijn Hesselink, Mehmet Cetik, the participants of the HiiL-workshop in Dublin, 16–17 June 2010, and of the seminar on *Transnational Private Regulation: Fundamental and Practical Challenges* at Tilburg University, 20 October 2010, for their valuable comments on earlier versions of this article. The usual disclaimer applies.

1 See the introduction to this volume, pp. 1–19.

many different policy sectors and areas, including financial markets, food regulation, consumer protection, product safety, data protection, environmental protection, and so on. On the contemporary map of governance (and as this special issue shows), the private role in regulation is no longer a matter internal to nation states[2] but increasingly, both in scope and intensity, a matter for the transnational (and supranational) levels of governance. Transnational private regulation (TPR) differs from traditional domestic forms of private regulation: its scope is broader and often less specific, it rarely takes the form of formal and informal delegation of rule making by public entities, and it uses a broad range of regulatory devices that may be of a rather 'soft' legal nature (at least initially), such as codes, or of a 'hard' legal nature, such as contracts.[3] The legalization that is taking place in the transnational sphere brings with it a changing relationship with public governance and public actors.[4] The distinction between private and public regulation is, in any event, blurred and unclear, with traditional *public* administration becoming ever more 'unbounded' as outside actors become involved to varying degrees.[5] In the transnational sphere there may sometimes (in international agreements or through the medium of international organizations) be a formal delegation of state public power.[6] On the other hand, different constellations of public and private actors may simply in practice adopt rules, implement and enforce them outside any formal context of delegation.

The question is whether ultimately the private sphere implies a different relationship between legitimacy and accountability because there are different instruments, different actors, different processes, and different addressees. Yet, as Kelsen noted, the 'private' law created in a contract is, 'no less the arena of political power than the public law created in legislation and administration'.[7] In other words, private law is public law in the sense that private regulation is part and parcel of democratic self-rule by a collective.[8] At the level of the nation state, the link between law (both public and private), politics, and society is established in the sense that private actors also operate in 'the shadow of' the political level or 'government' and not simply as free-standing actors. The problem with private rule making

---

2 See J. Freeman, 'The Private Role in Public Governance' (2000) 75 *New York University Law Rev.* 543–675.

3 See F. Cafaggi, 'New Foundations of Transnational Private Regulation' in this volume, pp. 20–49.

4 id.

5 See, too, M. Shapiro, 'Administrative Law Unbounded: Reflections on Government and Governance' (2001) 8 *Indiana J. of Global Legal Studies* 369–78.

6 See, further, C.A. Bradley and J.G. Kelley, 'The Concept of International Delegation' (2008) 71 *Law and Contemporary Problems* 1–36.

7 H. Kelsen, *Introduction to the Problems of Legal Theory* (1994) 95–6.

8 See, further, for this argument with regard to private self-regulation, H. Lindahl, 'Zelfregulering: Rechtsvorming, democratie en reflexieve identiteit' (2006) 167 *Rechtsgeleerd Magazijn Themis* 39–48.

beyond the level of the nation state is its legitimacy as the claim to authority is not derived from *state* legislation and administration and there may be no substitute at the transnational level.

'Accountability' is clearly related to legitimacy; it is a sub-component, alongside authorization and representation[9] but we eschew in this contribution a general discussion of legitimacy in favour of the more manageable sub-component 'accountability'.[10] In line with existing work with political science colleagues, this contribution will highlight a dual conceptual foundation for more detailed empirical research into the meaning and practice of accountability across a range of policy areas – and one that is not solely focused on the possible role of representative democracy at the national level. This approach highlights two different approaches to the conceptualization of accountability that can be discerned in the literature: both can be placed within a broader democratic and constitutional perspective of checks and balances (see, further, section III).[11] The first conception of accountability is as a normative concept, a set of standards for the evaluation of the behaviour of (public) actors. Accountability or, more precisely, 'being accountable', is thus seen as a *virtue*, as a positive quality of organizations or officials. Hence, accountability studies often focus on normative issues, on the assessment of the actual and active behaviour of public agents.[12] Accountability in this broad sense of virtue is an essentially contested and contestable concept,[13] because there is no general consensus about the standards for accountable behaviour. Some principles – for example, transparency, authorization, representation, and participation – have been identified as part of a growing body of global administrative law based on patterns of commonality[14] where global administrative law functions as a mechanism of constraint and control.[15]

9 D. Beetham and C. Lord, 'Legitimacy and the European Union' in *Political Theory and the European Union, Legitimacy, Constitutional Choice and Citizenship*, eds. A. Weale and M. Nentwich (1998); M. Bovens, D. Curtin, and P. 't Hart (eds.), *The Real World of EU Accountability: What Deficit?* (2010).
10 For this approach, see Bovens et al., id.
11 Including M. Bovens, 'Two Concepts of Accountability: Accountability as a Virtue and as a Mechanism' (2010) 33 *West European Politics* 946–67.
12 M. Dubnick, 'Seeking Salvation for Accountability', paper presented at the Annual Meeting of the American Political Science Association (2002); J. Koppell, 'Pathologies of Accountability: ICANN and the Challenge of "Multiple Accountabilities Disorder"' (2005) 65 *Public Administration Rev.* 94–108.
13 W.B. Gallie, 'Essentially Contested Concepts' in *The Importance of Language*, ed. M. Black (1962) 121–46.
14 S. Cassese, B. Carotti, L. Casini, M. Macchia, E. MacDonald, and M. Savino, *Global Administrative Law: Cases, Materials, Issues* (2008).
15 R.W. Grant and R.O. Keohane, *Accountability and Abuses of Power in World Politics* (IILJ Working Paper 2004/7, Global Administrative Law Series), at: <http://www.iilj.org/oldbak/papers/2004/2004.7.htm>); R. Stewart, 'Accountability and the Discontents of Globalization: US and EU Models for Regulatory Governance', draft

The second use of accountability is more narrow and descriptive and implies a focus on the institutional arrangements in which an actor can be held accountable to a forum. Accountability in this second sense is seen as a social *mechanism*, as an institutional relation or arrangement in which an actor can be held to account by a forum.[16] Here, the locus of accountability studies is not the behaviour of public agents, but the way in which these institutional arrangements operate. And the focus of accountability studies is not whether the agents have acted in an accountable way, but whether they are or can be held accountable after the fact by accountability forums.[17] This narrower definition of accountability has at its core the obligation to explain and justify conduct, implying a relationship between an actor, (the accountor) and a forum (the account-holder, or accountee).[18] It provides an analytical framework that is not dependent on the existence of a principal/agent relationship nor even a formal delegation of powers.

To what extent may it be helpful to borrow and apply to varying degrees a specific concept of public accountability to private governance especially at the transnational level? Or is the exercise doomed to failure from the start, a chimera or mirage that disappears once one tries to give it concrete substance and operationalize it in some form? Or may we discover that there are different mechanisms more tailored to the specificity of private governance? In considering these underlying questions we adopt a three-stage approach. First we consider further the nature of private governance and, in particular, the elusiveness of a strict distinction between the public and the private and whether accountability is considered an issue at all in the context of TPR regimes (section II). In section III we analyse and define the concept of public accountability and place it in both a democratic and a constitutional perspective. In section IV we explore why it is relevant to develop further an

paper presented at the NYU Hauser Colloquium on Globalization and its Discontents (2006), at <http://www.iilj.org/courses/documents/Stewart.Accountabilityand Discontents.091206.pdf>.

16 P. Day and R. Klein, *Accountabilities: Five Public Services* (1987); C. Scott, 'Accountability in the Regulatory State' (2000) 27 *J. of Law and Society* 38–60; R. Mulgan, '"Accountability": An Ever-expanding Concept?' (2000) 78 *Public Administration* 555–73; T. Schillemans, 'Accountability in the Shadow of Hierarchy: The Horizontal Accountability of Agencies' (2008) 8 *Public Organization Rev.* 175; M. Bovens, T. Schillemans, and P. 't Hart, 'Does Public Accountability Work? An Assessment Tool' (2008) 86 *Public Administration* 225–42; A. Meijer and T. Schillemans, 'Fictional Citizens and Real Effects: Accountability to Citizens in Competitive and Monopolistic Markets' (2009) *Public Sector Management – An Interactive J.*, at <www.spaef.com/file.php?id=1114>.

17 This is an admittedly limited approach and does not deny that it may indeed be possible to introduce forms of accountability on each of the discrete phases of rule-making procedures, also *ex ante*. See, further, for example, O. Perez, 'Using Private-public Linkages to Regulate Environmental Conflicts: The Case of International Construction Contracts' (2002) 29 *J. of Law and Society* 77–110.

18 C. Pollitt, *The Essential Public Manager* (2003).

166

understanding of accountability as a virtue of TPR and give a 'first cut' of specific work in functional areas where it appears that accountability is, in one form or another, already considered a salient and at times an urgent issue. In section V we apply the understanding of accountability as a mechanism to TPR, considering in what way this is distinctive from transnational public regulation. TPR may involve the delegation of powers from public to private actors but it also comes about as a result of a range of other processes, not entailing any form of (institutionalized) delegation. The question then is: do accountability forums exist at any (or several) levels of governance to make this an interesting avenue to pursue in the context of TPR? Finally, we conclude with some observations on the extent to which public accountability of TPR is a chimera or is, or could be, further turned into a reality.

II. THE TRANSNATIONAL PRIVATE-PUBLIC DICHOTOMY

The concept of accountability is often used as a synonym for many loosely defined political desiderata, such as good governance, transparency, equity, democracy, efficiency, responsiveness, responsibility, and integrity.[19] Accountability expresses primarily the belief that public institutions should render account publicly for the use of their mandates and the way in which they spend public money,[20] or that public power exercised by office-holders should be checked and balanced by forums that enjoy popular trust,[21] thus conveying a sense of control over the exercise of public power and of trustworthiness, transparency, and responsibility. Accountability has become a central notion for addressing certain legitimacy aspects of public regulation and regulators, given the exercise and delegation of power it involves. Where such power has been lost on the nation-state level and gained on the transnational and international levels, such as in the framework of the EU and the WTO, accountability has become a particular concern on those levels as well.[22] But also outside the public regulatory domain, including that of non-conventional regulatory institutions and TPR, accountability has become a concern where it involves such loss or transfer of power.

Public regulation is in principle imbued with a developed notion of control and subjects all relevant parties to its remit in a compelling and legally binding way. Public regulation will generally be adopted either for

19 Mulgan, op. cit., n. 16; R.D. Behn, *Rethinking Democratic Accountability* (2001) 3–6; M. Dubnick, 'Sarbanes-Oxley and the Search for Accountable Corporate Governance' in *Private Equity, Corporate Governance and the Dynamics of Capital Market Regulation*, ed. J. O'Brien (2007) 226–54.
20 D. Curtin, *Executive Power of the European Union: Law, Practices, and the Living Constitution* (2009).
21 Bovens et al. (eds.), op. cit., n. 9, p. 26.
22 See Curtin, op. cit., n. 20.

technical reasons (such as monopolies, externalities or public goods) or for socio-political reasons (such as the public interest, competition for power, private interest). Private regulation is, on the other hand, dominated by a high sense of freedom, namely, the choice to opt in or to opt out of a certain sphere, analogous to the freedom of contract.[23] Private regulation may also be resorted to for technical reasons even if in practice it is (far) more driven by private interests than by public interests. As regards TPR, this distinction is not black and white but comes in many shades of grey. TPR may thus in reality be far less characterized by freedom and voluntariness than generally assumed, as business and consumers may not always have the possibility in practice of opting out of private regulation. This is the case for many technical or other standards in different areas (food safety, electronics, and so on) that are de facto compulsory for market actors, whether promulgated by individual firms (such as Microsoft) or from standardization bodies (for example, ISO). The call for the accountability of such regimes may be more acute where the private standards have been adopted in an insufficiently open manner, within the framework of a standardization process that has entailed barriers to entry. The same goes for private standard setting that has initially been adopted as international soft law, but has then been redeployed by international organizations and implemented through hard law at the regional (EU) or state level, through contract law and/or tort law in particular.[24] Such later 'redeployment' processes mean that the norms in question acquire a compulsory de iure status at a later stage in time.

Furthermore, increasing globalization – economic trade, environmental, criminal, migration problems, and so on – has put a strain on national public regulation as an instrumental tool to steer economy and society, while transnational public structures and mechanisms for decision-making are not sophisticated enough to tackle these effectively. Self-regulation may then be resorted to out of sheer necessity or public actors may have to fall back on or cooperate with private actors to tackle a cross-border problem effectively, by bringing about some form of regulation, monitoring, and compliance mechanisms. As a result, transnational regulation is very hard to define as either (predominantly) public or private and the public-private distinction seems to be even more elusive on the international and transnational level than on the national plane.[25] It can be argued that there are no real centres of decision-making as such: rather, we find a find a variety of actors – public

---

23 Compare HiiL, 'The Added Value of Private Regulation in an Internationalised World? Towards a Model of the Legitimacy, Effectiveness, Enforcement and Quality of Private Regulation' HiiL Working Paper (2008), at <www.hiil.org>.
24 See, further, Cafaggi, op. cit., n. 3.
25 Regarding the national level, see, for example, G. Teubner, 'After Privatisation? The Many Autonomies of Private Law' (1998) 51 *Current Legal Problems* 394–5; Freeman, op. cit., n. 2.

168

and private – adopting multiple decisions in a web of negotiated relation-ships, marked by a certain level of interdependence.[26] TPR thus often represents some hybrid mix of public-private elements (see Cafaggi in this volume, pp. 20–49) and issues of accountability arise from the very fragmentation of responsibility these regimes entail in the regulatory state.[27]

The underlying argument is that *all* power-wielders within *any* regulatory regime should be accountable to those affected by their rule making,[28] regardless of whether they are to be qualified as public or private. If a regulatory regime is a 'sustained and focused attempt to alter the behaviour of others according to defined standards or purposes in order to address a collective issue or resolve a collective problem',[29] the demand for the accountability of an agent by some person or group can be justified not only by reason of (formal) authorization and financial or political support but also because of the impact the regime has. Agents whose actions have a considerable impact on the lives of people and are 'choice-determining' for them should be accountable and under a duty to report to those people and be subject to sanctions from them.[30] This means that there is a wider obligation of public accountability to those whose lives are affected by those who adopt the rules or standards.[31] This wider group owed accountability will include not only producers and companies but also citizens in their various capacities, either as consumers (for example, food and product standards), employees (collective labour agreements), recipients of services (profes-sional codes), economic investors (codes of conduct in financial markets), or as subject bearers of fundamental rights (for example, data protection and outsourcing/privatization of public security and military services), and so on. Whether the regulatory norms in question actually generate influence or impact will depend on the extent to which the norms crystallize in daily reality. This in turn will, as Casey and Scott argue in this volume (pp. 76–95), depend upon the processes of legitimation. Regulatory norms will only be legitimate if they are accepted by their addressees; the latter will only act

---

26 Freeman, id., p. 673; Scott, op. cit., n. 16; J. Black, 'Constructing and Contesting Legitimacy and Accountability in Polycentric Regulatory Regimes', LSE Working Paper 2/2008 (2008) 9, and literature references in fn. 22. Compare, also, M. Bovens, *The Quest for Responsibility: Accountability and Citizenship in Complex Organisations* (1998) 5, who prefers to speak of 'complex organizations' instead of distinguishing between public and private organizations.
27 In this sense, see Scott, id.
28 R.O. Keohane, 'Global Governance and Democratic Accountability' in *Taming Globalization. Frontiers of Governance*, eds. D. Held and M. Koenig-Archibugi (2003).
29 Black, op. cit., n. 26, p. 8.
30 Keohane, op. cit., n. 28, under reference to D. Held, 'Law of States, Law of Peoples: Three Models of Sovereignty' (2002) 8 *Legal Theory* 1–44, at 26. See, also, D. Held, 'Democratic Accountability and Political Effectiveness from a Cosmopolitan Perspective' (2004) 39 *Government and Opposition* 364–91.
31 Keohane, id.

according to the norm if there is congruence between the norm and the actors' 'beliefs or expectations or ... interests'.

A further question is to what extent there is a correlation between the nature of values and interests a TPR affects and the level and forms of accountability that are claimed. Governmental authorities and public regulation are generally guided by both classic and social human rights: this is far less the case at the transnational level where TPR may in fact represent a threat, to a greater or lesser extent, to classic fundamental rights (where, for example, the right to life or the prohibition of torture is at stake)[32] and/or to social rights (for example, where the right to employment is concerned). What is the consequence of this potential clash with human rights in terms of the accountability demand such regimes impose and does it vary according to the type of right(s) that is/are at stake? For example, might we not argue that there is a greater need for accountability of regulatory regimes that involve the use of force against individuals or affects their subsistence in any other fundamental way than with regard to regimes that affect the rights of people in a less immediate way[33] and in respect of which a less constraining form of accountability might be sufficient? In the transnational context, this issue becomes even more salient because of the fact that certain issues may be considered to involve human rights in certain jurisdictions and regions and not in others – a case in point is data protection. In the United States, this is considered an issue to be dealt with by corporate actors and self-regulation, whereas in Europe the protection of personal data is perceived as a human right of privacy. The right of privacy is recognized in the ECHR and in the case law on fundamental rights of the European Court of Justice.[34] Clearly, the United States and the EU have a fundamentally different starting point in regulating data protection. It is the distinction between the freedom of market actors and private regulation, on the one hand, and control by state actors and public regulation on the other.

This discussion suggests that the private role in governance requires more than the delineation of a threshold test to determine when a private actor is performing a sufficiently public function. An appropriate response to shared (public/private) governance requires a highly contextual, specific analysis of both the benefits and dangers of the different arrangements. This arguably also requires a willingness to look for other, informal, non-traditional and non-governmental accountability mechanisms. It seems that one may well need to go beyond traditional approaches towards ensuring accountability and look for and identify context/area/sector-specific elements that may

---

32 See F. de Londras, 'Privatized Sovereign Performance' in this volume, pp. 96–118.
33 Held, op. cit. (2004), n. 30, seems to hold this view, distinguishing between different levels of impact.
34 M. Herdegen, 'Legal Challenges for Transatlantic Economic Integration' (2008) 45 *Common Market Law Rev.* 1581–777.

170

contribute to enhancing accountability.[35] But first let us look more closely at how we understand further the concept of accountability and why we adopt an approach labelling it as 'public' accountability.

III. *PUBLIC* ACCOUNTABILITY: DEMOCRATIC AND CONSTITUTIONAL PERSPECTIVES

1. *Publicness*

The very words 'public accountability' imply that account-giving processes take place in the public domain. 'Public' can refer to the object of the account to be rendered in the sense of the spending of public funds, the exercise of public authority or the conduct of public institutions.[36] But 'public' can also be used more profoundly to refer to different links to the public eye and more generally to a commonality or 'common world' in the sense used by Hannah Arendt.[37] A 'common, shared world' provides the background from which public spaces of action and deliberation can arise and this is the deeper backdrop to an understanding of the centrality of publicness. 'Public' may also be used to mean 'openness' in the sense of what comes under the public eye. This requires processes of account giving not be rendered discretely or behind closed doors but to be open to the general public. By opening up to the general public (through whatever medium) a link can be made to an understanding of the public sphere. The public sphere has a triadic character with a speaker, an addressee, and a listener (or audience). Understanding accountability as a social mechanism involving a relationship between an actor and an accountability forum and an audience (the public) fits within this understanding of the public sphere and feeds into it in the sense of a network of communicating information and points of view (even if public accountability can go further in terms of imposing consequences). Public accountability can also be understood as a virtue shared by certain organizations/actors if they fulfill certain characteristics (for example, transparency or participation). The presumption is that these characteristics force what happens inside to the outside, with the public as general audience. Publics may be both weak (the general public) and strong (for example, a parliament).[38]

---

35 Freeman, op. cit., n. 2, p. 665, who has captured this under the term 'aggregate' accountability. Scott, op. cit., n. 16, has used the term 'extended' accountability to denote this.

36 M. Bovens, 'Analysing and Assessing Accountability: A Conceptual Framework' (2007) 13 *European Law J.* 447–68.

37 See H. Arendt, *The Human Condition* (1958).

38 N. Fraser, 'Rethinking the Public Sphere' in *Habermas and the Public Sphere*, ed. C. Calhoun (1992) 109–42, especially 132–4; J. Habermas, *Faktizität und Geltung* (1992) 373–82.

171

Accountability may indeed be traditionally applied within public law but that does not mean that publicity and general account giving to the public is not relevant to private law and private regulation. The term accountability, to quote Mulgan,[39] 'has come to stand as a general term for any mechanism that makes powerful institutions responsive to their particular publics'. The reality is that outside of the confines of the territorial nation states, public or private actors are only to a very limited extent held to account for their actions and inactions. The role of national parliaments is under challenge in this context when actors as a matter of practice are engaged in a non-hierarchical and disaggregated governance process. National *public* actors operate to some extent outside their own national political and constitutional level but are still in theory, and generally in practice, responsive to their domestic institutions (government/parliament). Private actors, on the other hand, are accountable to their constituencies, which may be domestic when there is a federation of *national bodies* (for example, the ISO) that will be constitutionally embedded in some form, but will be transnational when representation is interest-based (for example, the FSC or the IASC). The latter context is problematic as there is no transnational 'public' nor any institutions in place.

2. *A democratic perspective*

What can be designated the original or 'core' sense of accountability is that associated with the process of being called 'to account' to some authority for one's actions. Such accountability has a number of features: it is external, it involves social interaction and exchange, and it implies rights of authority, in that those calling for an account are asserting rights of superior authority over those who are accountable, including the rights to demand answers and to draw consequences, possibly including the imposition of sanctions. This sense of accountability is in line with the broad sense that Keohane and Grant describe 'accountability' as involving the justification of an actor's performance vis-à-vis others, the assessment or judgement of that perform-ance against certain standards, and the possible imposition of consequences if the actor fails to live up to applicable standards.[40]

In the context of a democratic state, the key accountability relationships in this core sense are those between citizens and the holders of public office, and within the ranks of office holders, between elected politicians and bureaucrats. At the end of the accountability chain are the citizens who pass judgement on the conduct of the government and can, if they so wish, 'throw the rascals out'. Such accountability relationships are based upon representa-

39 R. Mulgan, *Holding Power to Account: Accountability in Modern Democracies* (2003).
40 R.W. Grant and R.O. Keohane, 'Accountability and Abuses of Power in World Politics' (2005) 99 *Am. Pol. Sci. Rev.* 29–44.

tive, electoral systems and are obviously familiar terrain for (public) lawyers at the national level, much less so at the international or transnational level. Internationally, the principle of democracy has made only a limited entry at the level of the international legal order itself. International lawyers have traditionally focused on well-established legal principles such as state responsibility, and the operationalization of a broader concept of accountability in the sense of an actor being held to account in an iterative and interactive process is still nascent. In recent years it has been in the context of the European Union, in particular, that a rather explicit discussion has taken place on core democratic accountability issues such as how voters can make their elected representatives answer for policies, how legislators (at both the national and the European levels) can scrutinize the actions of (European and national) public servants and make them answerable for mistakes, and so on. In fact, that discussion even goes so far as to enable Walter van Gerven, a prominent European legal scholar, both a public lawyer and a private lawyer, to ask, rather provocatively, 'Which form of accountable government for the European Union?' [41] One can hardly envisage asking an equivalent question for any other international organization or indeed at the transnational level.

Much less effort has gone into studying other manifestations of the internationalization of policy at other levels than that of the EU. The 'backstage' politics of international and informal policy preparation (committee processes, bureaucratic politics, horizontal networks) and implementation remain under-explored relative to their importance in shaping the process and content of such public policy making.[42] In many national systems, specific democratic/political accountability regimes have evolved over decades/centuries to accommodate the various modes of political choice and action. But how do these national regimes adapt when at least part of the political and legal action has moved to the transnational or international level and how can the democratic voids created by these shifts in governance be filled? First, the challenge may be to democratize at the level of the transnational system itself; secondly, at the level of the national political system and thirdly, the often intricate interactions between the two. This description

41 See, W. van Gerven, 'Which form of Accountable Government for the EU?' (2005) XXXVI *Netherlands Yearbook of International Law* 227–58.
42 See, for example, M.P.C.M. van Schendelen, *EU Committees as Influential Policymakers* (1998); J. Richardson, *European Union: Power and Policy-making* (2000); T. Christiansen and E. Kirchner, *Committee Governance in the European Union* (2000); M. Rhinard, 'The Democratic Legitmacy of the EU Committee System' (2002) 15 *Governance* 185–210; H. Kassim, 'The European Administration: Between Europeanization and Domestication' and E.C. Page, 'Europeanisation and the Persistence of Administrative Systems', both in *Governing Europe*, eds. J. Hayward and A. Menon (2003) 132–60, 162–76; D. Gerardin et al., *Regulation through Agencies in the EU: A New Perspective of European Governance* (2005); M. Egeberg (ed.), *Institutional Dynamics and the Transformation of Executive Politics in Europe* (2007).

173

already indicates that there is unlikely to be a single solution for the democratic challenge at any level since national democracies are not only different but have been affected in critically different ways by ongoing processes of transnational regulation. The mere 'uploading' of a conception of national democracy to the transnational (and also the supranational) level is likely to remain a non-starter and further conceptualization of trans-national democracy requires, in the view of some, a major revamping of democratic theory.[43] The real issue remains how to institutionalize mech-anisms that do not simply try to extrapolate from electoral mechanisms in national democracies. In any case, any transnational institutionalization of democracy would have to find novel ways of dealing with two core questions: (i) who counts as an interested member of the polity, who should participate in one way or another in lawmaking or rule making? (ii) what counts as the common or joint interest? In further elaborating both of these questions (which is beyond the scope of the present contribution), the twin understandings of publicness in the sense of the public eye and the common shared world are crucial.

At first sight, the purely democratic perspective in its traditional con-ception does not seem to be all that helpful in taking the issue of public accountability further in the specific context of TPRs. After all, it is clearly an illusion to imagine that a system of democratic accountability for what takes place at the transnational level can rely on a (future) system of transnational parliamentary elections. One can argue therefore that there is, if anything, an even greater need for the public accountability of TPR regimes than of public regulation precisely because TPR lacks – or is weak in terms of – political and hierarchical accountability processes. Given the heterogeneity of TPR regimes, accountability deficiencies may, however, be (far) more acute for some regimes rather than for others, depending on their particular nature, characteristics, and the overall context. Extending our argument in section II, we submit here that there will be a greater need to ensure democratic accountability if a regime is or has become more compulsory, has more external effects,[44] a higher impact on people's lives[45] or involves the exercise of public power or a public function. We argue that there is not one fixed level of democratic accountability with which each and every TPR regime must comply but, rather, that we can approach the issue of accountability in terms

43 See, for example, J. Bohmann, *Democracy Across Borders: from Demos to Demoi* (2007).
44 Compare, also, HiiL, op. cit., n. 23, p. 13: 'It could be argued that there is a sliding scale that determines when legitimacy becomes important, depending on the quantitative and qualitative effects on third parties.' It further suggests a distinction between internal and external legitimacy; if private ordering is at stake that has 'spill-over effects' on third parties, external legitimacy is at stake and accountability becomes an important issue.
45 See approaches developed by Keohane, op. cit., n. 28, p. 141, and Held, op. cit. (2004), n. 30, p. 373.

174

of sliding scales. It is beyond the scope of this paper to flesh out the content of such sliding scales in detail but one of the central issues is clearly the kind of effect there should be on third parties with a view to identifying the actual demand for democratic accountability. When does a TPR regime affect a population to the extent that its democratic entitlements are potentially threatened? Macdonald and Macdonald have considered this to be the case whenever the political impact that some responsible power-wielder has upon a population implicates the autonomy and equality of affected individuals. They have thus identified a considerable need for democratic accountability in the area of core labour standards, where power-wielders have a significant impact on important aspects of workers' lives.[46] Such political impact may be deemed higher in the case of private regimes that involve the privatization or outsourcing of tasks and functions that traditionally have been regulated within the exclusive sphere of the state or government.

3. A constitutional perspective

The main concern of what can be termed a constitutional perspective on accountability as opposed to a democratic one is preventing the tyranny of absolute rulers or an expansion of 'privatized' executive power.[47] The separation of state powers has been a central concept of modern constitutionalism ever since Montesquieu[48] and has been intricately tied up with attempts to delimit the scope of executive power, among other things. The separation of the executive from the legislature, in particular, was used as a means to avoid tyranny, denying the executive the privilege of law making and ensuring that the legislative power serves the rule of law and not ambitious men. The primacy of human legislative power was devised in order to ensure the sovereignty of the rule of law.[49] The most relevant aspect of the general principle of separation of powers as it has evolved over time and abstracted from any one specific political system is this idea that one

46 T. Macdonald and K. Macdonald, 'Non-Electoral Accountability in Global Politics: Strengthening Democratic Control within the Global Garment Industry' (2006) 17 *European J. of International Law* 89–119, at 91.

47 Bovens, op. cit., n. 36, p. 463.

48 See, for example, M.J.C. Vile, *Constitutionalism and the Separation of Powers* (1967); E. Barendt, 'Separation of Powers and Constitutional Government' (1995) 21 *Public Law* 599–619. A clear expression may be found in Article 16 of the French Declaration of the Rights of Man of 1789: 'Any society in which the safeguarding of rights is not assured, and the separation of powers is not observed, has no constitution.' The principle of the separation of powers was also discussed extensively in *The Federalist Papers* and is reflected in Articles I (legislative power), II (executive power), and III (judicial power) of the US Constitution. This organic understanding of the separation of powers is also found in various other constitutions around the world, both written and unwritten.

49 See, further, H.C. Mansfield, *Taming the Prince: The Ambivalence of Modern Executive Power* (1989).

branch of government will be checked and balanced by the action of another.[50] A system of 'checks and balances' does not presuppose a radical division of government into three separate parts, with particular functions neatly parcelled out amongst them. Rather, 'the focus is on *relationships and interconnections*, on maintaining the conditions in which the intended struggle at the apex may continue.'[51] The relational and balancing aspect is of particular importance to the point where one may speak more of a *balancing* rather than of a *separation* of powers. A balancing of powers would, however, be unintelligible unless the powers that engage in checks and balances with each other can be viewed as powers that are competing with a view to determining the *common* interest, and which therefore can be viewed as powers within a *single* community. In other words: no *division* of powers absent the presupposition of the *unity* of power. In this minimal sense a *demos*, even if by no means the kind of demos to which we have become accustomed in national democracies, seems to be a condition of the possibility of accountability in a transnational framework.[52]

The remedy against overweening power in a constitutional perspective is the organization of countervailing power, of a system of checks and balances. This generally entails the construction or design of a system with largely autonomous public institutions other than those related to electoral and democratic accountability, such as a court system, an Ombudsman, or financial supervisory institutions with the power to insist that account be rendered in and to the public for the authority exercised. The constitutional perspective thus puts emphasis on other forms of accountability, including legal, judicial, financial, administrative, and the like (see, further, section V below). Social forms of accountability, such as that exercised by the media or social networks may be of help, too, in creating checks and balances.[53]

TPR seems to be devolving important public authority and power onto private actors who are able to operate outside the traditional public account-ability mechanisms designed for public servants.[54] The blurring of the private/public distinction at the transnational level has obvious legitimacy challenges but also offers new opportunities.[55] If such regulation was pre-

50 See G. Marshall, *Constitutional Theory* (1971).
51 See P. Strauss, 'The Place of Agencies in Government: Separation of Powers and the Fourth Branch' (1984) 84 *Columbia Law Rev.* 573–669, at 578. Author's emphasis.
52 See, further, Bohmann, op. cit., n. 43.
53 See, further, J. Mashaw, 'Accountability and Institutional Design: Some Thoughts on the Grammar of Governance' in *Public Accountability: Designs, Dilemmas and Experiences*, ed. M.W. Dowdle (2006) 115–56.
54 M.W. Dowdle, 'Public Accountability: Conceptual, Historic and Epistemic Mappings' in Dowdle, id., p. 1.
55 See, in general, K. van Kersbergen and F. van Waarden, 'Shifts in Governance: Problems of Legitimacy and Accountability',White Paper for the Netherlands Organization for Scientific Research (2001), at: <http://www.uu.nl/uupublish/content/NWOShiftsinGovernanceDefText.PDF>.

viously taking place within the context of democratic nation states (by public or private actors), then the shift in level will at any rate involve a challenge for democratic accountability because of the simple fact that national-level parliaments are fenced into their own national constitutional systems and cannot control where power has migrated to. Moreover, the regulation may be both legislative and executive in nature and effect but taken by actors disaggregated from the state context. Unlike in the purely national context it is difficult to resurrect a type of 'non-delegation doctrine' that constitutionally embedded legislatures cannot assign rule-making power to outside actors.[56] Rather, when private actors have effectively jumped the fence of national constitutional constraints, the question is whether there is any restraint emerging at the transnational level to compensate for this shift in governance.[57] As we will see from the discussion in section IV below, there are some compensatory mechanisms emerging that fit within a constitutional perspective on public accountability.

IV. THE ACCOUNTABILITY OF TPR AS A VIRTUE

Accountability has become a keyword in the debate on global regulation and governance, one possible cause for this being also a growing discomfort with the more general term 'legitimacy'.[58] Dubnick and O'Brien have observed that Williams's keyword approach to the creation and legitimization of everyday discourses has special meaning in the politics and governance arena, as here words and phrases do not merely 'represent' and/or 'shape' meaningful discussions, but are also linked to power relationships. They recognize an important discursive and policy-influencing role for accountability, exemplifying this by the role it has played in the discourse on the global financial market's crisis as either the cause or the cure for the market's problems. As a causal factor, the focus of the discourse is on the absence or the failure of effective accountability. As a cure, the focus is on how to deal with such failure, for example, by introducing substantive norms for the behaviour of actors.[59]

This double role is also expressed in the Global Accountability Framework, developed by One World Trust, a charity that conducts research on practical ways to make global organizations more responsive to the

---

56 See, for example, the discussion in the United States context by Freeman, op. cit., n. 2.
57 See, in general, van Kersbergen and van Waarden, op. cit., n. 55.
58 As noted by E. Meidinger, 'The Administrative Law of Global Private-Public Regulation: the Case of Forestry' (2006) 17 *European J. of International Law* 47–87, at 83.
59 M.J. Dubnick and J.P. O'Brien, 'Retrieving the Meaning of Accountability in Financial Market Regulation', paper delivered at the Annual Meeting of the American Political Science Association, Toronto (2009), referring to R. Williams, *Keywords: A Vocabulary of Culture and Society* (1985).

people they affect, and on how the rule of law can be applied equally to all.[60] While it is difficult to come up with a general definition of accountability as a virtue because the standards for what constitutes accountable behaviour differ, depending on role, institutional context, era, and political perspective,[61] the Global Accountability Framework (GAF) represents one of the more successful attempts to operationalize accountability as a virtue. It establishes an active notion of accountability, identifying four core dimensions that make an organization more accountable to both its internal and external stakeholders: transparency, participation, evaluation, and complaint and response mechanisms.[62] Each of these four dimensions is formulated as a standard for accountable behaviour. The debate on the (assessment of) behaviour of certain actors is thus not only framed in terms of accountability understood as a virtue, but through the use of this notion it is also sought to improve existing practices and behaviour and to identify pathways for bringing this about.

The extent to which one will identify accountability deficits in certain TPR regimes will depend upon the democratic and constitutional expectations one cherishes vis-à-vis such regulation and on the accountability standards that are set and their scope. What may be considered adequate and sufficient accountability from the constitutional perspective may not be the case from the democratic perspective, and vice versa. Schepel's observation as to the level of due process, wide and meaningful consultation, and institutionalized debate one requires from private governance such as standardization is illustrative here:

> Representation of diffuse interests is attractive in this light not because of the shallow idea that 'interests' need to be 'represented' for decisions to be made 'democratically', but because it enhances deliberation, and only in the measure it does so.[63]

Although there are not many empirical studies on TPR that address its accountability or otherwise, the few that do focus on or mention two of the aforementioned GAF standards as 'institutional proxies' – transparency and participation – to ensuring accountability on the *ex ante* side during the process of rule making.[64] We will now explore a number of examples in this regard.

The forerunner is clearly transnational forestry rule making. Meidinger is, on the whole, positive about the both formal and informal public participatory processes in forestry policy making, including, for instance, a

---

60 M. Blagescu, L. de las Casas, and R. Loyd, *Pathways to Accountability: The GAP Framework* (2005).
61 See Bovens, op. cit., n. 11.
62 See, further, Blagescu et al., op. cit., n. 60.
63 H. Schepel, *The Constitution of Private Governance: Product Standards in the Regulation of Integrating Markets* (2005) 413.
64 Meidinger, op. cit., n. 58, p. 81.

notice-and-comment procedure. Yet, transparency still remains limited in this area and is very much a work in progress.[65] Another issue that can be considered problematic here is that, for a long time, the FSC principles and criteria were not consistently reviewed. A first review and revision process was only initiated in recent years and will not be concluded until 2011. In the area of international environmental law more generally, the process within the framework of the International Organization for Standardization has been described as opaque and involving little public participation. It is a process dominated by business representatives. In order to enhance the legitimacy of this regime, it is suggested that certain mechanisms, such as the introduction of administrative procedural requirements, should be included.[66]

The Codex Alimentarius, created by intergovernmental organizations (FAO, WHO), provides another example. It incorporates minimum food standards and general principles that have to be implemented on the state level through public legislation but are also implemented on the trans-national level by private actors.[67] These standards are further often complemented by stricter private standards in agreements and contracts concluded by retailers and suppliers. National government experts, assisted by industry advisors, play a leading role in drafting these acts and codes.[68] Consumer and environmental associations or NGOs can only have observer status, but national delegations include some non-governmental representatives of various NGOs and corporate representatives.[69] Participation rights are thus not very well defined across the board. At the same time, *ex-post* mechanisms of legal accountability such as judicial review and liability of the private regulators that could enhance their accountability may be very limited. While (at least) procedural review might be a possibility via the WTO dispute settlement mechanism,[70] Cafaggi concludes in this volume that the current design of the Codex Alimentarius 'implies a trade-off between higher effectiveness and lower accountability'.[71]

---

65 id., pp. 81–3. See, also, the website of the Forest Stewardship Council, at <http://www.fsc.org/pcreview.html>.

66 D. Bodansky, 'The Legitimacy of International Governance: A Coming Challenge for International Environmental Law?' (1999) 93 *Am. J. of International Law* 596–624, at 619.

67 F. Cafaggi, 'Private Regulation, Supply Chain and Contractual Networks: The Case of Food Safety', EUI Working Papers no. RSCAS 2010/10 (2010).

68 Bodansky, op. cit., n. 66, p. 619.

69 E.E. Smythe, *In Whose Interests? Transparency and Accountability in the Global Governance of Food: Agro-business, the Codex Alimentarius and the World Trade Organization* (Paper presented at the annual meeting of International Studies Association, Chicago (2007), at <http://www.allacademic.com/meta/p180399_index.html>.

70 M.A. Livermore, 'Authority and Legitimacy in Global Governance: Deliberation, Institutional Differentiation, and the Codex Alimentarius' (2006) 81 *New York University Law Rev.* 766–801.

71 Cafaggi, op. cit., n. 67, pp. 9–10.

Another example in a completely different area concerns private security companies (PSC) which provide a broad range of services, such as guarding, detention, training, advice, interrogation, and intelligence gathering in a transnational context on behalf of states and non-state actors.[72] Non- or under-regulation of the private security sector may be considered morally problematic, in particular if a PSC resorts to the use of force for its own financial benefit. If force is used, then the risk is that important public law values, including human rights norms, norms against corruption, and democratic process values may be affected.[73] While such values protect individuals from governmental misconduct in the case of security and military activities, those norms are not often seen as applicable to private security actors and the question that immediately emerges from this is how to hold PSC responsible for misconduct or illegal conduct. A multi-stakeholder initiative with the participation of states, NGOs, and companies resulted in the so-called Voluntary Principles on Security and Human Rights (VPSHR) which attempts to ensure that some of these values are protected in the private context. However, the inclusiveness of the VPSHR is itself problematic as is its transparency: the PSC themselves have only been included to a very limited extent.

These examples illustrate that, whereas TPR raises problems from an accountability perspective, the nature and scope of the deficits differ from one subject area or regime to another. At the same time, these examples also reveal a certain consensus that transparency and participation are relevant standards that enhance the accountability of such regimes and reinforce the fact that further mechanisms need to be put in place in order to achieve this objective. There is also some (still limited) empirical evidence that transparency can indeed play a useful role in furthering the accountability of these regimes.[74] In conclusion, it seems that a number of TPR regimes already put some emphasis on transparency and participation mechanisms. However, from the limited empirical evidence available, they far less frequently include complaint-response and evaluation mechanisms (see further, however, in section V). This is an area requiring further study.

72 S. Percy, 'Morality and Regulation' in *From Mercenaries to Market: The Rise and Regulation of Private Military Companies*, eds. S. Chesterman and C. Lehnardt (2007) 13.
73 L.A. Dickinson, 'Public Law Values in a Privatized World' (2006) 31 *Yale J. of International Law* 383–426, at 400.
74 T.N. Hale, 'Transparency, Accountability and Global Governance' (2008) 14 *Global Governance* 73–94.

V. THE ACCOUNTABILITY OF TRANSNATIONAL PRIVATE REGULATION AS A MECHANISM

1. *Multiple accountability relationships*

Having considered the normative dimension of accountability of TPR as a virtue, we now turn to view TPR through the conceptual lens of accountability as a mechanism. How can we perceive of and develop the notion of accountability as a mechanism within the context of TPR and how distinctive is it vis-à-vis transnational public regulation? With a view to this, we take as our conceptual understanding the following description of accountability as a mechanism, containing seven constitutive elements for a social relation being qualified as a practice of accountability:

> a relationship between an actor and a forum (i), in which the actor has an obligation (ii) to explain and to justify (iii) his or her conduct (iv), the forum can pose questions (v) and pass judgment (vi), and the actor may face consequences (vii).[75]

This conceptualization can be applied from a democratic perspective (for example, to parliaments or hierarchical accountability between a minister and civil servants) but it can equally be applied from a constitutional/checks-and-balances perspective (including courts, Ombudsmen, and so on). The underlying questions are who is accountable, to whom, and for what exactly? It should be understood that we do not seek to give a comprehensive answer to these questions. This would be impossible given the heterogeneity of individual regimes and the amount of empirical work that would be required and the little that is already available. Rather, we seek to contribute in a modest initial way to the development of a framework for engaging in such empirical investigation and to do so in a comparative way. What issues arise then when we try to operationalize these building blocks and underlying questions in the specific context of TPR? Is there something distinctive about it?

The first building block is a very fundamental one. Its operationalization with regard to a specific regulatory regime will determine to what extent the subsequent building blocks can be put in place. Moreover, it will determine the answer to questions such as what (the nature of) the obligation of explanation and justification actually entails, what conduct of the actor is subject to scrutiny, and what consequences (perhaps even sanctions) it may face upon being judged negatively. Different types of relationships can thus be envisaged. The actor or accountor can be either an individual, or an organization, such as a public institution or any other entity involved in a private regime or arrangement, including enterprises, standardization bodies, professional bodies, and so on. Generally speaking, the significant other, the accountability forum or accountee, can be a specific person, such as a

---

75 Bovens et al., op. cit., n. 9, p. 37.

superior, a minister, or a journalist, or it can be an agency, such as parliament, a court, the audit office, an NGO but also specific public groups (consumers). Even at the level of public regulation, the relationship between the forum and the actor does not necessarily have to have the character of a principal-agent relation. While such a relation is often present with political (forms of) accountability (representatives, parties, media), this is not the case for other forms including legal accountability (courts), administrative accountability (auditors, inspectors, controllers), professional accountability (associations, peers), and social accountability (interest groups, charities, other stakeholders). These different forums obviously also apply their own set of criteria; for example, parliaments applying ministerial accountability requirements, courts legal requirements, auditors procedural and financial requirements, professional bodies ethical-professional standards, NGOs a combination of process/procedural and substantive standards, and so on. As a consequence, the more forums a specific regulatory regime or actor is required to answer to, the more aspects of its conduct are subject to scrutiny as well and the higher the exposure to consequences or sanctions. The case of transnational forestry regulation provides an illustration of a fairly accountable regime, having put into place quite successfully a variety of accountability mechanisms, including forms of political, legal, administrative, judicial, and financial accountability.[76]

In the context of TPR, the identification of an accountability relationship is nonetheless complicated first of all because of the problem of the many hands.[77] In its original conception, this problem referred to the multiplicity of officials contributing in many ways to decisions and policies of government, as a result of which 'it is difficult even in principle to identify who is morally responsible for political outcomes'.[78] This problem presents itself with even more force in transnational contexts with regulatory regimes that are of a diffuse, hybrid public-private nature and include many different (public and private), organizationally often disconnected, actors at various moments in time. One example is that of supply-chain contracts in areas such as food regulation and the garment industry.[79] This makes it more difficult to identify those that are responsible for certain detrimental consequences of the regimes at issue – such as food crises and child labour – and those to be held accountable.[80]

---

76 Meidinger, op. cit, n. 58.
77 D.F. Thompson, 'Moral Responsibility of Public Officials: The Problem of Many Hands' (1980) 74 Am. Pol. Sci. Rev. 905–15; Bovens et al., op. cit., n. 16; Y. Papadopoulos, 'Problems of Democratic Accountability in Network and Multi-level Governance' (2007) 13 European Law J. 469–86.
78 Thompson, id.
79 Macdonald and Macdonald, op. cit., n. 46, p. 98.
80 See G. Teubner, '"So ich aber die Teufel durch Beelzebub austreibe …": Zur Diabolik des Netzwerkversagens' in Ungewißheit als Chance: Perspektiven eines produktiven Umgangs mit Unsicherheit im Rechtssystem, ed. I. Augsberg (2009).

A second complication concerns the problem of the many eyes.[81] Public institutions are subject to forums involving some form of political accountability, but this is far less the case for private regulators[82] who more often face the problem of being accountable to a plethora of different forums which may not always be easy to identify. This links with the issue discussed above regarding the impact TPR generates for and on certain groups. Where private regulators wield a huge impact on people's lives or exercise public power, the question becomes very pressing as to whom exactly they should be accountable.[83] While it has been established that the greater the effects on third parties, the greater the need for accountability,[84] this does not answer the question as to whom accountability should actually be entrusted and for what exactly. In some cases, the effects may be limited to (potentially) specific, more or less identifiable groups of persons. An example of the latter is professional codes for lawyers stipulating standards and rules for their (ethical) behaviour vis-à-vis their clients. Such standards are monitored and enforced by professional supervisory and even discipli-nary bodies on the basis of peer review. This could be qualified as a rather internal accountability relationship. Multinational corporations are also in such internal accountability relationships with their stakeholders. Many regimes that can be categorized as TPR, however, potentially affect much wider groups, for example, investors but also workers and consumers. The global garment industry constitutes a case in point.[85] While investors will tend to be focused on the way in which their money has been spent, and thus on financial accounting, workers will probably like to hold the private regulators involved accountable for the way in which their economic and human rights are affected, whereas consumers could be concerned with different issues, including not only the quality of the product but also the protection of human rights in the production process.

The conclusion is that in relation to many TPR regimes it will be possible to identify *multiple* accountability relationships. This means that the identifi-cation of both the actor and the forum will determine the answers to the questions for what aspect of conduct the actor will be held accountable and what forms or mechanisms of accountability (can) come into play in this regard. With a view to the identification of both the accountability problems and the appropriate accountability mechanisms, it is thus essential first to clarify in each and every case the actors involved and the actual forums of

---

81 Bovens et al., op. cit., n. 9, pp. 41–6.
82 K. Strøm, 'Delegation and Accountability in Parliamentary Democracies' (2000) 37 *European J. of Political Research* 261–89; K. Strøm, 'Parliamentary Democracy and Delegation' in *Delegation and Accountability in Parliamentary Democracies*, eds. K. Strøm, W. C. Müller, and T. Bergman (2003) 55–108.
83 Held, op. cit. (2004), n. 30, p. 373.
84 See sections II and III, and HiiL, op. cit., n. 23, p. 13.
85 Macdonald and Macdonald, op. cit., n. 46.

the TPR at issue. One should also note that, for the sake of avoiding 'accountability paralysis', this determination requires prioritization both as regards the forums that are most significantly affected by the TPR regimes – both internally and externally – and the most pressing issues on which the actor should be held accountable.[86] Obviously, these issues can only be addressed through empirical analysis of specific TPR regimes. The same goes for claims that there is a need to enhance the accountability of TPR and for putting certain mechanisms into place for this. It may thus transpire that there are sufficient mechanisms for ensuring the internal accountability of a specific regime, but not for ensuring external, public accountability.[87]

2. Is there an obligation?

Having discussed above the fact that TPR should in principle be accountable, it is a different question whether there is in fact an obligation imposed upon the actors involved in TPR to explain and justify their conduct. Public officials will often be under a formal obligation to render account on a regular basis to specific forums, such as supervisory agencies, courts, or auditors. Public officials can be forced to appear in administrative or penal courts or to testify before parliamentary committees when those forums have reason to believe these officials are involved in (or responsible for) wrongdoings, mismanagement, policy failures, and other failings. But the obligation can also be informal, as in the case of press conferences and informal briefings or even self-imposed, as in the case of voluntary audits.

While, in the case of TPR, *political* accountability mechanisms will mainly be absent, this is certainly not to exclude the possibility that TPR regimes may entail certain formal or hard administrative and/or legal obligations of account giving. An example is where private regulators are subject to compulsory reporting and/or audits or may have to appear before a court or tribunal. The scope of judicial review of decisions of private bodies is, as such, not necessarily limited to individual litigation in the framework of contract law or tort law but may also be a matter of administrative law.[88] Yet, it seems likely that informal, voluntary or even moral[89] obligations as softer forms of accountability, in particular of a professional and social nature, will be most feasible and more relevant for TPR. There may therefore not be a hard obligation for any account giving, but there may be, for example, voluntary inspection or audits, the establishment of public panels, and so on. Again, one can identify a pressing need for further comparative, empirical study in this regard.

---

86 Blagescu et al., op. cit., n. 60, pp. 20–1.
87 Compare Keohane, op. cit., n. 28, p. 20.
88 In the context of English law, see the decision of the Court of Appeal in *R (Datafin plc)* v. *Panel for Takeovers and Mergers* [1987] Q.B. 815.
89 Dubnick, op. cit., n. 19.

3. Fully fledged account giving?

The relationship between the actor and the forum, the actual account giving, usually consists of at least three elements or stages. First of all, it is crucial that the actor is obliged to *inform the forum about his or her conduct*, by providing various sorts of data about the performance of tasks, about outcomes, or about procedures. Often, and particularly in the case of failures or incidents, this also involves the provision of explanations and justifications.[90] Account giving is more than mere propaganda, or the provision of information or instructions to the general public. The second stage is *debate*. There needs to be a possibility for the forum to interrogate the actor and to question the adequacy of the information or the legitimacy of the conduct – hence, the close semantic connection between 'accountability' and 'answerability'. Thirdly, the forum may *pass judgment* on the conduct of the actor. It may approve of an annual account, denounce a policy, or publicly condemn the behaviour of an official or an agency. In passing a negative judgment, or as a result, the actor may face certain consequences including, in certain cases, the imposition of sanctions.

Looking through this lens at TPR, a few issues need further consideration and analysis. First, it appears that it is, in particular, with a view to enabling the actual account giving that the standards of transparency and participation come into play in the context of an accountability relationship. While these standards may have their own intrinsic democratic or constitutional value, in this context they are instrumental prerequisites enabling any accountability mechanism or arrangement to function adequately. There cannot be any meaningful explanation and justification of conduct and debate if the forum does not have access to all relevant information and is not somehow involved in the actor's functioning. Secondly, it is clear that ensuring accountability requires more than realizing transparency and participation; the element of passing judgment presupposes evaluation and, depending on the outcome and institutional context, the possibility of imposing consequences. Without this, a relationship between an actor and a forum cannot be qualified as an accountability relationship. This also ties in with the approach developed within the framework of the Global Accountability Framework mentioned above, emphasizing the elements of evaluation and of complaint and response mechanisms. Evaluation is said to encompass:

---

90 M. Bovens et al., 'The Politics of Blame Avoidance: Defensive Tactics in a Dutch Crime-fighting Fiasco' in *When Things Go Wrong: Failures and Breakdowns in Organizational Settings*, ed. H.K. Anheier (1999) 123–47; K.M. Hearit, *Crisis Management by Apology: Corporate Response to Allegations of Wrongdoing* (2005); C. Hood, W. Jennings, and B. Hogwood, with C. Beeston, 'Fighting Fires in Testing Times: Exploring a Staged Response Hypothesis for Blame Management in Two Exam Fiasco Cases' (LSE/ESRC Research Centre Discussion Paper 42 (2007), at: <http://www.lse.ac.uk/collections/CARR/pdf/DPs/Disspaper42.pdf>.

185

the processes through which an organization, with involvement from key stakeholders, monitors and reviews its progress and results against goals and objectives; feeds learning from this back into the organization on an ongoing basis; and reports on the results of the process.

More concretely, it would mean that TPR regimes have policies in place that ensure such an evaluation process.[91] Independent and credible complaint-and-response mechanisms are critical building blocks without which accountability remains a dead letter. Complaints should be possible not only against outcomes, but also against practices and policies. It is thus essential that TPR regimes also include policies for dealing with complaints from stakeholders. Complaint mechanisms can clearly be of varying degrees of formality. Most importantly, where informal mechanisms are not effective, the stakeholder should be able to access a mechanism through which a complaint can be lodged formally.[92] Stakeholders should thus have the opportunity to do more than merely engage in protests and boycotts (naming and shaming), but also to have recourse to non-judicial means of dispute resolution and, ultimately, formal judicial redress.

In the context of TPR, the existence and scope of the most significant external, social or public accountability relationships may not be very easy to establish. The extent to which manifestations of such relationships can be qualified as fully fledged accountability mechanisms remains still very much an empirical question – and there is a dearth of empirical material in this area.[93] There may be interest groups, NGOs, associations of clients or consumers and activists to which private regulators respond in the form of issuing public reports or by the organization of public panels or otherwise, but the question is to what extent these devices can be said to encompass the possibilities of debate, passing judgment, and the imposition of consequences. This requires further analysis of the evaluation and complaint-and-response policies and mechanisms that have actually been put into place.

VI. CONCLUDING REMARKS

The hypothesis underlying this contribution is that the traditional democratic processes at national level (the role of national parliaments in particular) simply cannot keep up with the migration of power and authority to the transnational level.[94] It seems equally naive to imagine that the transnational level can be 'easily' democratized, mainly by using national models of democracy and applying them beyond the state. The debate on the EU shows

91 Blagescu et al., op. cit., n. 60, pp. 34–6.
92 id., p. 37.
93 Compare Bovens et al., op. cit., n. 9, p. 44 on this problem in relation to the accountability of the EU.
94 For an opposite view, see A. Moravcsik, 'Is there a "Democratic Deficit" in World Politics? A Framework for Analysis' (2004) 39 *Government and Opposition* 336–63.

186

that even at this level, where there are putatively representative institutions in place and a system of direct elections to the European Parliament, this is by no means the case. There seems to be little evidence at this stage to suggest that the even more remote and under-institutionalized transnational level lends itself in any realistic way to this kind of approach, particularly as regards forms of purely private governance. Finally, there is some evidence with regard to wider transnational processes that democracy can simply not be transposed from the national to the transnational arena and that other 'compensatory mechanisms' need to be found *instead* of traditional, electoral democracy.[95] A 'democracy-striving approach' acknowledges the difficulty and complexity of democratizing transnational governance yet insists it is necessary, and identifies the act of continuous striving as the source of legitimacy and accountability. The question is whether this argument and approach is equally applicable in the context of transnational private governance (or one of its hybrids) as opposed to transnational public governance.

TPR is considered to have a bias towards regimes (of industrialized countries) that have more advanced regulatory traditions, exemplified also by the under-representation of certain regions in it.[96] This underscores not only the relevance of the democratic perspective but also that of the constitutional perspective to the desirable or expected effects of accountability in this context, that is, that it should help to mitigate the risk of the abuse of power by those that hold it.[97] The Global Accountability Framework understands accountability as referring to:

> the processes through which an organisation makes a commitment to respond to and balance the needs of stakeholders in its decision-making processes and activities, and delivers against this commitment.

Today's global governance arena is not considered to be defined by unaccountable organizations but, rather, by organizations that are either accountable to the wrong set of stakeholders or focus their accountability on one set of stakeholders at the expense of others. The key challenge is thus deemed to be the creation of more balanced accountability, in which the interests of the most powerful stakeholders do not overshadow the voices of those most affected by an organization's activities. Accountability is thus perceived as a power-balancing process between the organization and its stakeholders as well as between an organization's various stakeholder groups.[98]

---

95 See, in particular, G. de Búrca, 'Developing Democracy Beyond the State' (2008) 46 *Columbia J. of Transnational Law* 221–78.
96 K. Ronit and V. Schneider, 'Global Governance through Private Organizations' (1999) 12 *Governance: An International J. of Policy and Administration* 243–66, at 249. Compare, also, V. Haufler, *A Public Role for the Private Sector: Industry Self-Regulation in a Global Economy* (2001) 118–19.
97 Grant and Keohane, op. cit., n. 40; M. Koenig-Archibugi, 'Accountability in transnational relations: how distinctive is it?' (2010) 33 *West European Politics* 1142–64; Bovens, op. cit., n. 36.
98 Blagescu et al., op. cit., n. 60.

In view of the rather impossible mission to enhance the democratic account-ability of TPR on the basis of a traditional, political-electoral approach, there is a growing consciousness that alternative approaches need to be developed to realize this. At the same time, it has been established that in the short(er) term it seems more promising and feasible to develop further the constitutional perspective on the accountability of TPR regimes as an avenue to enhance their public accountability. Despite the complications identified earlier in this article, it does not seem impossible to make the public accountability of TPR a reality. The improvement of external, social and public accountability mechanisms in the framework of a checks-and-balances (and learning) approach can potentially make a valuable contribution to enhancing the democratic accountability of TPR as well. Different studies provide a starting point for looking deeper into this potential, for example, the possible contribution of social accountability devices to bringing about a non-electoral form of democratic accountability,[99] including also the development of global civil society as a political presence in international life, and of its capability to push forward key initiatives in the international arena.[100] In addition, the argument that supragovernmental regulatory regimes compete for business and legiti-macy and as such are under constant pressure to improve their accountability mechanisms is novel and merits further exploration. Such processes of competition may thus actually function as 'vehicles of an emergent form of democratic politics'.[101] Moreover, there is some evidence that the increased controversiality of decisions will lead to a widening of the interested publics.[102]

The question at the transnational level remains, what public? The communities involved are plural, partial, and emergent. While the problem of the many hands might suggest that all these communities should be made part of the accountability process, this would exacerbate the problem of the many eyes, and work against the cure of prioritization. Bringing the public back in should thus be a balanced exercise. While this and many other issues need to be fleshed out in more detail, there is already sufficient prospect of accountability as discussed in this article to conclude that it is neither a chimera nor a full-blown reality; its current status is fledgling and 'in between' but with clear growth perspectives. More empirical research is badly needed with a view to defining the nature and scope of public accountability in normative terms and as a matter of practice.[103]

99 Macdonald and Macdonald, op. cit., n. 46.
100 R. Falk and A. Strauss, 'On the Creation of a Global Peoples Assembly: Legitimacy and the Power of Popular Sovereignty' (2000) 36 *Stanford J. of International Law* 191–220.
101 E. Meidinger, 'Competitive Supragovernmental Regulation: How Could It Be Democratic?' (2008) 8 *Chicago J. of International Law* 513–34, at 518.
102 See, further, P. Schmitter, 'Three Neofunctional Hypotheses about Institutional Integration' (1969) 23 *International Integration* 161–6.
103 Eleven case studies in the areas of consumer protection, financial markets and human rights are currently undertaken within the HiiL research project on TPRERs: Constitutional Foundations and Governance Design.

188